NEW DIRECTIONS IN ECONOMIC ANTHROPOLOGY

Anthropology, Culture and Society

Series Editors:
Dr Richard A. Wilson, University of Sussex
Professor Thomas Hylland Eriksen, University of Oslo

NEW DIRECTIONS IN ECONOMIC ANTHROPOLOGY

SUSANA NAROTZKY

Pluto  Press

LONDON • CHICAGO, IL

First published 1997 by Pluto Press
345 Archway Road, London N6 5AA
and 1436 West Randolph
Chicago, Illinois 60607, USA

British Library Cataloguing in Publication Data
A catalogue record for this book is available from
the British Library

ISBN 0 7453 0717 5 hbk

Library of Congress Cataloging in Publication Data
Narotzky, Susana,
    New directions in economic anthropology/Susana Narotzky,
        p.   cm. — (Anthropology, culture and society)
    Includes index.
    ISBN 0-7453–0717–5 (hardcover)
    1. Economic anthropology. I. Series.
    GN448.N37   1997
    306.3—dc21   96–48054
                                                           CIP

Designed and produced for Pluto Press by
Chase Production Services, Chadlington, OX7 3LN
Typeset from disk by Stanford DTP Services, Milton Keynes
Printed in Great Britain

A José Antonio, sólo

CONTENTS

ACKNOWLEDGEMENTS

Some years ago, Richard Wilson, editor of this series, suggested that I write a book on economic anthropology. The challenge was appealing because the book was meant to be both an introductory university level textbook and a thought-provoking work at the scholarly level as well. It has taken a long time for me to write a book that, I hope, comes close to the initial intentions. I have done my best and I alone am responsible for the results. Many people, however, have made this book possible often without being aware of it.

I want to thank my first teachers who contributed early on to give me a certain turn of thought: Mercedes Molleda, J.P. Kloster and Jean Feutray. I also want to thank very specially some university professors who where crucial in my development as an anthropologist: Jesús Contreras, who introduced me to economic anthropology; Rayna Rapp, who pointed to the significance of feminist and gender issues in anthropology; William Roseberry, who introduced me to a particularly enriching perspective of the Marxist tradition in anthropology.

But many other social scientists, teachers, friends and colleagues, have to be thanked: Dolors Comas, Joan Frigolé, Alberto Galván, Maurice Godelier, Marcial Gondar, Elizabeth Handman, Nieves Herrero, Ubaldo Martínez Veiga, Lourdes Méndez, Paz Moreno, Isidoro Moreno, Pablo Palenzuela, Reyna Pastor, Juan Luis Pintos, Gonzalo Sanz, all of them gave me the opportunity to develop my thoughts in seminars and discussions.

Finally, I want to thank very specially those friends who have read or discussed parts of the book: Roberto Blatt, Jesús Contreras, Gavin Smith and Ignasi Terradas. I am also deeply indebted to Richard Wilson who has been a very patient and thorough editor and without whom the book would not exist. Both his and Jeff Pratt's suggestions have been a great help in the revision of the final manuscript.

My family, José Antonio, Bruno and Lucas, my parents, Mercedes and Norman and my sister Viviana, have been a constant source of support and happiness and many other things. I thank them all.

INTRODUCTION: BEYOND ECONOMIC ANTHROPOLOGY

First, a word of caution. This is not a book on the History of Economic Anthropology. It is not an exhaustive presentation of the theoretical perspectives that have been associated with the 'economic' field of study within the academic discipline of Anthropology (for a view on these see Ortiz 1983; Clammer 1985, 1987; Kahn and Llobera 1981, Moniot 1976, Roseberry 1988). Most theoretical perspectives will be clarified along the route, however.

This book intends to be a journey. It wants to bring closer to a wider public the main concepts, debates and questions that have been relevant to the understanding of how people organise themselves for the production and reproduction of the material goods and services that make life possible. Its aim is threefold: first, to provide the conceptual tools necessary to follow most of the 'economic' anthropology debates; second, to present some of these debates; third, to put forward my view of what the present challenges are in 'economic' anthropology.

In this chapter I will try to define, briefly, the scope of the term 'economic' in anthropology as it has developed in academic discussions during the last fifty years. This will be followed by an attempt to narrow the area of discussion to a context where local and global material processes are embedded in historical concrete social relations. More specifically, the subject of this book will be presented as the drive toward an all-inclusive approach to material, life-sustaining processes, through the use of the concept of 'social reproduction'. The reasoning behind the emphasis on social reproduction is that it contributes to bridging dualisms such as those between micro and macro approaches, material and cultural perspectives and, more generally, between 'economy' and 'society'. Indeed, these dualisms have become a major obstacle to social scientists' understanding of life-sustaining processes.

1

But first let us try to get a rough idea of how anthropologists have been trying to deal with realities encountered in the field, realities that relate to the material facts of living in any society and to how these are organised through social relations in a regular although changing way.

The domain of 'economic anthropology' and the definition of the 'economy' by anthropologists has generated much debate for over fifty years. For R. Firth (1970) economic anthropology focuses primarily on resource allocation and product distribution and rests on the 'acceptance of the view that the logic of scarcity *is* operative over the whole range of economic phenomena'. Moreover:

> while the material dimension of the economy is regarded as a basic feature, the significance of the economy is seen to lie in the *transactions* of which it is composed and therefore in the quality of *relationships* which these transactions create, express, sustain and modify. (1970:4)

This view of the scope and method of economic anthropology termed 'formalist' has been criticised on the grounds that it applies theoretical criteria developed from the analysis of capitalist societies (scarcity of resources, alternative allocation processes, marginal utility motivation) to all societies all over the world, past and present. Although *relationships* between individuals are highlighted as the significant aspect of the economy to anthropologists, these are conceived in a 'transactional' mode (Blau 1982). The basic problem of this perspective is that social relations are perceived as an *exchange* of social 'values' or, alternatively, as attributes of exchange acts, being therefore treated as 'utilities' to be maximised in the same framework of scarcity and alternative allocation as any other resource.

Another view of what economic anthropologists should focus on is suggested by Polanyi (1957) and his followers. They propose two distinct meanings of the concept of 'economy'. One is the 'formal' meaning which is a theory of rational action involving choice between alternative uses of scarce resources (Firth's definition). For them, however, this meaning can only be applied in a society where the market mechanism is the dominant means of allocating land, labour and goods. The *real* (or *substantive*) concept of economy should be meaningful for any society, whatever its form of allocation (or distribution) is. Accordingly, in the 'substantive' sense the economy can be defined as:

> an institutionalised interaction between man and the environment that provides a sustained provision of material means for the satisfaction of wants.

Satisfaction of wants is 'material' when it requires the use of material means to obtain the ends. (Polanyi 1957:293; see also Dalton 1971a [1965]:31)

This definition remains within a means–ends/wants–satisfaction logic which seems to refer implicitly to an abstract demand/supply motivation for economic activity and this renders 'universal' and 'natural' – not historical and social – the conditions of production, distribution and consumption of material goods and services. It presents, however, several interesting points: first, the focus on *material* needs and means; second, the idea of the economy as a *process* that sustains *social continuity*; and third, that this is done in an institutionalised and therefore *socially structured* way. Moreover, Polanyi and his followers pointed to the fact that in non-market integrated societies, the economy is *embedded* in other social institutions and cannot be analysed as a separate realm.

Godelier takes over most of the substantivists' propositions and redefines them within a Marxist framework. The economy is defined then as a series of social relations present both in a specific domain of activities – that of the production, distribution and consumption of material goods – and as a 'particular aspect of all human activities that do not belong in themselves to that domain but the functioning of which involves the exchange and use of material goods' (1974:140).

In Godelier's view, it is the social structure of a society, the 'logic of its social relations', the 'realisation of the socially necessary ends', 'the better functioning of all social structures, kinship, politics, religion, etc.' that sets material 'needs' and the means of 'satisfaction' in a concrete social ground. The historical conditions of emergence of a particular social context are not explicitly integrated in his theory, however (Khan and Llobera 1981:299). Social relations become the centre of economic analysis within a context of social reproduction.

If *that which* is produced, distributed and consumed depends on the *nature* and on the *hierarchy* of needs in a society, then economic activity is organically tied to the other political, religious, cultural, family activities that compose with it the contents of life in that society and to which it gives the material means of realisation. (Godelier 1974:147)

However, although in Godelier's view all sorts of social structures might have an 'economic' aspect, the economy should be analysed starting from the social relations obtaining in the properly economic *domain* of production, distribution and consumption (1974:151).

Critiques of Godelier's view (Kahn and Llobera 1981; Asad 1974) have pointed out several problems with his approach. First, it is claimed that *history* is not taken into account. The concrete conditions of production of an existing social structure, the way in which present 'bundles of relationships' relate to past ones has no place in his theory. Second, their critique underlines a problem concerning anthropology more generally: that is, the assumption of the universal relevance of some categories such as 'economy', 'kinship', 'politics', 'religion' that have become bounded domains of study of the academic discipline. This leads to the assumption that 'a distinct field of social activity which can be carved out of the totality of social relations' exists and can be studied in isolation (Kahn and Llobera 1981:309), later to be related to the other categories in a 'structured', 'organic' or 'systematic' way. One of the perennial issues in anthropology is unquestionably the discussion about the status of the categories that social scientists have forged in the course of academic debate as compared to other 'common-sense' categories that they encounter or to the real lived relationships that they must explain. The last critique might appear as a paradoxical formulation of the former ones; that is, Godelier's *relativism* (Asad 1974:214) where each society is conceived as an autonomous system setting its needs and hence organising economic activity in a manner unrelated to other societies' logics. This is particularly relevant because, as Wallerstein (1974, 1980), Frank (1967), Wolf (1982) and others have shown, the logic of accumulation that originated in Europe and set forth the organisation of economic activities in specific ways reached directly or indirectly all over the world and profoundly transformed whatever social structures or economic systems might have existed previously and whatever relations might have obtained between relatively distinct polities or groups.

Other French Marxist anthropologists have been more preoccupied by the reality of the impact of Western capitalist economies in non-capitalist societies through colonial and neocolonial processes (Meillassoux 1982 [1975]; Rey 1971; Terray 1969). Their view is that in these social formations (that is, concrete historical realities) several modes of production (that is, abstract structured totalities) are articulated in a hierarchical way: the capitalist mode of production subordinates the non-capitalist modes.

The main theoretical question which arose revolved around the *status of autonomy* of the distinct socially organised life-sustaining processes (termed 'modes' or 'forms' of production) that were articulated in a concrete 'social formation' (that is, a real, complex, historical society). Put simply, the question was whether the different modes or forms of production retained an autonomous distinct path for organising their continuity, or whether their articulation implied *necessarily* a common, interdependent and mutually transforming path of social reproduction. As I will briefly point out later, the debate was embedded in a broader philosophical argument dealing with abstract models and concrete realities of society, and with the interface between the abstract and the concrete.

Two aspects of the French Marxists' debates should be highlighted here. On the one hand I want to stress their increasing theoretical preoccupation with social reproduction or the 'laws of motion' of social totalities. On the other hand, the problem of thinking *in the abstract* concrete historical social realities continues to be, in my opinion, an unresolved methodological issue. The fascination with abstract models is directly related to Althusser's reading of Marx (Althusser 1969, 1974; Balibar 1969) in a structuralist fashion where a mode of production's structure is a set of *fixed* connections between agents of production and means of production which can be defined as relations of production. In order to exist in the *concrete*, the structure requires a superstructure of political and ideological relations. But because these relations are deemed *necessary* to the *concrete* existence of the structure they also have to be accounted for in the abstract model. There is then an opposition between the abstract and the concrete expressed in the base/superstructure model and in the need of an abstract predefinition of a concept of 'the economic' as an autonomous instance (or level) of any social structure.

The model poses beforehand a set of predefined social relations (economic, political, ideological) that appear as conceptual objects, and thus it achieves the reification of 'localised' and 'bounded' regions (levels, instances). These 'levels' are subsequently, but necessarily, articulated in a totality which is historical (Althusser 1969:192–3). Althusser and his followers, however, also felt strongly the need to transcend this fragmentation through the emphasis on 'reproduction' of the totality (Balibar 1969:282–3, 289). I do not wish to enter more deeply here into the Althusserian debate. I will just point to its influence in Marxist anthropology on the one hand through its excessively theoretical emphasis on abstract structures which are then treated as objects; on the other hand, paradoxically, through its idea of the fundamental role of 'overdetermination' by non-economic instances (ideological, political, etc.) in all concrete historical formations (Althusser 1974:112–13, 240–1). And, following Banaji I will propose that:

modes of production are impenetrable at the level of simple abstractions. The process of 'true abstraction' is simultaneously a process of 'concretisation' of the definition of specific historical *laws of motion*. (Banaji 1977:9)

Thus, I am more interested in highlighting social reproduction, the movement through which a concrete historical social reality sets the conditions for its continuity and contains transformations within the limits of a dominant logic.

Up to this point I have briefly presented the main debates that shaped the field of economic anthropology: the formalist/substantivist debate and the debate within Marxist anthropology. Now I will focus on the basic ideas that form the context in which my own theoretical perspective is embedded.

I want to briefly present two currents of thought that will be more fully dealt with in Chapter 4. The first current centres around the work of E.P. Thompson and R. Williams who developed a certain strand of Marx's and Gramsci's thoughts. Their emphasis on human experience and agency points to the materiality of consciousness, to the importance of culture and of the personal environment in the construction and transformation of the social relations that make life-sustaining processes possible.

The second current deals with the tension between local and global material processes. In this respect it should by now be clear that a capitalist logic of accumulation has reached the farthest corners of the world. How, in this several centuries long process, it has transformed the ongoing local and regional logics should be the main interest of present-day 'economic' anthropology. From this perspective the dispute about whether exchange relations in a worldwide context (Frank 1967; Wallerstein 1974, 1980) or production relations in a local context (Laclau 1971) are the key to conceptualising 'capitalism' and thus asserting the degree of penetration of the capitalist logic into a social formation, seems to me now a vain and casuistic exercise. Moreover, capitalist relations of production might find expression in multiple concrete forms drawn to capital accumulation but different from the 'classical' free wage labour relation (Goodman and Redclift

1982:54) and this should also be understood as part of the concrete processes (creative and/or resistance forms) that take place. As Wolf (1982) has shown in *Europe and the People without History*, we must think both globally and locally if we want to understand what happened all over the world, we must think *historically*. Wolf says of his book that:

It hopes to delineate the general process at work in mercantile and capitalist development, while at the same time following their effects on the micro-populations studied by the ethnohistorians and anthropologists. My view of these processes and their effects is historical, but in the sense of history as an analytical account of the development of material relations, moving simultaneously on the level of the encompassing system and on the micro-level. (1982:23)

And this is what I think 'economic' anthropologists should deal with in the concrete cases they study (C. Smith 1983:344–7).

What, then, is the framework I propose for this 'economic' anthropology? On the one hand, the rejection of the idea of a separate economic level or bounded region of economic social relations or activities seems to me a first and necessary step. On the other hand, I feel it is useful to narrow the scope of the 'economic' to the social relations involved in the production and reproduction of material life, through the organised interaction of humans and nature. And, last, I would want to put forward the idea that for human populations material relations cannot be theoretically separated from their cultural expressions which, in turn, are materially produced and embodied.

I propose, then, to take a somewhat paradoxical route that will start with the 'classic' analytic division of the economic process into the distinct moments of production, distribution and exchange, and consumption, and will end in the all-encompassing field of social reproduction. At every point I will present the concepts and issues that have been addressed in 'economic anthropology' and I will try to show how the original self-enclosed categories break down and give way to one another in concrete historical social processes.

1 PRODUCTION

This chapter will begin by presenting what is often thought of as the most inescapably material and objective part of the production process: the environment. The argument will develop eventually into a critique of the naive ahistorical notions of a 'given' natural environment. I will support instead the perspective that the environment is *always* the product of social historical processes. A similar critique will be presented for 'technology', the very material mediation between humans and their environment. The last two sections of the chapter will focus on social relations that effect differentiation around 'production'. Here also I will try to show, for example, that gender-linked divisions of labour are not natural. The chapter will end with a long discussion about the concept and the realities of 'work' in contemporary societies. This will bring us unhesitatingly, I hope, to the conclusion that the bounded region of 'production' should give way to a more wide-ranging framework.

THE ECOSYSTEM

Space; resources; populations

Economic activities are those which are directed toward the satisfaction of material needs in human populations. This perspective presupposes the existence of a given 'natural' context, an environment, where human groups dwell, which is there to be acted upon and from which they can extract what is needed for a living. The environment in turn will respond to human action triggering feedback responses affecting in one way or another the different species that share a defined space. From this perspective humans are mainly treated as just one species interacting with other species in space and through time. Exchanges of energy

8

are the link which relates living beings, and these occur in a certain, predictable way. The methodological framework is that of a *system*, where clearly distinguishable elements are related in what is meant to be a functioning totality. The underlying idea is that, left to itself, the system tends toward equilibrium, although not static equilibrium. It follows from this that the species adapts in the *ecosystem* to environmental changes brought about by the effective energy exchanges through time and the unpredictable catastrophes – discontinuities – that can befall any system. *Adaptation* to the changing environment leads to a renewed unstable equilibrium. Transformation is thus part of ecosystems. It is *regular*, however, because the effects of elementary exchanges can be described, and quantitative variations thereof may then have predictable results in the overall system. These assumptions should be thought of as the most materialistic pole of an approach to economic anthropology. It is both a useful starting point and a methodological device. We will see in the following chapter how, in fact, the context that constrains and is acted upon by human beings in their search for a livelihood is a social and historical one, where cultural and material forces are entangled in a dialectical process of continuous transformation.

From this human ecology perspective, then, the environment can be defined as a space where human and other species' populations exchange energy. For humans, this exchange becomes a matter of harnessing resources. What is understood as 'space' and 'resources' must be related to *human populations*, that is, social processes – as distinct from any other species' populations – if the ecological approach is to be meaningful in economic anthropology.

For human populations *space* is not so much a given objective material fact as a lived experience. Geographical barriers can become paths of communication with the use of certain technological knowledge. A river, for example, might either be an isolating obstacle or a waterway enabling transport over long distances. A chain of mountains is not the same sort of obstacle for a human society that masters aviation techniques as for one that does not. Distance in a flat country depends on the means of transportation available, etc. The material constrictions of space for human groups must be related to the knowledge and availability of technology (that is, material artefacts derived from human intellect). For economic anthropology, therefore, space cannot be devoid of human interaction.

Something similar happens to *resources:* a resource is not one until it is *known* to be one by a human group. For example, the mere existence of some mineral in the inhabited realm of a human group does not make it a resource. First, its presence must be known, second, its useful aspects for human life must be understood, third, the means to harness this aspect must be discovered and fourth, the social organisation of society must permit the exploitation of the resource. All of these conditions may not be present simultaneously in a human group. Moreover, probably they will not be shared homogeneously throughout the group and the differential access to resources will express political and economic differences. On the other hand, although resources are located in space and would therefore seem to be ascribed to the human populations inhabiting a particular space, this is not generally so. For example, we could consider the many instances in which Western industrial societies have exploited resources located in Thirld World countries. Once again, technological knowledge and relations between human societies, dwelling in different spaces but always mobile and interactive, must be taken into account. Demands on resources and stress on the limiting factors of an environment must therefore be approached as a complex political economic process.

Humans get energy from resources – other species and material elements in space – but humans also produce energy and might be themselves sought after as resources by other humans. The control of human labour is one of the main forces in the organisation of societies.

An important aspect of the ecological perspective is the influence of space and resources on human *populations*. A population can have different rates of growth or decline as a result of the availability of resources in a certain location. On the one hand, population growth may trigger the expansion of a human group into neighbouring areas when resources become scarce. This might encroach into some other group's established location and will result in conflict. However, if a human group is severely constrained by geographical barriers, population growth might lead to technological change in order to harness local but hitherto unattainable resources (Carneiro 1970). On the other hand, the availability of certain nutritional resources affects female fertility. A certain ratio of fat in body weight must be attained in order to get regular ovulation cycles. This will depend not only on the general amount of food intake but also on the proportion of fat to other nutrients in the diet.

Therefore we must account for variation in fertility rates among different societies but also *within* the same society, depending on differential access to food resources. This means we should explore political issues in order to understand much 'ecological' variation. Moreover, an important aspect of human populations is that growth might be consciously controlled in several ways. We must bear in mind that control might refer not only to practices *restricting* but also to those *enhancing* population growth. Among those restricting population growth, prolonged lactation periods after each birth seem to be a fairly common method. Two factors seem to contribute to decreased fertility during lactation: the lower ratios of fat to body weight and the presence of the hormone prolactine. Other restrictive methods include delaying marriage age for women; ritually prohibiting intercourse during prolonged periods; infanticide (especially female infanticide) and warfare.

Practices enhancing fertility include nutritional habits aiming at lowering the age of menarche; shortening lactation or suppressing it altogether through the use of food substitutes or wet nursing; early marriage age for women; certain forms of marriage such as monogamy (as opposed to polygyny) which increase the chances of intercourse occurring during the fertile period of ovulation cycles. Emphasis on prolonged lactation periods in many societies may also aim at increasing the chances of survival of babies in environments where substitute food is unavailable or scarce.

Human populations, then, respond to environmental factors such as scarce or bountiful resources but never in an 'objective' mechanical way. We must think in terms of a *politics of populations* which will take into account the structure of power influencing fertility, morbidity, mortality, migration, expressing differential access to local resources and the control of space.

Energy input/output; the question of productivity: ecological value vs. economic value

Human ecology seeks to explain the relations between resources and populations in a given space. The relation is expressed in terms of energy exchanges. The amount of energy that a human group spends in subsistence and other activities is balanced against the amount of energy obtained for subsistence and other social purposes. This has permitted quantitative studies measuring human energy input in subsistence activities against output retrieved among different societies, an interesting asset for comparative reasons. The detailed study of time allocation to diverse activities shows difference in work loads following gender and age lines within all societies, to which class, ethnic or national divisions must be added in some cases. Energy input/output analyses present, on the one hand, work energy expenditure in reference to the energy produced, showing thus if any definable group is more energy-efficient. On the other hand, work energy expenditure in reference to the energy allocated to different activities, and consumed and controlled by different groups of people (that is, adult male, adult female, elderly and youngsters, etc.) can be assessed. Measuring energy exchanges gives us interesting 'hard' data on a number of factors relating to the social organisation of economic processes in societies. Some drawbacks should be mentioned, however. In most anthropological studies the energy accounted for is only related to the obtaining of food, neglecting such crucial activities as food processing, shelter construction and maintenance, dress, pottery and other instrument manufacture, as well as infant care, which are necessary to the material reproduction of any human group.

One of the very interesting aspects of the human ecology energy exchange perspective has been to question the concept of *productivity*. It is a central theoretical concept in most economic models. Moreover, it has become the measure of economic development as expressed by increased productivity through technological innovation in Western industrial societies. This position might be questioned in the light of an 'energy' model. On the one hand, productivity of labour should be differentiated from land productivity in agricultural systems, for instance. Productivity is defined as an input/output ratio, but while produce – measured in energy or otherwise – is generally taken as the output unit, the input unit can be human energy or total energy, but also time, land or money (Jochim 1981:65–90). Increases of the input/output ratio will express alternatively rewards to average labour expended, total energy expended, or to the amount of time, land or money used. Different interpretations of economic relations will result from stressing efficiency in relation to different measure inputs. As a rule, 'people tend to work no harder than they have to at production unless constrained by overriding shortages of time, land or money' and, thus, labour efficiency seems to be 'a major decision objective when neither land nor time seem to be limited' (Jochim 1981:72).

On the other hand, if we think about energy productivity we will get a ratio of total energy spent (including human, chemical, mechanical energy) against total energy retrieved. Where 'classical' productivity indexes might point to an increase (of output per acre in agriculture, or product per work hour in industry), thus expressing 'economic development'; a total energy productivity index might show a sharp decrease, therefore implying an involution in the effective use of energy. For example, agriculture produces a higher output per acre when employing irrigation, chemical fertilisers, pesticides, specific genetically engineered species, etc. The resulting cost/benefit monetary value, that is, a strictly market-oriented definition of 'economic productivity', might improve, especially if long-term soil regeneration and water supplies are not included as costs and depletion of non-renewable energy sources such as fuel are not taken into account. However, from an *energy* input/output viewpoint, where it is not the market value of energy inputs and output that counts (we must take into account that many energy inputs are not marketed) but the total energy balance (whatever its market value), the more technically 'developed' an agricultural system is, the lower its total energy productivity seems to be (Jochim 1981:34).

Productivity is a complex and ambiguous concept which appears strongly related to the idea of 'economic development', that is, the expression of a more efficient way of gaining access to material goods. For every account of 'development', however, we might ask a few questions: which input/output ratio is being stressed – time, money, energy – and why? Whose definition of material well-being is being used as the aim to be attained? Why should 'efficiency' – that is, getting to the goal with 'economy of means' – be posited as a universal drive at all? The ambiguity of the concept of productivity shows that it is highly loaded with political implications. The use of such a concept in a mechanical, abstract way obscures in fact the fields of power, local and global, within the community and between nations that construct the aims of a group of people as being those of all. A clear example of the problem of applying mechanical efficiency models to human societies can be seen in the concept of 'carrying capacity'.

Carrying capacity; technological efficiency

Human populations use resources localised in space. There is a relationship between populations, resources and space which is mediated by technology. The concept of carrying capacity tries to study that relationship and to point at factors specifically significant in a given society. The technological efficiency index tries to measure the energy input/output ratio for subsistence activities in societies using different technologies. Societies can then be compared from a human ecological perspective, seeking to understand the transformations of populations, resources and the use of space within a systemic model of energy exchange (Harris 1986:194–214, Ch. 11).

The capacity of the resources located in a given area to carry a maximum size of human population is the *carrying capacity* of that geographical space. Resources depend on technological achievement. When population increases above the carrying capacity of the area, resources are depleted and returns to labour diminish. Moreover, the environment is substantially transformed. Some resources are considered *limiting factors* because populations cannot survive if deprived of them below a certain limit, for a certain time. Water is such a limiting factor in many societies; protein resources or land for cultivation might be limiting factors in other environments. The *minimum availability* of limiting factors during the annual seasonal variation cycle sets the maximum population that an environment may carry given the technological achievement of the society considered.

Human populations will try to react when reaching the carrying capacity of their environment. Several strategies have been used, alone or in combination. Restriction of population growth through various techniques is one. Expansion into neighbouring spaces to increase the absolute amount of resources or the crucial availability of a limiting factor is another strategy. Temporary or definitive migration of some of the population is yet another possibility aiming at re-establishing the previous population/resources balance. Other options, however, seek to adapt to environmental transformation through technological innovation. This implies the use of old resources in a new way and the discovery of new resources in the old environment. Both these processes generally result in an intensification of labour and a different organisation of social relations. Historically, the adoption of slash and burn agriculture first, and later the intensification of agriculture through irrigation and manuring techniques, seem to be technological adaptations in response to population pressure on the carrying capacity of a given environment (Boserup 1965; Cohen 1977). The restriction of population mobility due to geographical barriers might have been a co-determining factor in the search for and adoption of more labour-intensive techniques. Technological innovation is thus related to the need to overcome a limiting factor in a given environment. However, as critiques of the carrying capacity concept point out, pressure over resources might be a result not of population increase but of production increase due to market demands (Martinez Alier 1992). Technological innovation should not be confused with greater technological efficiency.

Energy efficiency may not increase with technological innovation. In fact, as previously mentioned, some new technologies might be energetically inefficient. Moreover, the capacity for a society to maintain a larger population is not a sign of a greater technological efficiency nor is it a self-evident positive value.

Of particular relevance are the critiques that point to the limited understanding of a society that an exclusive ecological perspective might produce. The best example is the study by Lee (1979) of the Kalahari !Kung San as compared to the study by Wilmsen (1989) on the same area. Lee's is a thorough and detailed ecological study where the environment – considered as an ahistorical given context – and its use by the !Kung people are extensively described. The caloric and protein content of foods made available by foraging and hunting is compared to the energy requirements according to age/sex and work load needs and a positive energy balance is found on average (1979:269–72). Although some nutritional stress is acknowledged, it is found to be much smaller than that of agriculturalists and is related to the lack of mobility of some people at the main waterhole after a period (dry season) of intense use of the surrounding resources, when better resources are now (rainy season) to be found by dispersion at temporary waterholes (1979:301–2).

In a conclusion, a model of foraging adaptation is proposed where 'size of groups, use of space and work effort are systematically interconnected' variables (1979:443) and 'the constant, or given, in this simple model is the productive system: the tools, knowledge and organisation necessary to make a living in that environment' (1979:444). Moreover, 'the collective, nonexclusive ownership of land and

resources: widespread food sharing within and among local groups'
(1979:117) should be added to this 'system of subsistence' together
with the fact that mobility 'sets limits to the amount of material wealth
a family can possess' (1979:117). Thus, foraging is not only a 'mode
of subsistence' (that is, a technique, a system) but a 'mode of production',
a 'full fledged way of life' (1979:116–17).

The impression one gets is that !Kung foragers have been basically
isolated from other forms of subsistence provision and organisation,
from other peoples' social, political and economic endeavours. The
!Kung's way of life appears strictly as a product of ecological adaptation
to 'nature' – an ahistorical environment – which produces an egalitarian
form of access to and distribution of resources. Only in two moments
(1979:76–86 and 401–31) is this impression challenged. First, when
speaking of 'a history of contact' Lee situates 'early contacts' around
the 1870s when the Tawana, Tswana-speaking cattle people settled
nearby and Lee tells us that '!Kung-operated cattle posts in the interior
was the main business of the period 1890–1925' and 'according to the
!Kung version of events, it was they who played an active role in bringing
cattle to the interior on a year-round basis' (1979:79). Moreover the
!Kung seem to have been involved in the Tswana sharecropping
mafisa system (1979:79–80).

The second occasion is when speaking of the 'economic and social
change in the 1960s and 1970s'. Here we are surprised to learn that
these ecologically well adapted foragers were, by the time Lee did his
first fieldwork (1963), doing *mafisa* work in cattle posts, planting crops
(up to 55 per cent of men prior to 1966 had been at some point involved
in agriculture), owning some cattle, working for wages, hunting with
(borrowed) firearms (1979:403–12). None of this has been taken into
account when describing the !Kung's *foraging* way of life! When,
finally, these multiple and complex economic, social and political
'non-foraging' relations come up, they are presented as the sudden
effects of change, of the transformation of a 'foraging way of life' that
has 'remained the same' for 'thousands of years' (1979:438). Even as
mafisa-type relationships in herding have been acknowledged since the
beginning of the twentieth century (1979:79), the 1960s and 1970s
situation is presented against a background of an all-foraging system.
Hence, the contradictions that can be observed between !Kung 'who
have begun to farm and herd' and those who '*continue* the foraging life'
is presented as a result of the tension between 'two ways of life': farming

and foraging (1979:412–13, my emphasis). This inhibits the possibility of looking at this 'contradiction' as the outcome of differential access to resources and the different positions of !Kung people in the complex set of relations of production present in the area.

Wilmsen's (1989) critique is based on two main points. On the one hand he stresses the fact that, according to the area's archaeological and written records, the relations of the Kalahari people with other groups in the region go back a thousand years or more. Also, there is evidence of pastoral economies for as long a period, together with social and economic differentiation (1989:64–75). By the nineteenth century the area was being integrated in the European trade routes for ivory, feathers and cattle: 'San participation in the rapidly expanding mercantile economy was by no means limited to the role of guide ... they became probably the principal producers of both ivory and feathers as well as pelts' (Wilmsen 1989:119, 121). At the same time, Tswana polities were achieving domination throughout the Kalahari and structuring new forms of differentiation. Wilmsen points to the fact that the impression of remoteness might have been a result of the collapse of the ivory trade and the rinderpest that wiped out most cattle at the end of the nineteenth century, together with the local decrease in labour demand (1989:123–7, 133, 157).

On the other hand, Wilmsen points to the fundamental flaw of understanding social relations as the egalitarian result of energy flows. He points at the differentiation existing in the present (1975–80) among Zhu (San) homesteads and how it is related to local land tenure rights favouring people with the longest history of residence which, in turn, is a result of kinship relationships and alliance strategies. This differentiation is expressed in the varying capacities of homesteads and individuals within them to access not only foraging and hunting resources, but also livestock, horses, rifles and employment for wages as well as subsequent investment in stockholding (1989:195–271). Thus:

The assumption that resources are readily available to all Zhu under projected conditions of equality is inappropriate to the actual conditions of stratification that are a salient feature of Zhu social relations. (1989: 254)

Moreover:

advantage is thus acquired through historically mediated advantageous political position in place, which allows hereditary owners to appropriate economic opportunities for themselves to the nearly complete exclusion not only of nonkin but of collateral rivals as well. (1989: 255–6)

Wilmsen's critique shows that an ecological perspective should always be part of the wider framework of relations of production: that is, access to resources and the distribution of power. Moreover, the environment should not be taken as an ahistorical given. History is inscribed in the environment. Past relations between individuals, groups, communities and larger polities are expressed in the environment and in turn become elements constricting future relations.

TECHNOLOGICAL PROCESSES

Instruments; knowledge; operative chains

Often, in a naive but misleading way, speaking of a society's technological achievement assumes that technology is a device evenly and homogeneously diffused through society. This is seldom so, however. The way in which technologies are put to use in different societies tells us about the social organisation of production, and more generally about the social relations within which people have to manage their livelihood.

Technology is not only a material instrument or even an intellectual device but also a social process. We should think of *technological processes* as including various instruments, knowledge and people (human energy) articulated in space and time in sequences which are under the control of particular individuals or groups at different points in the total process.

Instruments are the semantic core of our concept of technology, yet they are inseparable from human knowledge. Knowledge is necessary when conceiving the use and design of an instrument; when materially creating the instrument (knowledge of the material's resistance, of efficient movements ...) and when using any instrument, for there is no 'natural' use of even the simplest axe.

The aim of a concrete technological process is obtaining and/or transforming a specific product. In the process several instruments might be used by one or more people. The use of an instrument requires the knowledge of several minute movements coordinated in time. Each specific movement can be described as a *technical action* which must be learnt and mastered. Several technical actions are coordinated towards a significant qualitative result, such as drilling a hole. This is described as a *technical sequence*. In turn, several technical sequences are articulated in an *operative chain* that leads to the completion of a production stage. Generally, the technological process leading to the desired end-product is the sum of a number of operative chains where different people cooperate, spending their energy in different technical sequences and mastering the necessary knowledge to keep the process going (Balfet 1975). It is interesting to note that specific characteristics of the primary produce or raw material being processed might narrowly condition certain aspects of the technological process (Narotzky 1988c). This will result in stressing as particularly crucial certain points in the operative chains. Moreover, variations in the primary produce or raw material will probably affect the technological process attached to it. For example, the level in the soil where a mineral is to be found in a specific location, as well as the distinct qualities of the various minerals that provide coal, will determine concrete differences in the technological processes of extraction. This, in turn, will affect the organisation of production and the relations of production in the mine.

In the olive oil producing community of rural Catalonia (Spain) where I did fieldwork, the ripening cycle of the olive is important in order to understand some technical constraints of production that have economic and social consequences. The quality of the oil obtained and therefore its price in the market is related to the different moments when the olive is harvested and processed. Olives are ready to harvest at the end of November and the harvest generally ends in January or February but it can extend up to March. During this period olives can be classified in four different categories:

(1) Olives are still green; their output of oil is less and the flavour is bitter and spoils its quality.
(2) The fruit is ripe with its oil content at its maximum.
(3) The fruit is over-ripe, has a greater fat content but less oil; it loses water and may suffer from frost. All of this negatively affects the flavour of the oil.
(4) Olives picked from the ground make the last category; the fruit is usually spoiled and this contributes to fermentation, which results in a higher degree of acidity in the oil and therefore lower market value.

After the harvest, lengthy storage in sacks should also be avoided because it accelerates the fermentation process. In order to avoid storage and its negative consequences, the rhythm of oil production at the oil mill where olives are ground and pressed, should be continuous and in accordance with that of collection.

The degree of control over the oil mill will, then, be a crucial element in the setting of production relations in the area. At the turn of the century a few private oil mill owners had a monopsony over all the olive crop produced in the area (that is, were the sole buyers). Small and medium landowners, as well as sharecroppers, had to sell their olives to the mill owners at whatever price they were willing to pay. Also, small landowners who worked as day labourers for large, mill-owning, landowners had to delay their own harvest until after their employer's crop was harvested. Their olives were by then over-ripe or on the ground and fetched very low prices. Medium landowners, on the other hand, had enough production to remain independent, but were barred from the oil market where profits could be obtained, and instead were forced to sell olives at monopsony prices to mill owners. In order to bypass the control that oil mills had over the production process and the oil market, medium landowners founded an oil mill cooperative in 1914. They were then fully integrated in capitalist market relations as independent producers of the marketable commodity, oil.

Ownership of the oil mill, the means of transforming olives into a marketable commodity, was therefore fundamental. It determined relations of production in the wider frame of a capitalist market economy. It established the mill owner as the only one who had control over the product of labour, regardless of whether land was or was not his property. He decided how much to pay the producers according to 'quality' standards based on the ripening cycle of the olive and the time of storage it had endured before being brought to the mill. To the extent that independent peasants' production was captive in the local product market for olives, the producer's labour was 'dependent' labour in regard to the oil mill owners (Narotzky 1989).

The loci of control: the ownership of instruments, the transmission of knowledge; the design of the labour process

Technology, then, is a complex process combining resources, human beings, their labour knowledge and instruments in an articulated relationship. The technological process expresses in many ways the social organisation of a society. Instruments, for example, may be easy or difficult to manufacture, and this may be done individually or cooperatively; they may be circulated among exchange partners, or at ceremonial occasions, etc. Instruments in and of themselves embody a wide set of social relations. When part of a technological process, instruments are important points where control might be exercised. There are two basic means of control: ownership of the instrument and knowledge of its use. Both might or might not be attributes of the same people, both express power over different aspects of the production process. Moreover, within a specific technological process, different instruments will probably be controlled in different ways by different people. Crucial points in the operative chains, those that significantly compromise the outcome of the total process, will usually concentrate more power. Thus, for example, a mill might be owned by a cooperative but knowledge of its use might be the privilege of an individual, a 'specialist'. Then, although the rights of access to the mill are shared among co-owners, they all depend for the transformation of their produce on the individual who controls the knowledge of its use.

Ownership of instruments falls into two basic categories which in turn have many variations, all of them with significant consequences for the relations of production. Instrument ownership is either private – when access is *restricted* to a particular person or group of people – or common – when access is *open* to all the members of a community. However, the degree of institutionalisation of ownership varies among societies. Some have very fuzzy definitions of ownership, others have punctilious and explicit regulations. Within societies, moreover, it may vary according to the importance of specific instruments in concrete technological processes. Also, the same instrument may be 'owned' in different ways by different people. This happens for example where use rights are distinct from property rights whether explicitly or implicitly.

Knowledge is the other crucial factor in the control of instruments. On the one hand knowledge can be 'owned' to the exclusion of others, or it can be widely shared within a society. On the other hand, *de facto* knowledge must be distinguished from *socially recognised* knowledge. The way in which transmission of knowledge is effected expresses social relations in a society. And the effective control of knowledge is the battlefield of many conflicts concerning relations of production. The use knowledge of a loom, for instance, can be shared in some societies by all men and women without distinction, whereas in other societies only men will know how to use it, and in yet another society just a small group of artisans following very strict apprenticeship regulations will be allowed into use privileges, and will occupy positions along a hierarchy of knowledge grades which in turn might influence their capacity for owning certain instruments.

Transmission of the knowledge needed to operate instruments can be realised in a continuum spanning from very formal to very casual ways. Generally, the more casual the transmission the more open is the access to knowledge; the more formal, the more restricted. Not infrequently, similar knowledge is transmitted in different ways within different social institutions, and this will affect the *social value* of knowledge, which may in turn be expressed in the market value of that knowledge (in societies where the market institution is hegemonic). The knowledge mastered by girls who are taught by their mothers at home how to design, make and cut patterns, mount and sew garment pieces, might probably be very similar to that mastered by young male apprentices formally learning in a tailor shop. The latter, however, may receive social recognition for their knowledge while the former may be considered socially devoid of knowledge. It is interesting to note, as feminist scholars have done, that knowledge transmitted within the family in an informal way, is generally *not* recognised as added qualification but is instead subsumed under *natural* qualities, for example, aptitude for monotonous work or 'nimble fingers' dexterity for girls in most societies (Phillips and Taylor 1980; Elson and Pearson 1981). Much of the knowledge women acquire in the domestic group from a very early age through training in household chores and abilities such as cooking, cleaning, caring for the young, ironing, sewing, etc. are of this type. These qualifications are naturalised and cannot be valued as skills in the market. Therefore, although much of the employment offered to women specifically requires such knowledge and training (service and health care jobs, apparel or electronic industry, etc.), women enter into the market labelled as 'unskilled' labour.

Ownership of the instruments needed in a technological process and knowledge of their use are important assets in the control of the production process. Yet it is interesting to keep in mind that different people may hold these *loci* of power and this will cause *conflict* over the control of the labour process. Taylor, the proponent of Taylorism or scientific management which was set as the model for the organisation of production in industrial manufacturing at the beginning of the twentieth century, clearly points to the problem affecting factories in those times: workers had thorough knowledge of the instruments they used and of the overall labour process. This gave them the power to control production rates and production quality on the shopfloor. Moreover, technological and organisational improvements of the labour process rested mainly in their hands (Taylor 1970 [1911]; Braverman 1974). In this situation, resistance against owners and managers' interests was easier to effect. Scientific management wanted to counter these problems by expropriating workers from their knowledge, transferring it all to management. Without the knowledge, workers would be devoid of power and would become mere 'hands': human energy.

However, even when workers retain some knowledge, this is forced into the framework of a specific *design of the labour process*. Those who control this aspect of the production process have the key to overall control. For some labour processes, design might be of an immediate character, largely dependent on environmental conditions, with little planing and great flexibility: this is mostly the case with foraging where, moreover, instruments and knowledge are widely available for most members of a group, although sometimes with distinctions along gender lines or around differential access to resources. A certain capacity to design the labour process might be mastered by a recurrently successful hunter or by older women whose extended experience of local resource variation is an acquired knowledge yet to be mastered by younger gatherers. Greater control might be in the hands of the 'owners' of land resources, those with the longest recorded residence (Wilmsen 1989). This will undoubtedly give some power to those able to control, however fleetingly, the design of the labour process. This circumstantial control and power will rarely become institutionalised but might increase differentiation and will probably influence the possibility of getting access to a wider range of resources.

The design of classical industrial labour processes, on the other hand, requires the articulation of cooperation in a highly hierarchical and rigid – stable and predictable – manner. Although recently 'flex-ibilisation' of labour processes is being proposed this rarely eliminates a rigid control hierarchy. Therefore, how the technological process is to be organised, which technical sequence precedes another, which activities might be carried out in parallel, which part of the process sets the pace for the rest and so on, are crucial matters. In turn, these might shape control nodes of foremen, production department managers, etc. More generally, the aim is to set work activities in a strictly predefined framework controlled by management. Labour capacity and autonomy is therefore restricted from the outset by its ascription to specifically predefined sequences in the technological process. It is also defined as 'skilled' or 'unskilled' not so much according to its inherent capabilities but according to its position in the technological process.

The question of 'skill'

'Skill' is the *socially recognised* knowledge incorporated in labour. It is knowledge about the use of instruments. Managerial knowledge is spoken of as 'qualification'. There is always something manual in the common use of the term 'skill'. The concept in fact derives from medieval artisanal organisation of production, where progressive mastery of 'skill' – general knowledge of the labour process – was the key to the hierarchical institutional power of the guilds. *Ownership of skill* was thus not only the knowledge mastered but the institutional assessment of the achievement of a certain predefined category within social relations of production. It differentiated workers along institutionalised knowledge categories. It also established solidarities among those sharing the same 'skill' status, therefore sharing an equivalent position in relations of production. 'Ownership of skill' was, during the nineteenth century, the core ideological concept used by workers to organise the first unions. Only after the Taylorist battle to expropriate 'skill' from workers did other concepts for the organisation of solidarity acquire force.

Specific and general knowledge of the labour process is different from the concept of 'skill' as it is used by economists, sociologists and policy makers. While the former is merely descriptive of technical capacities, the latter implies the institutional acknowledgement of technical capacities. Without the latter, the social and economic valuation of technical capacities is hampered. The acknowledgement of technical capacities is not homogeneous in a society, however. It expresses lines of struggle over social relations of production. In Western industrial societies, for example, workers might recognise technical capacities of fellow workers, might institutionalise social rituals and sanctions which explicitly attribute specific knowledge categories, while management and capitalists deny any 'skill' to those workers' activities. Male workers might acknowledge 'skill' in the technical activity of fellow male workers while denying it for the same activity to female workers. The state might recognise 'skill' formally acquired in any licensed institution while employers might deny 'skill' to those having learned in some of those schools. We must therefore pay attention to the fact that 'skill' is not an 'objective' quality incorporated in labour, but that it expresses the struggle over the access to and value of knowledge as a means of production. Indeed, the construction of power relations in the labour process is often expressed in the language of 'skill'.

An interesting consequence is that only 'skill' can be 'owned', only 'skill' is 'capital' – as in the 'human capital' concept. Only 'skill', in market societies, has exchange value. This is important to bear in mind when thinking about the 'skilled'/'unskilled' opposition that segments the labour market and guides government policies and union strategies. We must ask ourselves: whose categories of 'skill' are being used, and how do they relate to the social relations of production at work? Are those deprived of 'skill' deprived of acquired technical capacities necessary to fulfil the activities demanded of them? Is 'skill' being used as an ideological arena in the struggle to set forth definite material relations of production? The dialectics of 'skill' are at once ideological and material, and therefore crucial to the understanding of the social relations of production. However, 'skill' can only be a valuable conceptual tool if clearly distinguished from technical capacities and specific and general knowledge of a labour process.

ACCESS TO RESOURCES

Differential access to space, technology, energy sources; cooperation vs. competition

Access to resources is the main factor determining the organisation of production. It sets the stage for specific relations of production between those participating in a production process. In any society we will find distinctions as to who has rights over one resource or another.

Generally, there is not a consistent and single pattern of access to different resources. Land, for example, might be appropriated in different ways for different uses, as when private cereal parcels are open to communal use as animal fodder after harvest, or when private olive groves are open to anyone in the community for the collection of olives fallen and left on the ground. Also, full property rights might be distinct from use-rights, as when a surviving spouse holds use-rights to the deceased's property although full property rights have been transferred to the children. On the other hand, different resources necessary to the production process might be appropriated by different people, who might then hold distinct power positions in reference to the organisation of production and to the implementation of diverging strategies within it.

The way in which access to space – land, sea, air – and the resources within it are organised in a society expresses the relations of production present in that society. There are four main ways in which resources are appropriated.

First, *free access* refers to that situation in which there are no rules governing the use of a resource and no restriction to its access. Air is presently such a resource and the attempt to regulate its use by international organisations is meeting with widespread resistance. Deep sea fisheries used to be another such resource, but their use and access has been increasingly regulated by international committees.

Second, *private property* refers to the restriction of rights of access to an individual or a group of individuals – that is, a corporation. Rights are alienable and transferable without limitation by those holding them. The state, however, might set general rules impinging on the absolute rights to the use and transfer of private property, setting therefore a legal framework to which private property must conform. On the other hand, use-rights are not coterminous with full property rights and should be distinguished. They can be transferred following diverging lines. Use-rights are different from full rights of alienation, and both might be privately held and transferred by one and the same or by distinct individuals or groups. Agricultural land in many societies is presently held as private property, and so are most of the instruments and facilities used in industrial production in Western market societies.

Third, *communal property* refers to the regulation of the access to and use of a resource by a community, and should be clearly distinguished from free access. Rights over a resource are collectively assigned and the main restrictive factor is definition of the rules of inclusion in the community. 'Belonging' to the community is generally based on criteria such as effective or putative kinship ties to long-standing members, residence and other ideological references to space such as filiation with sacred lineages and shrines, etc. The application of these diverse criteria of membership will in many cases result in a clear differentiation and hierarchisation of community members, and this in turn will affect their power to regulate the communal access to resources, and probably also their effective right of access to those resources. Communal property is open to the members of a community under specific regulations. It is generally inalienable because, ultimately, property rights are ascribed to an atemporal and transcendent group of people, while physical individuals hold only use-rights. Although differentiation must not be excluded when communal property is said to be present, collective regulations of access and use of resources and strategic manipulation of community membership criteria by individuals and/or domestic groups tend to the equalisation of use-rights among community residents. Rights over pasture land in pastoral and mountain communities are often described as communal property. Such is also the case of agricultural land and coastal fisheries in many societies.

Fourth, *state property* refers to resources over which the state holds and regulates access and use-rights. Many of these resources are managed for public use under certain conditions – such is the case with tap water, roads, public gardens, etc. Others are managed as 'private' enterprises belonging to the state 'corporation', with profits and losses affecting the state budget and only indirectly the citizens' livelihood. Still others are transferred as concessions that grant to a private individual, a corporation or a community, the privileges of use-rights and exploitation of the resource.

These four main ways of appropriation of resources must be considered an abstract typology serving as a guide towards the understanding of the complex systems formally and informally regulating access to resources. Several factors should be taken into account, moreover. These forms of access are not exclusive, and in most societies several systems will coexist. Many societies do not have any 'property' concept equivalent, and regulation of access to and use of resources may be blurred, and may alter according to such variables as group size, environmental conditions, etc. Also, different people – individuals, corporations, communities, the state, etc. – might hold

different access and use-rights over the *same* resource. The multiplicity
of regulated and unregulated, explicit and implicit, formal and informal,
modes of access and exclusion to resources sets the arena for conflict
and cooperation among individuals and groups in the context of
changing historical circumstances.

The Indian tribes around the Great Lakes in North America present
an interesting example of the historical transformation of a mainly
communal access to resources into a basically restrictive access in
relation to specific resources. Before the penetration of the fur trade
(eighteenth century), these tribes had a pattern of individual or family
hunting of caribou in the winter, when this animal tended towards
dispersion and solitary pasturing. In spring and early summer and
autumn, when caribou and salmon migrated in large groups, collective
hunting and fishing was practised. And again, a more autonomous,
dispersed, domestic group pattern of resource use occurred in summer,
when edible vegetables and berries as well as various animal species
were widespread and plentiful. Access to resources located in the area
where the tribe ranged were open to members and visiting residents,
range borders were blurred, and cooperation – not competition –
amongst smaller or larger groups expressed the unrestricted relationship
to resources. With the penetration and extension of the fur trade,
commercial deals were individually arranged with the European trader.
As a result, individual hunters competed against each other for fur
animals, and access to fur animals became restricted within a clearly
bounded family hunting land. It is interesting to note that this restriction
of access affected only fur animals for the trade and that communal
patterns persisted for subsistence matters (Wolf 1982; Leacock 1978).

Agents and means of production; the construction of divisions of labour

Space, technology and energy sources when geared towards obtaining
a specific output or product, are *means of production*. We should not
forget that labour, the intelligent application of human effort, is
undoubtedly the most crucial element in the process of production.
The knowledge and energy in labour are essential to any production
process, whether we focus on the material aspects of the technological
process or on the social aspects of the relations of production.

Social relations of production are the purposeful organisation by human individuals or groups, of labour, land and instruments with the aim of producing a specific output. Access and control over the means of production and the diverse forms of cooperation or resistance structure the relations of production. Various coercive or consensual methods of compliance with a predefined labour process might be at work. Indeed, individual or collective interests might be driven at through real or fictive ascription to the aims of those dominating the production process, or through challenge and conflict aiming at transforming the production structure.

Differential access to resources takes on a particular meaning when considered from the viewpoint of the production process which involves concrete people situated in different relations with regard to the means of production. This perspective creates a model highlighting production as the crucial process engendering the structure of societies. This model stems from Marx's writings, and stresses the basic need, for all societies, to organise the means for material subsistence. Although interesting critiques have transformed and enriched this position (as we will see in the following chapters), production remains the most telling process for the understanding of the 'economic' questions structuring social relations.

Access to the land, labour and instruments necessary in a production process might be appropriated freely, or communally, or privately, or by the state, in the explicit, implicit or blurred manner we have described, with the frequent superimposing of various different rights over the same resource. Differential control of the means of production by particular individuals defines the distribution of power along the process – the capacity to make and carry out decisions concerning the process, the ability to forward particular interests, etc. – as well as the issues over which friction and conflict are more likely to occur. Access and control of labour might be attained through the use and manipulation of real and fictive kinship ties enabling elders in a pastoral lineage society, for example, to use the labour power of younger members (Meillassoux 1982 [1975], 1978). Control of labour is generally associated with exclusive control over some crucial resource, such as water, land or information.

Peasant domestic groups in Western societies such as rural Catalonia, for instance, might separate transmission of property and use-rights over land. In Catalonia the son/daughter inheriting property at marriage does not have use-rights, and therefore full control, until both his/her parents are dead. A man's labour (that of the son or the daughter's husband) is therefore tied to the land by a legacy which does not yield decision-making capacities until many years later. Informally, however, the heir's responsibility for direct control of the labour process increases as his father's energy and abilities are affected by old age. Non-inheriting siblings are excluded from any position of control, except maybe those directly referring to their specific knowledge of the technological process. Their labour is controlled by those owning the means of production but it is not tied into the structure of the production process. Migration in search of better labour opportunities is a very frequent strategy for those deprived of inheritance rights over land. In this situation, conflict arises between those holding use-rights vs. those holding property rights (father/heir); and between those holding some rights vs. those holding none in the same generation (heir/siblings), especially when no alternative income opportunities are available. Power and conflict arising from differential control over the means of production are clear in this example (Narotzky 1989, 1991).

In most societies some sort of division of labour is embedded within the general organisation of society and is legitimated and reinforced by ideological and cultural constructs. Gender and age criteria for the construction of divisions of labour are widespread: women are meant to do certain things and not others, while men are also channelled and restricted in their range of activities; young men/women are banned from doing some jobs which are restricted to older people. Legitimation is often based on the naturalisation of specific chores: for instance, because women give birth and breast-feed, they are 'naturally' meant to clean, cook, take care of older children and adults, etc.; older people have lived longer and therefore have more experience, knowledge and information to make important decisions, whilst younger people are physically stronger and can do the hard work. Although undoubtedly women give birth and breast-feed, older people have lived longer and younger ones are generally fitter, the use of generic criteria to construct divisions of labour is *always* a *social*, not a natural, creation. For, even if all women give birth, not all of them breast-feed. Substitutes for breast-feeding are available in many societies. Not all women give birth and, moreover, the life cycle of any woman has fertile and unfertile periods. Often, the chain of logic is faulty and there are non sequiturs, as when sedentariness, cleaning and cooking are deduced from birthing and breast-feeding. Therefore the extension of specific, socially circumscribed attributes, to an abstract general category of people should not be taken as the description of 'natural' or universal 'characteristics' inherent in these categories. Rather, they should themselves be seen as the expression of social and political forces within the realm of discourse and culture. These ideological constructs can become dominant and ingrained in a society to the point of being accepted as 'natural' by those affected by them. But we must try to unveil how these constructs are negotiated, effected, resisted and transformed by the groups of people situated at different points in the structure of a given society, placed within different cultural and material fields of force.

The division of labour is generally conceived as a set of criteria homogeneously affecting the total organisation of a society in its productive and reproductive endeavours, in its material as well as in its cultural aspects. Originally, it is a functionalist concept developed by Durkheim linking work specialisation to the 'integration of the social body' (1933:60–2):

It is possible that the economic utility of the division of labour may have a hand in this, but in any case, it passes far beyond purely economic interests, for it consists in the establishment of a social and moral order *sui generis*. Through it, individuals are linked to one another. Without it, they would be independent, instead of developing separately, they pool their efforts. They are solidary... (Durkheim 1933:61)

The concept is interesting because it is broad and considers as 'labour' a number of activities which are not directly part of the production process, such as domestic work. However, the homogeneous projection of these 'divisions of labour' as constituting the core structure of society as a whole, tends to overlook, or render 'exceptional' differentiation *within* these broadly organisational 'divisions'.

The 'division of labour' concept also refers to specific production processes and the assigning of individuals or groups to positions within the process. Cooperation is needed between individuals or groups in charge of different parts of a given production process, in order to articulate and complete the process. The contribution of effort into a specific production process might be delivered willingly or may be forced, or there may be a combination of both elements. 'Need', the urge to get hold of subsistence goods, is an example where compliance depends on a lack of alternatives (that is, force) but is generally perceived as an autonomous, free and voluntary decision.

Forms of control over the means of production – whether land, labour, instruments, knowledge or 'skill' – will be determining factors in the designation of particular individuals or groups in the 'division of labour' and in the greater or lesser constraints over the effective contribution of work effort into the production process. Hierarchical or horizontal forms of cooperation might be devised according to the structure of the 'division of labour' in the production process and according to the power attributed to those occupying certain positions within it. These 'divisions of labour' will also tend to be sustained through ideological discourses by those holding positions of power, and attempts to challenge and subvert them will rest not only on material but on ideological – cultural and moral – justifications.

Social relations of production; the labour process; regulation and the state

The *organisation of production* is the analytical unit referring to the entire production process leading to a desired product. It generally comprises several distinct units of production articulated as a working totality but internally organised in an autonomous or semi-autonomous manner. The organisation of production of, say, motor vehicles, should take into account all production processes and units related with the end product, including mineral extraction at one end and marketing systems at the other. This global perspective is necessary if we want to understand the social relations of production at work in the particular production units, in the entire production process and in the economic system as a whole. Therefore the study of subcontracting networks, of trade agreements with suppliers of production inputs, of specific state regulations affecting production in any part of the global process is extremely important. However, the detailed analysis of the units of production articulated in the total process is also important to the comprehension of social relations of production. A *unit of production* might be defined as the space where organised relations of production result in producing a desired output. Space is continuous as in a factory, or discontinuous as when homeworkers are part of decentralised units of production. In each unit of production one or several *labour processes* might take place, and will be organised in a specific manner through the implementation of decision-making capabilities. Moreover, coordination of the different labour processes in a production unit will also have to be managed. Either hierarchical or horizontal decision-making processes are generally used, and in many production units such as some automobile factories, a combination of both systems is present: work groups are supposed to have direct control over the labour process and to arrive at horizontal, consensual decisions about achieving optimal performance and quality. The setting of objectives and the control of labour process remain, however, tied to a hierarchical chain of command that descends down to the work-group 'leader'.

Agricultural production in many societies combines labour processes organised in many different ways. The account given by Malinowski (1977 [1935]) for the Trobriand Islands, for example, shows how general cleaning and preparation of the cultivated area is done in large groups by the whole community under the direction of the magician. Planting, cultivation and further maintenance are done by the domestic group which has been assigned a particular plot by the clan or lineage elder. Work within the domestic group follows a division of labour along gender lines which seems to be related, as Weiner (1976) explains in her study of the Trobriand Islands, to the total – material and symbolic – reproduction process of the society. Production relations are then included in the reproduction of the society as a whole. Finally, the collection of the tubers is done by the entire domestic group, often with the help of extended family members, recruited through networks of reciprocal favours.

Social relations of production result from how cooperation (willing or coerced) and coordination are effected between those contributing in one way or another to the production process. Access to the means of production and its corollaries of control and decision-making power are the main elements in the construction of relations of production. Social relations of production should be observed at the detailed level of the labour process as well as at the general level of the organisation of production. The analysis of the labour process can help us understand the everyday experience of work: how people manage their energy, how they interact in an organised or spontaneous manner, how constraints limit their capacities, how they manoeuvre to enhance their power, how resistance and cooperation are accomplished, how individual and collective interests are constantly being redefined and strategies carried forward or obstructed, etc. Labour recruiting by a factory, for instance, may be achieved at some point through informal networks relying heavily on kinship and targeting specific communities. This will build patronage relationships within the factory while creating clusters of dense 'economic' and 'non-economic' social relations, affecting life in and out of the factory. At another moment, management might try to shift towards a more formal system of recruitment in order to break non-managerial control and power circles. Tamara Hareven (1977b) gives such an example for a New England textile factory at the turn of the century.

Through the analysis of the organisation of production as a whole the social relations observed at the level of the labour process take on a significance affecting the total organisation of the society. The appropriation of the means of production, whether in a fairly open or a more restricted form, will force people to enter the production process in certain positions. Their ability to control production will then be limited accordingly.

Generally, all societies regulate access to crucial means of production such as land and water. Members of the society must comply with defined norms. In many societies, physical force is the warrant of regulations affecting the access to the means of production. Whether privately or publicly controlled and managed, force sets the limits of interpretation and transgression of norms. Hunter-gatherer societies, such as the Kalahari !Kung, seem to have fewer regulations, and then affecting mostly limiting ecological resources, such as water and food. Enforcement is largely carried out through diffuse social pressure and strategic alliance patterns. The need to maintain extended social networks in a context of high environmental variability, however, is balanced against the positive benefits to be gained by some through restricting access to resources (Lee 1979; Wilmsen 1989; Weissner 1982). Nowadays, the politically hegemonic form of the nation-state sets the framework for regulations concerning access to the means of production, as well as for normative enforcement policies (which can be monopolised by the state or shared between public and private means). This, however, does not preclude the existence and operation of autochthonous regulations, locally produced, formal or informal, restricted to areas such as a community or a region. The dominant mode in which access to crucial means of production is regulated and enforced sets a general pattern of relations of production. Private property, or the restriction of access to the means of production, excludes many people from the direct control of their livelihood in its more material aspect, subsistence, and thus *forces* them into specific positions of dependence in the production processes designed and controlled by others.

THE QUESTION OF 'WORK' IN WESTERN SOCIETIES

A problem of definition: beyond 'employment' and 'dependent' relations

Separation from the means of production has excluded many working people from directly earning their livelihood. Dependent wage relations have increased in agriculture and industry as common land and more competitive technologies have been appropriated by private individuals. In Europe, for instance, work relations became more dependent as access to such necessaries of life as firewood, small game hunting, thatching hay, etc. which used to be open to common use, were enclosed and restricted for private use, banning cottagers and day labourers from needed sources of livelihood.

The tendency towards generalisation of dependent wage relations between labour and capital owners has been posited as the mark of contemporary industrial relations of production and, by extension, of social relations of production in Western societies as a whole. At the same time, income has been equated with wages. Obtaining the necessities of life relied, purportedly, on wages provided for those entering into dependent labour relations.

On the other hand economic models have tended to emphasise the production process, while the consumption process, which refers more directly to people's livelihood, has been approached mostly as constituting the demand pole of production. Generally, what people did to secure the necessities of life and to organise the consumption process was considered as an 'economic' question only inasmuch as it pertained to or affected the production process. Therefore *work* as an economic concept in Western societies, came to be strongly related with 'employment' and 'dependent' labour relations.

Economic anthropologists, feminist scholars and, more recently, those studying the 'informal economy', have contributed to a richer and more complex concept of work. Non-Western societies studied by anthropologists such as Malinowski and Firth, had to be approached with a flexible concept of work appropriate to all sorts of activities connected with subsistence and the reproduction of a society as a whole. Domestic work was considered 'work' of equal 'economic' standing. Also, activities such as the maintenance – through ceremonial or ritual activities – of social networks were approached as work from an 'economic' point of view. Indeed, networks have proved to be an important tool in securing labour or other resources at certain points in the annual economic cycle or along the domestic or the individual's life cycle. As anthropologists increasingly turned to the study of more industrialised and industrialising societies, and as they became aware of the articulation of 'Western' and 'primitive' societies – capitalist and pre-capitalist modes of production in Marxist terminology – this openness of the concept of work was generally carried over to their economic perspective.

Feminist scholars have confronted directly the problem of women's work. The economic relevance of invisible work such as housework, and of devalued work such as homework or 'unskilled' service work, has been demonstrated by analysing the material and ideological articulation of such work within the context of social reproduction as a whole. 'Reproductive' activities – including procreation, child care and care of the elderly, consumption organisation and realisation, household maintenance and other domestic chores – have attained a standing parallel to 'productive' activities in feminist economic approaches. Also, the need to see the process of obtaining a livelihood as including both productive and reproductive processes in the context of the state, has become one of the main agendas of feminist research on social relations in Western and non-Western societies.

The awareness of the existence of a large part of production unaccounted for in official statistics has impelled many economists, anthropologists and sociologists working in Third World and Western 'developed' societies towards the study of the 'informal' or 'underground' economies. Much of this informal production follows wage work patterns although labour/capital relations are thickly woven into other 'non-economic' (kinship, friendship, neighbourhood), non-contractual, trust relationships which create a different context for the enforcement of cooperation. Yet other informal economic activities are related not so much to 'production' but to the earning of the necessities of life, whether this means getting a wage for labour, receiving food stamps from the state, building a house, fixing a plug, being helped with child care, cooking or dishwashing, etc. This perspective also expands the meaning of work to include 'reproductive' activities.

This triple strand of research and theoretical writing – anthropological, feminist and informal economy perspectives – has contributed to an understanding of the need to consider work, beyond 'employment' and 'dependent' labour relations, as part of a larger economic field including productive and reproductive social relations in the process of the material reproduction of a society.

Accounting for invisible work; work vs. leisure or work during leisure?

A further problem, once we adopt the larger concept of work, is how to value work that does not enter directly into market relations. Women's housework has been approached time after time in the attempt to deal with the question of value. Two perspectives are generally found: one considers housework as having exchange value – that is, value referred to market transactions; the other maintains it has only use value – that is, value referred to need satisfaction. The debate leads to the question of whether housework can be thought of as generating surplus value – that is, excess value generated by the difference between the value necessary to reproduce the labour power and the value obtained for the goods produced. How can housework have exchange value if it does not respond to supply and demand, or to free market competition? How do we account for sentiments such as love, or other motivations tied to gender identity in the valuation of women's activities? We will enter more fully into the 'domestic labour' debate in another chapter.

The problem of value affects not only women's housework but all other activities which take place outside market exchange but are clearly part of the work necessary to the material reproduction of a society. Such is the case of non-monetary exchanges of labour and voluntary community services. The first case has been very common in small farming and peasant agriculture, where the labour force necessary at certain points of the agricultural cycle was recruited through exchanges of work outside the labour market. Exchanges of work are inserted in 'non-economic', 'non-market' social relations such as friendship or kinship, and have a wide range of application. At one end we can see very 'informal' or 'casual' *help* given without accounting when a close relative is in need. At the other end we have very 'formal', regulated *work* accounted for in work-hours or work-load, sometimes even referred to labour market prices for equivalent activities, but which bypasses the market and monetisation.

In Western societies many of life's necessities are often procured through non-market exchanges of labour: such is the case of habitation – construction and home refurbishing – and infant care. These can be considered as 'reproductive' activities, where the product is directly consumed and thus labour might be said to hold only 'use value'. However, many non-market exchanges of labour are referred for accounting purposes to production for the market, as is often the case in agriculture. And then, the problem of 'exchange value' emerges with force. Work activities in market agriculture also highlight the question of self-employment: is it the work or the product entering the market? Do the energies consumed by the self-employed or small family entrepreneur in the production of a marketable product or service have 'exchange value' or just 'use value'? And, therefore, can surplus value be created and appropriated by capital through market exchange? This brings up the problem of commoditisation of labour, and whether work in capitalist economies can only be exploited through direct market relations. It also stresses that non-market social relations of production based on kinship, friendship or propinquity networks, and on qualities such as trust, affection or mere frequentation, should be analysed as a crucial part of the production processes of market economies.

Moreover, the necessary articulation between production and reproduction re-emerges now in the light of labour/capital relations and the organisation of production as a whole. Take, for instance, voluntary community services and self-provisioning – where labour is only consumed – or direct marketing network strategies – where labour enters market relations. While these are very different activities with distinct moral motivations (altruism, egoism or gain), they share the fact of being carried out in a time–space framework defined by society as non-productive, barely reproductive, or 'leisure'. Therefore they are excluded from the category of 'work'. This marginalised, invisible human effort refers directly to work that contributes to the particular and general well-being of societies' members. Indeed, social services are increasingly provided through voluntary community organisations. Home appliances and maintenance are obtained through

Do-It-Yourself (DIY) activities. And many consumer products (Avon, Tupperware) are marketed through non-professional housewives' networks as a tea-party activity procuring a nest-egg. Not only is this work effort necessary for the reproduction of society as a whole, but concretely for the reproduction of a specific organisation of production, where labour relations in the 'visible' realm of 'production' include and depend on social relations taking place in the 'invisible' realms of 'reproduction' and 'leisure'.

A shift of emphasis: towards the 'means of livelihood' thesis

Social scientists have been increasingly aware that provision of the means of livelihood occurred not only in the connected realms of market production and consumption, but also in the realms of reproduction, leisure and non-market exchanges of goods and services. Many of these scholars perceive this situation as emerging from the breaking down of post-Second World War state economic regulations and the welfare state. They see a general trend towards deregulation and flexibilisation of social relations of production and the transferring of social services to private and communal hands (Pahl 1984; Gershuny and Miles 1985). Thus, personalised, informal, non-market economic relations have expanded to occupy spaces of production (and reproduction) previously covered by market relations and state subsidies. The family, relatives and friends, neighbours and the local community have been stressed as networks of economic relations, covering formal and informal production processes.

Moreover, this awareness has brought about an interesting shift of emphasis in the study of economic processes. The economic organisation of Western societies was structured around production processes taking the market as the nexus between production and personal consumption. The new emphasis, instead, proposes to think about people first, about their ways of earning a livelihood. The 'means of livelihood' theses point out how people manage to get the necessities of life. Formal, market-mediated, economic relations such as employment and informal, non-market systems for getting hold of resources are considered on an equal methodological standing. At the same time, the concept of personal or family income has expanded beyond its usual reference to monetary wages, to include not only goods constituting payments in species still referred to market values, but also transfers of goods and services occurring in a non-market environment referring to values such as friendship and filial solidarity. As a result of this perspective the part of formal, market-mediated, relationships in the livelihood strategies of most people has appeared to shrink dramatically in recent analyses. On the one hand, the weakening of the state's regulation of labour relations – mainly protection and welfare benefits – and the fragmentation of previously integrated production processes (decentralisation, contracting out), has been described as the transformation of Western economies towards a more flexible organisation of production. And this has resulted in greater ambiguity and ambivalence in the definition of labour/capital relations loosely mediated by markets, and therefore of people's work identities. On the other hand, massive unemployment has forced people to seek alternative means of earning a living.

By focusing on how people manage to earn a living, in fact, 'production' has become an epiphenomenon of 'reproduction' processes. Microanalyses of family economies and local social relations have come to the forefront. This perspective is interesting because it uncovers a wide range of non-market 'economic' social relations previously neglected in social science analyses. The 'means of livelihood' framework enriches our understanding of economic processes and focuses on human agents and their everyday social relations in a daily struggle for livelihood.

However, the 'means of livelihood' theses with their emphases on what people do to earn a living, tend to forget that life necessities must be procured in a context where capital accumulation is the driving force organising the material reproduction of most societies. We should then take into account in market as well as non-market-mediated economic relations the constricting force of the drive towards capital accumulation. For example, the rise of DIY furniture manufacture (or in general home refurbishing) has been related, by proponents of a 'means of livelihood' perspective, to an increase in income level capacity for the household at a time when cash is scarce (Pahl 1984), but *not* to the organisation of production in the furniture industry. However, a specific structure of social relations between labour and capital depends on the existence of the DIY consumer market. Capital (that is, furniture firms) extracts surplus value by including future labour in the price of unfinished goods (a table-kit is sold as *a table*), that is, including as labour costs labour which in fact will be realised by the consumer. Thus, the consumer not only does the work himself without being paid for it, but also pays the firm for the work he will have to do (!!). This, however, allows the firm to lower prices and expand the market, to produce standard products (the parts to be assembled) and benefit from economies of 'scale', without forgoing customisation of the final product (by giving customers the possibility of choosing certain combination of parts, colours, etc.) and benefit from economies of 'scope' or small series, customised production. Moreover it transfers responsibility for final product quality to the consumer-worker. Finally, some labour/capital relations in the production process will appear as final consumer/purveyor relations and social relations of production which are exploitative will be subsumed in the 'reproductive' realm of 'self-provisioning', 'means of livelihood' and 'domestic work'.

2 DISTRIBUTION AND EXCHANGE

This chapter explores a region of the 'economy' which, like 'production' has generally been very rigidly defined within tight limits. The purpose of this chapter, then, is to unravel the concepts of 'distribution' and 'exchange' in order to open them to the wider field of forces of social reproduction. The approach will attempt a critique of concepts such as 'reciprocity', the 'market', 'money', 'value', 'embeddedness', etc. This will help to clarify the general use of such terms in anthropological literature. At the same time I will try to show that economic processes should necessarily be conceived as part of a wider set of social relations where meaning – not only matter – is an inescapable aspect of the material conditions of any life-sustaining process. As an example, the last section discusses the controversial argument that a 'market culture' was the crucial element in the construction of a capitalist system in Europe.

FORMS OF RECIPROCITY AND REDISTRIBUTION

Mauss: the gift, a social bond

Distribution is a function of allocation, exchange (or circulation) is a function of movement and substitution. Although analytically distinct, both appear generally as indistinguishable in the movement mediating production and consumption. Together they describe the process by which things produced get into the hands of the final consumers. However, many objects are not consumed in the sense that they are destroyed during a final use; many objects are entangled in processes of 'consumption' with the aim of creating and recreating social bonds through continuing transactions. In both cases, transactions are the movement of products between people and generally some kind of transformation of their meaning arises during the process. Things acquire meaning because they embody social relations of production and because they produce and reproduce social relations during distribution.

Marcel Mauss was a French sociologist and anthropologist, and a disciple of Emile Durkheim. In 1923–4, he wrote an essay on *The Gift: The Form and Reason of Exchange in Archaic Societies* (1990 [1923–4]) which had a lasting influence in economic anthropology. The origin of his study was his interest in contracts, in the nature of the bond that constitutes human transactions, together with his interest in exchange. Thus from the start both material and moral aspects formed the core of his research. He used the comparative method ranging from 'primitive' contemporary societies such as Melanesian and Polynesian or American west coast groups, to Ancient European societies. Mauss tried to explain, first, why the gift created an obligation to be returned: what was the norm of right and interest (moral and material) that engaged the recipient in a reciprocal transaction, and, second, what in the object enforced reciprocating action. The gift appeared as a form of transaction very different to the acts of exchange taking place in our society. Indeed, in Western contemporary societies, people appeared separated from their social context and confronted as individuals during transactions; things were severed from people in an autonomous realm of exchange.

In Mauss's analysis, the gift appeared as a 'transitional' form of exchange placed between *total prestations* (as in the west coast potlatch where the social group as a whole is involved in a phenomenon embracing religious, economic and social intent) and the 'pure individual contract' existing in market systems. Thus the gift form appears in an evolutionary framework of exchange forms, although Mauss points that the moral and economic entanglement associated with it is 'still constantly at work today in our societies in an underlying way ...'. In the gift, as in total prestations, things and persons are intertwined and reciprocally constitutive of their values. In total prestations, moreover, all the realms of society are reproduced simultaneously through the transaction.

The analysis of the gift transaction describes three 'obligations' associated with it: to give, to receive, to return. However, the particularity of the gift in Mauss's view, as opposed to other forms of exchange, is that apparently voluntary and disinterested acts of generosity involving the transfer of goods are in fact to be seen in the context of social constraints that make giving, as well as receiving and returning the gift, into an obligation. But what is the nature of the constraint? Two hypotheses are offered: first, that the social relations existing between people are expressed in the material bonding of the gift; second, that the material object transferred as a gift embodies in such a way the person(s) of its previous holder(s) that it pulls back toward the giver and creates a return-gift field of force. On the one hand, the gift is based on symmetrical norms regulating transfer movements: giving–receiving and returning–receiving. This symmetry is defined as *reciprocity*. On the other hand, the force that impels the movement is based on the nature of the gift where things and people, material relations and social (and spiritual) relations cannot be dissociated. Speaking of the *kula* exchange in the Trobriand Islands (the best example of gift transactions), Mauss writes: 'Sociologically, it is once again the mixture of things, values, contracts and men that is expressed' (1990:26). As a result the *kula* gift valuables create and transfer a multiplicity of rights of different people over one object, while the circulation of the gift object produces and embodies social bonds which define its value.

In contrast to societies where the gift system of exchange is a core institution (although not an exclusive one as the Trobriand example shows, for the exchange of 'valuables' occurs in the context of other types of exchange such as barter) our Western societies are based on a clear dissociation between people and things which is reflected in law in the distinction between *real* rights (over things) and *personal* rights (between people) (see also Durkheim 1933:115–25; Gregory 1982). For Mauss 'Such a separation is basic: it constitutes the essential condition for a part of our system of property, transfer and exchange' (1990:47).

Generalised, balanced, negative reciprocity and social distance

Malinowski had in 1922 described the 'mutual exchange of gifts' between partners belonging to different communities and tied by the institution of the *kula* ceremonial exchange of valuables. He had also described different forms of exchange, of gifts and counter-gifts, giving a typology including 'pure gifts', 'customary payments, repaid irregularly and without strict equivalence', 'payment for services rendered', 'gifts returned in economically equivalent form', 'Exchanges of material goods against privileges, titles and non-material possessions', 'Ceremonial barter with defined payment' and 'Trade, pure and simple'. He then suggested that 'It will be ... interesting to draw up a scheme of exchanges, classified according to the social relationship to which they correspond' (Malinowski 1961 [1922]: 176–94). Mauss's elaboration of Malinowski's and other ethnographers' descriptions of primitive exchange presented a theory of the gift as the central institution of the primitive exchange systems. His analysis and abstract rendering of the form of this transaction explicitly proposed 'reciprocity' as the actual structure of the exchange: a movement impelled by the social and moral forces binding people and things. From then on, anthropologists studying transactions in non-Western societies increasingly used the concept of reciprocity as particularly suited to economies strongly embedded in the fabric of social life and lacking a generalised market-price system for establishing equivalence of value.

However, specific definition and finer development of the concept did not emerge clearly until the 1960s, mainly through the efforts of Gouldner and Sahlins. Gouldner (1960:170) defined 'a generalised moral norm of reciprocity which defines certain actions and *obligations* as repayments for benefits received'. Moreover, the *value* of the benefit received and thus of the obligation incurred is related to 'the recipient's need at the time the benefit was bestowed, the resources of the donor, the motives imputed to the donor, and the nature of the constraints which are perceived to exist or to be absent' (1960:171). Reciprocity, then, is defined as a *moral norm* structuring the giving and returning of *help*: 'If you want to be helped by others you must help them' (1960:173). Two variables are important in the discussion of reciprocity: *equivalence of value* as defined by those involved in the transaction; and *time* elapsed between gift and return movements.

Following the insights in Malinowski's Trobriand exchange typology and its correspondence with social relationships, Sahlins (1965) puts forward three main types of reciprocity which he then associates with *social distance*, that is, the distance between people according to their location in the social structure of the tribe. His proposal is meant for lineage tribal societies such as that described by Evans-Pritchard, in *The Nuer* (1940), but has in fact been used as a universal typology of reciprocity forms. In *generalised reciprocity* equivalence of value is not stipulated. Need of the recipient seems to be the impelling force setting the transfer's movement and content, in a context where the moral norm of reciprocity is very strong – within the closely knit social fabric of the domestic group, or the small local community. Help is given and is expected if need arises, but there is not a one-to-one relation between gift and return movements, nor between value of goods transferred. Also, time between transfers in opposite directions is undetermined and need is once again the basic criteria for returning past help. Generalised reciprocity describes transfers in a social context where people are all more or less in debt with each other. In fact the ambiguity and indeterminacy of transfers strengthens the social obligation and subsumes material interest to it. In this context giving is always returning some help received some time by someone close. Following Sahlins's typology, generalised reciprocity is associated with the closest kinship and spatial relations, that is, with the minimum social distance: the domestic group and the local lineage segment. Gouldner had previously suggested that generalised social indebtedness might be a function of the reciprocity norm: by delaying repayment and inhibiting complete equivalence reciprocity generates stability in the social system. In generalised reciprocity, moreover, goods are entangled in the social fabric in such a way that they appear as extensions of personal obligations and never seem to acquire the autonomy necessary for establishing equivalences of value.

Balanced reciprocity takes place in a less closely knit social ground where social ties are clearly distinct from material interests. Transfers of goods are therefore regulated by exchange partners as to the equivalence of value and the delay admitted for the return movement. Following Malinowski's description of 'gifts returned in economically equivalent form', Service (1966) defines the '"perfect type" of balanced reciprocity' as 'a simultaneous exchange of identical goods'. This sort of immediate and identical exchange, however, seems to stress in fact the creation of symbolic and social ties between individuals or groups *through* material items, although it is the equivalence expressed in the material item's value and the negation of indebtedness that establish the quality of the social bond. Generally, balanced reciprocity is used as a concept describing exchanges where give and return movements must compensate each other within a specific time frame. The material aspect of the transaction is still embedded in social relationships and frequently appears as a medium through which social bonds are produced and reproduced, but it is not subsumed by them. Transfer movements might result from material interests or social bonds, but are always closed give–receive/return–receive transactions that must be completed. Several such transactions might be conducted recurrently by the same actors, articulating different balanced reciprocity exchanges in a continuous and long-lasting social relationship. Such is the case of 'exchange partners' in many tribal societies. According to Sahlins, balanced reciprocity is associated with medium range social distance: distant kin, non-local tribe members, people who are situated at an intermediate social distance within the kinship and political organisation of lineage tribal societies.

Negative reciprocity prevails where social distance is greater and material interest is the sole motive of the transaction. Typical examples are theft, swindle, bargaining, where the negative social relation is a direct result of the material gain obtained by the opposing party. Transfers are initiated by a 'taking' not a 'giving' movement and are deemed completed when the goods sought are obtained. In its strongest forms such as war plunder it is a unilateral transfer. In milder forms such as bargaining, the opposing parties try to 'take' as much as possible. Negative reciprocity transfers might be 'returned' by the previous losers in a symmetrical but likewise independent and unilateral movement, 'taking revenge'. However, as in generalised reciprocity, negative reciprocity might involve recurrent transfers in the same direction without any predictable 'return' movement. Such is the case of colonial exploitation of resources by the metropolitan nations. Although material gain is the basis of negative reciprocity, it is also embedded in social relations. Enemies, competitors, colonial subjects are bound by social ties whose laxity – such as in bargaining – or negative intensity – such as in political antagonism and violent confrontation – are the ground that enable material interests to express themselves in an unbridled and dangerous manner.

Redistributive systems: Polanyi's typology and the integration of the economic process

Polanyi's (1957) contribution to economic anthropology is rooted in his definition of the concept of 'economic', where he distinguishes two separate meanings: *real* (or *substantive*) and *formal*. The first derives from empirical observation and refers to the relationships that human groups establish with their natural and social environment in order to provide material goods or services. The second derives from a general logic of rational action implying explicit ends and delimited means and the allocation of scarce resources between alternative uses. The formal meaning of 'economic' only coincides with the real meaning in market integrated societies, that is where 'the institutional complex which integrates the system ... is the supply–demand price mechanism working through a national network of labour, resource and product markets' (Dalton 1971b [1961]). All societies, however, give *unity* and *stability* to the *real* economic activity through which material goods and services are continuously provided. Interdependent and recurrent movements for the use of natural resources and the organisation of human cooperation form a structure that integrates economic processes in every society. This is defined by Polanyi (1957) as the *institutionalisation* of economic activity and it will follow different patterns of integration in different societies. According to Polanyi, who compares a wide range of past and present societies, three main patterns integrate the economies: *reciprocity*, *redistribution* and *exchange*.

Reciprocity as an integrative pattern of economic processes occurs in societies where given symmetrical structures – such as kinship moieties – organise movements between a group of people. *Redistribution* defines movements going first towards a central point and being distributed to diverging points from there. This pattern appears in societies with a centralised political structure such as chiefdoms, kingdoms, etc., where goods and services flow towards the centre through tribute or kinship obligations and are redistributed in feasts, during work parties or whenever there is a need to consolidate the power structure. It is important to keep in mind that these patterns of economic activity do not concern only the distribution of products but also production and the allocation of labour. For example, an elaborate division of labour such as that existing in the ancient kingdoms and empires of China, India, Peru, was possible because of the mechanism of redistribution (Polanyi 1971 [1944]):

These instances show that redistribution also tends to enmesh the economic system proper in social relationships. ... The production and distribution of goods is organised in the main through collection, storage, and redistribution, the pattern being focused on the chief, the temple, the despot, or the lord. (Polanyi 1971:52)

Exchange for Polanyi has three different applications. First 'the merely locational movement of a "changing of places" between the hands'. Second, a movement of appropriation at a set rate. Third a movement of appropriation at a bargaining rate (1957:254–5). In its second and third meaning, exchange implies the existence of equivalences between the goods and services exchanged. The equivalences can be fixed, regulated by some political instance such as the state, municipal or guild authorities; or they can be regulated by the exclusive dynamic of the market: supply and demand. It is in this last instance alone that the integration of the economy follows a market pattern and that we are confronted with a market system economy. The peculiarity of the market pattern of integration is that it is not structured by a social institution with functions in other realms of society, but by its own specific 'economic' institution: the market.

Ultimately, that is why the control of the economic system by the market is of overwhelming consequence to the whole organisation of society – it means no less than the running of society as an adjunct to the market. Instead of economy being embedded in social relations, social relations are embedded in the economic system. (Polanyi 1971:57)

These forms of institutionalisation of economic activity must not be confused with mere aggregate of interpersonal behaviour; rather, they must appear as the backbone structuring economic processes as a *system* within a society. In fact, a society whose economy is integrated by a redistributive pattern will probably harbour reciprocal and exchange behaviours as well, but not as part of an institution structuring society.

Polanyi's typology, therefore, is meant to dispel the universalist assumption that a logic of rational economic choice for the achievement of ends with scarce means is present in all economic processes. Methodologically, this *formal* definition is unable to explain *real* economic activities in societies other than those integrated by a market system. In other societies 'The human economy, then, is embedded and enmeshed in institutions, economic and non economic. The inclusion of the non economic is vital' (Polanyi 1957:250). Only in societies where the market system integrates economic activities does 'the economy' appear disembedded from other social relations. In fact, Polanyi shows in *The Great Transformation* (1971 [1944]) that the economy is embedded in other social institutions even in industrial capitalism.

A critique of the reciprocity concept: towards a 'reproduction' approach

In the last twenty years A. Weiner (1976, 1978, 1980) has constructed a critique of the models based on 'norms of reciprocity', and has proposed a 'model of reproduction' which seeks to integrate into wider time/space and material/symbolic frameworks the broad range of transactions occurring in a society. This theoretical perspective emerges from her own fieldwork in the Trobriand Islands, and her interest in transactions of valuables between women during mortuary ceremonies. The confrontation of her data and analysis with that of Malinowski (the origin of the gift/counter-gift exchange theories which developed into Sahlins's mechanical model of reciprocity) suggested that transactions among Trobrianders could not be understood as 'linear sequences basically concerned with discrete acts of giving and receiving' (Weiner 1980:71). Whereas Sahlins, following Malinowski, construed his model upon the different determination of equivalences in the return side of the transaction, Weiner defines the process of 'replacement' as the central one in transactions when considered from a long-term viewpoint. 'Replacement' occurs when a living person 'takes the place' of a dead person in order to prolong the deceased's claims, possessions and obligations. 'Replacement' and reclaiming practices knit a complex web of transactions and meaning.

Inherent in the replacement process is that payment received has long-range expanding effects. What one individual gives to another not only creates obligations between giver and receiver, but eventually involves other kin who must use their own resources to reclaim what has been given to a non-kin ... by someone else. ... The replacement process, on one hand, puts a drain on resources, but on the other hand, the process allows for long-term regeneration of intergenerational (and intragenerational) social relations, thereby giving the system a dimension of reproductive potential. (Weiner 1980: 78–9)

During mortuary ceremonies significant amounts of women's wealth are distributed as replacement or reclaiming actions related with transactions that occurred during the deceased's life or even before, but that *tied* his spirit in a web of social relations. At death the spirit must be released in order to become pure spirit and in that form create a new being by entering a woman's womb at conception. Reclaiming and replacement transactions taking place during mortuary distributions seek to release the deceased's spirit from his social obligations, while recasting those relations in terms of the living (Weiner 1976, 1978, 1980).

Thus, Weiner was able to link exchanges occurring throughout the life cycle and to elicit the *replacement* and *reclaiming* processes that integrate individual transactions into a cyclical system where 'human lifecycles' and the 'life trajectories of objects of exchange' are entangled in the process of reproducing social relations between individuals and groups, material and symbolic relations: 'In this way, the internal parameters of exchange illustrate the highly productive societal effort directed toward the production and regeneration of, not merely material resources, but human beings, social relations, and cosmological phenomena' (1978:177). In fact, Weiner's position echoes Mauss's description of total prestations where 'Everything passes to and fro as if there were a constant exchange of a spiritual matter, including things and men, between clans and individuals, distributed between social ranks, the sexes, and the generations' (1990 [1923–4]:14).

Although her critique is based on Trobriand data her central point is close to Polanyi's caution not to confuse particular transactions with a society's global economic integration pattern. However Weiner emphasises social reproduction including 'elements and relationships of human, social, material, and cosmological character [which] contain such value that a society attempts to sustain their reproduction generation after generation' (1978:175). By trying to explain transactions as a thread that creates and holds the social fabric in the *long term*, Weiner sets the problem of particular transfers and return equivalences in a framework that cannot be reduced to a one-to-one relation. Her position has wide-ranging theoretical consequences and it is interesting to keep it in mind, particularly when analysing market system societies (for a similar approach see Bloch and Parry 1989; Parry 1989). Indeed, the market form of transaction *appears* as a one-to-one relation, with equivalences regulated by supply and demand, while it *obscures* other material, political and symbolic transfers, which are in fact integrated in a long-range, complex social process (cf. Marx's 'commodity fetishism' in *Capital* vol. I, Chs 1, 4)

EXCHANGE

Marketplace and market system; information; central place theories

Since Polanyi, economic anthropology has tended to distinguish marketplace and market system. According to the criteria that different institutions integrate economic processes in different societies, the concept of market system is appropriate only where the market is the institution integrating the economy as a whole: production, distribution and consumption. On the other hand, societies where the economy is embedded in other institutions such as kinship or centralised political structures may have product exchange going on as well.

Bohannan and Dalton in their introduction to the work *Markets in Africa* define the difference between marketplace and market principle:

it is necessary to point out clearly the distinction between the institution of the market place and the transactional mode of market exchange. The market place is a specific site where a group of buyers and a group of sellers meet. The market mechanism, network, or market principle, on the other hand, entails the determination of prices of labour, resources, and outputs by the forces of supply and demand regardless of the site of transactions. (1971 [1962]:144)

A continuum of empirical situations may be found in which the market principle is more or less dominant or peripheral, is more or less integrative of the economy as a whole. (A further distinction is made between societies having and those lacking marketplaces.) Thus the concept of 'peripheral market' encloses both the idea of a local marketplace and of a peripheral market principle (1971:150–51) while the term 'market economy' describes societies where the market principle is dominant and where:

(a) sale at a money price is determined by impersonal supply and demand forces; (b) the buyers and sellers depend on such market exchange for livelihood; (c) the market prices for resources and finished goods crucially influence production decisions and therefore the allocation of resources, including labour, into different lines of production. (1971:152)

This last point is the crucial distinction: 'the peripheral market place is not integrated with production decisions' (1971:151).

On the other hand it is important to note that supply and demand forces *are* operative as well in peripheral markets, and although other elements such as kinship and a variety of social processes going on in the society might affect price formation, many case studies of peripheral marketplaces (Tardits and Tardits 1968; Ottenberg and Ottenberg 1968) show how supply and demand influence prices of food staples. In South Dahomey, for example, corn prices increase in June–July just before the harvest, when supply is scarce, and decrease in August just after the harvest when supply is plentiful. Prices of cooked food, an important commercial item, also follow supply and demand variations of prices linked with the agricultural cycle of the basic ingredient or with the accidental increase in demand related to ceremonial or other local social events (Tardits and Tardits 1968: 98–102). An interesting system of price control is described by the Tardits for South Dahomey marketplaces. Rather than increase market prices in relation to supply and demand, this system reduces the volume of goods offered for the same price: prices thus remain apparently stable. The example given is that of *akasa* (a corn paste consumed at every meal).

Akasa is commonly sold in small portions packed in banana leaves, the weight of which varies with corn prices and seasons. From June on, the prices of corn suddenly climb up during two months; from then on, *akasa* merchants are obliged to reduce stringently the volume of the parcel sold at an unchanged price.

In South Dahomey, 'the agency responsible for the price control operation is a men's secret association called *zangbeto*'. On request of the *akasa* sellers (women) the *zangbeto* association will publicly sanction the fact that:

the parcels of *akasa* be modified on account of the price rise. Later on, after the harvest, corn prices fall but most of the dealers still use the corn bought before the harvest and go on selling *akasa* as usual until *zangbeto* gives signal to decrease prices.

Offenders against the *zangbeto* regulations are publicly cursed and heavily fined (Tardits and Tardits 1968:101).

In fact the ethnographic record shows that all societies have some exchange relationships with other groups. This is generally motivated by a degree of local specialisation determined by especially useful or valued resources – such as salt, flint or obsidian in prehistoric times – not widely available, or by the development of certain skills such as pottery making in specific regions. Through exchange, local communities occupying different ecosystems and having access to different resources are integrated into a wider interacting system. The forms of exchanges, however, might vary widely from one society to another. There are two basic forms of organising exchange.

The first form is through a chain of individual *trade partners* who move the needed goods along a relay route that might cross enemy as well as friendly country. This is the case of the Papua New Guinea (PNG) Baruya described by Godelier, who trade salt for bark cloth capes, flint stone and weapons. It is interesting to underline as Godelier (1977:187) does that:

Because of this variety of essential functions (subsistence, ideology) *exchange is not a marginal activity*, an occasional appendix of the functioning of Baruya society, *but a strategic element of its structure*. To extremes, one may say that this society cannot subsist without exchanges.

Therefore, although not integrating the society as a whole, in Polanyi's terms, exchange is an integral part of this society's economy.

The second basic form of exchange is through the creation and protection of a privileged meeting place: the *marketplace*. Less formalised places of exchange exist, such as the Trobriand beach where barter occurs alongside gift-giving; or the border space limiting two communities of hostile strangers where *silent trade* has been reported to take place. Silent trade has been described as trade where the exchanging parties avoid speaking and/or directly encountering each other. The goods bartered are placed in succession near each other until equivalence is agreed upon and expressed by the fact that one of the parties carries away the other's trade goods. This type of exchange implies a difficult tension between distrust – which induces avoidance – and trust – which drives the parties to abandon their goods in the opponent's hands. Silent trade, however, although widely reported in classic texts, has not actually been witnessed by anthropologists in the field (Hamilton Grierson 1980 [1903]; Price 1980; Kurimoto 1980; Meijer and van Nijf 1992). Its theoretical interest as the proposed 'origin' of trade lies presumably in the extreme form in which *trust*, *fear* and the *bargaining* for equivalence appear. These three elements might be said to be present at the core of most exchange processes.

Economic exchange occurs within a field of *information*. Information about the goods that are available for exchange (quality and quantity), information about the people seeking and those offering the goods (their professional and social background as well as their control over the goods), information about similar ongoing and past exchanges. The greater the overall information available the easier it will be to reach a decision on the part of those involved in an exchange transaction. Generally, however, information is not readily and homogeneously available within an exchange system. On the one hand, information must be sought *at a cost* (it is always time-consuming and may have to be bought through securing access to specialised information cliques) and it must be publicised *at a cost* (social and/or market costs). On the other hand some groups of people control information that others don't get, and the exclusiveness of valuable information is one of the main strategic factors affecting speculative exchanges. At any rate, information sets the ground for *trust*, and *trust* is essential for the realisation of exchange.

Trust might be forthcoming as a result of the credibility of an institutionalised exchange environment. This is the case of market economies where the classic model of perfect competition, supply and demand trends towards equilibrium, generates a general ideology of stability, predictability and impersonal self-regulation movements. Within this setting information is supposed to be open and complete. The risk involved in transactions tends to a minimum, and therefore anyone may engage in exchange with anyone without much risk. This atomised, short-term, limited mode of exchange might be termed 'impersonal' and defined by 'closed-ended transactions' as opposed to an 'open-ended, personal mode of exchange' (Plattner 1989:211).

When the exchange environment is not highly institutionalised, or when information is monopolised by certain groups, trust must be constructed on personalised relationships that enable exchanges at presumably lower risk:

> knowledge of the other's personality, family, history, church, and so on *is relevant to the trust* one has that the exchange will be satisfactorily completed. The riskier the economic environment, the more traders need additional information about a partner over and above the specific facts of the proposed deal. (Plattner 1989:211)

Recurrent transactions, then, take place in the context of trading partnerships built on social relationships that are not solely economic.

It is interesting to note that in market economies as well, personalised exchange relationships often overlay the impersonal mode of exchange ideology.

Together with information, other costs (physical, social, monetary) should be taken into account when analysing exchange. 'Central place theory' is an attempt to make a deductive model of the location of exchange places, based on a series of cost-incurring factors and individual decision-making strategies seeking to minimise cost in the process of exchange. *Central place theory* was originally developed by the German geographer Christaller in the 1930s and was specifically proposed as a deductive model of spatial distribution of settlements according to their function as providers of goods and services. Christaller's model, further developed by Lösch (1954), Berry et al. (1988 [1967]) and Haggett (1965) has been relevant to economic anthropology through the studies of marketplaces done by Skinner (1985), C. Smith (1985) and Plattner (1985) among others. The basic elements of Christaller's central place model 'are developed ... under conditions of a uniform distribution of population and purchasing power, uniform terrain and resource localisation, and equal transport facility in all directions' (Garner 1971:307). Under these assumptions the model takes a regular lattice form where hexagons linking settlements of a same hierarchical order are nested within each other minimising population movement and maximising marketing benefits. The model presents a hierarchy of market settlements where

higher order places supply all goods of lower order places plus a number of higher order goods and services that differentiates them from, and at the same time sets them above, central places of lower order, and higher order places offer a greater range of goods and services, have more establishments, larger populations, trade areas and trade area populations and do greater volume of business than lower order settlements. The 'vertical' organisation has 'horizontal' expression in the following ways: higher order central places are more widely spaced than lower order places, and lower order central places, to be provided with higher order goods and services, are contained or 'nest' within the trade areas of higher order places according to a definite rule. (Garner 1971:307–8; see also Christaller 1966:17–22, 52–3)

Christaller took into account some possible deviations from his basic model, for example where transport costs would distort trade areas (Christaller 1966:72–80). Other assumptions, however, are essential to central place theory: the homogeneity of demand and the pervasiveness of marginal utility motivations of actors, that is, the willingness to incur an extra cost or effort in order to obtain an extra 'unit' of a good or service (Christaller 1966:52–3).

Central place theory has been enlarged to account for itinerant markets. Stine (in Garner 1971:320–1) develops a model where the willingness of consumers to purchase a particular commodity and the minimum demand necessary for a firm to be economically viable are spatially expressed as concentric circles or ranges. Under 'normal' conditions the viability threshold of a firm is within the larger range of potential demand and the commercial establishment will be fixed in a permanent location. In areas where transportation is difficult, time-consuming and costly, the relation might be reversed. 'When this situation pertains, there are two alternatives: (1) the firm cannot survive at a fixed location and so disappears from the landscape, or (2) the firm must become mobile and move from place to place' (Garner 1971:320–1) thus increasing the consumer demand range. This model, which adopts Christaller's purely economistic assumptions, is supported by Skinner's (1985) work on historical ambulant periodic markets in Szechwan, China, suggesting that central place theory might be a useful base for the analysis of marketplace functions and spatial distribution.

However anthropologists such as C. Smith (1985) analysing marketplace patterns in Guatemala are critical of the homogenising assumptions of Christaller's theory. Smith points out several important modifiers of central place theory for the Guatemala example. In the first place she addresses the significance of differentiating the function – retail or wholesale – of the marketplace. Second, the effect of the distinct economic position of particular ethnic groups – Ladino and Indians – in production, distribution and consumption is taken into account. Third, C. Smith stresses the fact that relations of production have to be considered together with relations of exchange. And fourth, the historical development of local and regional economic relationships (for Guatemala a plantation system and semi-proletarianised peasants) within the context of a worldwide expanding capitalist logic is assessed (C. Smith 1983, 1985). Thus, from an anthropological perspective, central place theory as such lacks the instruments necessary to account for the embedded nature of the economic processes in many societies where provision of goods and services, and demand for them, are strongly dependent on kinship, political, ethnic, religious and other social forces. Moreover, central place theory ignores the concrete historical forces that shape specific distribution patterns. Differentiation in the access to consumption goods and services (and to the factors of production), in turn, will push people into various forms of dependency and exploitation relations in order to sustain a livelihood.

The functions of money: special use vs. all-purpose money

Exchange can be carried out by means of *barter*, *money* or *credit*. Classical economists (A. Smith 1982 [1776]: 117–20) placed barter as the original form of exchange and indeed the motor of the division of labour. But once specialisation pervades a society, barter in practice obstructs the realisation of exchange:

In order to avoid the inconvenience of such situations [of barter: that is, the reciprocal need of the commodities which the agents of exchange want to dispose of], every prudent man in every period of society after the first establishment of the division of labour must naturally have endeavoured to manage his affairs in such a manner as to have at all times by him, besides the peculiar produce of his own industry, a certain quantity of some one commodity or other, such as he imagined few people would be likely to refuse in exchange for the produce of their industry. (1982:126–7)

... [Thus] Money has become in all civilized nations the universal instrument of commerce, by the intervention of which goods of all kinds are bought and sold, or exchanged for one another. (1982:131)

A. Smith's thesis on the origins of money stems directly from Aristotle's views in the *Politics* (Book I, 9) and the *Nicomachaean Ethics* (Book V, 5) and refers to two basic problems of transactions: first, comparability between the items being exchanged and, second, non-simultaneity of the agents' needs. Money, then, mediates in two ways the processes of exchange: as a *measure of value* and as a *medium of exchange*. The distinction is very clear in Aristotle, where the function of measure of value seems to take precedence over that of medium of exchange:

This is why all things that are exchanged must be somehow comparable. It is for this end that money has been introduced, and it becomes in a sense an intermediate; for it measures all things. ... All goods must therefore be measured by some one thing, as we said before. Now this unit is in truth demand, which holds all things together (for if men did not need one another's goods at all, or did not need them equally, there would be either no exchange or not the same exchange); but money has become by convention a sort of representative of demand ...

And further he adds:

And for the future exchange – that if we do not need a thing now we shall have it if we ever do need it – money is as it were our surety; for it must be possible for us to get what we want by bringing the money. (1971:380–1)

In a less clear reference in the *Politics* (Book I, 9, 1971:451) money appears to be primarily linked to long-distance trade as a medium of exchange and *need* is the concept mentioned as measure of value. As a medium of exchange: the *portability* attribute of money is mentioned.

In the fourteenth century, nominalist philosophers such as Nicolas Oresmes introduced interesting analyses of the material medium used as currency, and the political causes and consequences of its mutations: 'The mutation of monies ... can be effected in different ways: in the form or precisely in the type, in the proportion, in the price or denomination, in the quantity or weight and in the substance of the matter' (*Traité des Monnaies*, 1989:57). It is a critique of the Prince's (or state's) misuse of power regarding the medium of exchange and standard of value and of the gains that can be obtained by the state through the undue appropriation of the processes that fix and change money's value, as opposed to the claim that as a *social* convention 'Money belongs to the community and to every one person that composes it' (1989.55). The attribute of money that appears essential in his discussion is its *stability* through time.

A. Smith's discussion of money centres on its function as a medium of exchange and focuses on the most useful attributes of any common instrument of commerce: *durability*, *divisibility*, *recognisability* or 'trustability'. These explain the emergence of different metals as monies and further the emergence of coinage, that is to say the public recognition of specific measures of quantity and quality of the mediating commodity: money. Money, then, has generally been recognised in Western thought as defined by two main functions: that of measure of value and that of medium of exchange. When emphasis is given to the 'medium of exchange' function, the distinction is blurred and the 'measure of value' function is taken for granted as being a necessary quality of the instrument of exchange under consideration (be it oxen or metal). This automatic conflation of both functions of money has been, however, interestingly disproved by Grierson (1978), following

Polanyi, who shows that in many historical cases such as Homeric Greece or Pharaonic Egypt the standard of value did not function as a means of payment and thus could not be a medium of exchange. 'Pharaonic Egypt had no coinage, and used metal by weight as its standard of value. Actual payments, however, were made in goods' (Grierson 1978: 10). And more generally:

Such divergences between the money in which prices are reckoned and the commodities in which debts are discharged represent, it may be noted in passing, a fairly common phenomenon in history. They are found even in societies which use coined money, occurring either because coin is in short supply – this was frequently the case in early medieval Europe – or unusually unstable in value, or because the sums involved are inconveniently large and the merchant or contractor prefers the payment to be made wholly or partly in goods which he hopes to resell at a profit. The ratios will vary according to the state of the market ... . In such cases we should, I think agree that the goods in question are best not called money, but money substitutes. But where the ratio of such money-substitute commodities to whatever serves as the basis for valuation is fixed by law or custom ... they must be regarded as having crossed the boundary between money-substitutes and money, and become the latter. Money as a standard in fact lies behind money as a medium of exchange ... (1978:10–11)

He then goes on to search the possible origins of a standard of value and finds it in compensation payments or 'blood money' and more generally in compensations involving transfers of human beings such as women (bridewealth) or slaves in the Germanic context (1978:12–19). It would thus be 'a system of legal compensation for personal injuries, at once inviting mutual comparison and affecting every member of the community' that would lie behind 'the notion of money as a general measure of value' (1978:19; see also Polanyi 1957). Although this interpretation seems somewhat questionable it is interesting in that it presents the origin of money as a measure of value as stemming from the need of realising *payments* concerning human beings. The function of *payment* in the definition of money should be distinguished from that of medium of exchange. It is generally related to pressures exerted by a political (or religious) centralised institution with the aim of transferring wealth upward, through tribute or taxation, from smaller social units such as the individual, household or community.

However, what is more relevant to our discussion is Grierson's material distinction of money as first, a measure of value and, second, as a means of payment and a medium of exchange. This brings us back to Aristotle's original measure of value: *need*. It is the agent's needs that make things comparable and enable exchange. And need in turn remains tied to the personal and social contexts of the agents of every specific transaction. *Barter* is the form of exchange associated with the direct satisfaction of reciprocal needs. Barter occupies a paradoxical situation in the historical accounts of market economies. On the one hand it is perceived as the origin of the market principle. Something akin to a 'natural' instinct in A. Smith, but also in Polanyi 'a principle of economic behaviour ... a propensity to barter' which enhanced by a market pattern can give rise to a 'market society' (Polanyi 1971 [1944]:56–7). On the other hand, as a form of exchange barter is seen as 'primitive', as hindering the full development of a price-creating market. As a non-monetary form of exchange barter has been deemed inconvenient because it is assumed to require the simultaneous, bilateral balance of the value of traded goods.

In fact the difficulties of barter might be the result of implicitly applying money functions to the process of negotiating equivalences. Most important here is the frequent absence of a socially defined, overarching, measure of value which could be applied generally to all transactions. Objects therefore are not detached from their social context and from the agents of the transaction, they are not comparable goods *per se*. In barter, comparability, the reaching of equivalences, and thus exchange, are a function of specific social agents in specific contexts for a specific transaction of specific goods. Values, for example, can be 'measured' with very different 'standards' by each of the parties to the transaction, and this will not prevent the negotiating of an equivalence. Moreover barter is frequently associated with *credit* where the realisation of the full transaction is postponed, although equivalences are reached initially. Although barter appears as a self-contained, bilateral, autonomous transaction, ethnographic accounts seem to show the embeddedness of barter in trading partnerships (Casaverde 1981; Humphrey and Hugh-Jones 1992) and the importance of *trust* in the construction of long-term barter relationships. Access to information about the goods and qualities available at different possible trading *loci* is an element of barter as of any other exchange and will depend on a social field of personalised information networks.

Equivalences reached in barter tend either, to fixed ratios of specific goods, with very slight variation (perhaps linked to differences in quality) and persistence in time; or, to market-type, supply and demand ratios with high fluctuation. The first case is described by Casaverde (1981) for Peru, where highland pastoral communities producing meat, hides and wool trade with agricultural valley communities producing corn, wheat, barley and beans. The form of exchange is barter between long-standing partners. Bartered goods are referred to a common measure of value, the 'peso' (an ancient monetary value) which is only used in truck instances, and equivalences remain basically stable, although minor fluctuations occur in order to adjust for quality. This occurs in a context where the alternative of market exchange exists for all the products bartered. However, barter of these basic subsistence products through long-term trusted partnerships, enables both parties to obtain needed goods with low-risk, high equivalence stability and high provision of continuity. The benefit here is subsistence security.

The second case could be termed 'money-barter' (Einzig 1966:319; Curtin 1992:58–9, 228) and is widely described in long-distance trade between different communities. In the North American fur trade (Curtin 1992:228), for example, the modes of exchange between Indians and Europeans at the Hudson Bay Company (during the eighteenth and nineteenth centuries) are well documented. The unit of account was the 'made beaver' (MB), an abstract reference to the value of a good beaver pelt. In each trading post a different list of the 'standards of trade' evaluated import goods in terms of the 'made beaver' unit. On the other hand each post had a 'comparative standard' list evaluating each kind of animal pelt in terms of the 'made beaver' unit. Thus the 'made beaver' appears superficially as a fixed medium of exchange and standard of value and the exchange process recalls Polanyi's concept of *administered trade* at fixed prices. The real exchange process, however, presents a different picture. Curtin (1992:228) describes it as follows:

Neither standard represented actual exchange values of particular transactions. They were designed to serve as a guide to the factor and his superiors. The factor negotiated with Indian sellers as best he could. His objective was to obtain a total quantity of furs, by *gift and exchange* combined that would produce a difference between the MB value of goods sold and that of furs bought. That difference was called the 'overplus', and the size of the 'overplus' measured the success of the trading season. But it was an index, not a measure of the actual profit. The true profit depended on the European cost of trade goods, the sale value of furs, and the company's expenses. The actual bargaining at the trading post followed native American practice ...

The process opened with an exchange of *gifts* (including some pelts), followed by the 'bargaining over the equivalents of skins to trade goods' where 'the supply of furs had a low price elasticity' in market terms. This means that good prices for skins would not induce an increased supply, so that quality, instead of quantity fluctuations, seems to have been the determinant element in the setting of equivalences for prices. The negotiations ended with another round of gifts (Curtin 1992:228). This system is similar to that of 'assortment bargaining' described for the West African Coast where prices for export goods in local units of account were stable for decades during the eighteenth century, but the assortment of European goods taken in payment of the account unit varied widely with supply and demand in European and African markets (Curtin 1992:58–9). We may recall the Tardits's (1968) description of local Dahomey market ways.

'Money-barter' processes point to a complex form of exchange where different principles are at work (reciprocity, redistribution, market), where goods are comparable only in a specific social context and where values are often measured according to different social, cultural and economic criteria by the parties effecting the transaction.

Moreover, Bloch and Parry (1989) have warned anthropologists against an overly economistic tendency to treat money as a mere function of short term, material transactions. This, they believe, is a result of projecting our own (Western) cultural premises onto other societies. Rather, their concern is with 'the way in which money is symbolically represented in a range of different societies and, more especially, with the moral evaluation of monetary and commercial exchanges as against exchanges of other kinds' (1989:1) This preoccupation with the symbolism of monetary exchanges stems from a critique of the frequent polarisation between gifts and commodities (Gregory 1982) and to the mutually exclusive opposition of these distinct transactional modes' range of meanings. Their position, instead, points to the fact that monetised transactions cannot be abstracted from the social and cultural context of any given society as if they had a 'universal', functional, meaning. Rather, the meaning of different transactional modes is to be understood within the larger framework of social reproduction.

Through a comparative analysis, Bloch and Parry reach the conclusion that in most societies two distinct transactional orders can be found: one concerned 'with the reproduction of the long-term social or cosmic order', the other with 'short-term transactions concerned with the arena of individual competition' (1989:24). In an argument that echoes Weiner's emphasis on 'reproduction', they stress that procedures for transferring goods between the different transactional orders exist everywhere and that they are loaded with moral implications (1989:25–7). Money-mediated transactions, then, should be considered in the wider context of the social, cultural and economic processes where different modes of circulation are embedded.

As a result, this perspective drives us into confronting the problem of value, both as it has been developed in Western economic tradition, and more generally as a concept measuring some desirable attribute attached to meaningful goods or actions.

Use value and exchange value; 'commodity fetishism' and the labour theory of value

The question of what constitutes the value of things is one of the crucial problems arising with exchange. The goods being transacted must be comparable and their ratio of equivalence accepted by the parties in the exchange. The standard of value function of money is central to its definition, however, since Aristotle, money is perceived as a social convention substituting for the real measure of value. Aristotle saw *need* as being the measure of value. Following this path Marshall's concepts of *utility*, diminishing utility and marginal utility and their influence on demand are found at the core of his concept of value: *relative exchange value*. However, utility is not to be confused with *use value*, the former being a relation in exchange, the latter being independent of exchange (Marshall 1964 [1892]). A. Smith and after him Ricardo and Marx saw *labour* as determining 'the relative or exchangeable value of goods' (A. Smith 1982 [1776]:131). We might recall A. Smith's words:

The value of any commodity, therefore, to the person who possesses it, and who means not to use or consume it himself, but to exchange it for other commodities, is equal to the quantity of labour which it enables him to purchase or command. Labour, therefore, is the real measure of the exchange value of all commodities. ... What is bought with money or with goods is purchased by labour as much as what we acquire by the toil of our own body. That money or those goods indeed save us this toil. They contain the value of a certain quantity of labour which we exchange for what is supposed at the time to contain the value of an equal quantity. Labour was the first price, the original purchase-money that was paid for all things. It was not by gold or by silver, but by labour, that all the wealth of the world was originally purchased; and its value, to those who possess it and who want to exchange it for some new productions, is precisely equal to the quantity of labour which it can enable them to purchase or command. (A. Smith 1982:133)

Why is labour chosen as the measure of value? Because, of all commodities, labour alone:

at all times and places, may be said to be of equal value to the labourer. In his ordinary state of health, strength, and spirits; in the ordinary degree of his skill and dexterity, he must always lay down the same portion of his ease, his liberty and his happiness. The price which he pays must always be the same, whatever may be the quantity of goods which he receives in return for it. ... Labour alone, therefore, never varying in its own value, is alone the ultimate and real standard by which the value of all commodities can at all times and places be estimated and compared. It is their real price; money is their nominal price only. ... Its [labour's] real price may be said to consist in the quantity of the necessaries and conveniences of life which are given for it; its nominal price, in the quantity of money. (1982:136)

The price of commodities, according to A. Smith, is constituted of three different basic component parts: wages, profit and rent of land. This fact, however, does not invalidate the labour measure of value: 'Labour measures the value not only of that part of price which resolves itself into labour, but of that which resolves itself into rent, and of that which resolves itself into profit' (1982:153). A. Smith sets the basis for Marx's labour theory of value and we can understand the latter only as a critical development of the former.

For Marx 'that which determines the magnitude of the value of any article is the amount of labour socially necessary, or the labour time socially necessary, for its production' (1952:15). In Marx's theory, however, everything revolves around the distinction between use value and exchange value. Although this distinction appears in A. Smith when he first defines the concept of value he does not make it the pillar of his theory. In fact, one of the central differences between Marx's approach and that of the political economists before him, is the

definition of commodities as a product of labour conceived directly
for exchange. Because of this social circumstance only, the use value
embodied in all goods can be abstracted in exchange: 'As use-values,
commodities are, above all, of different qualities, but as exchange values
they are merely different quantities, and consequently do not contain
an atom of use-value' (Marx 1952:14).

It is the condition of commodities as such that makes labour the
only property 'common to them all'. Only 'by an exchange, we
equate as values our different products [and], by that very act we also
equate, as human labour, the different kinds of labour expended upon
them' (1952:32). *Only by equating all labour in society it becomes abstract
social labour and a measure of value.* This, in fact, is an important difference
from Smith who sees labour as 'the original purchase money that was
paid for all things' and, although he perceives that labour must have
a homogeneous character in order to become a measure of value, he
merely assumes an average or 'ordinary' degree of fitness, skill and toil
which suffice to equalise the labourers' expenditure.

From Smith's point of view, then, there would always – universally –
be some sort of average labour expenditure that would constitute in
a given society the measure of value of goods exchanged. Marx
explains that concrete labour which creates specific use value in all
things may only become a measure of exchange value when it is
abstracted from its concrete use value aspect. This happens when
most of the labour expended in a society is related through exchange,
entering thus a social labour pool. The big difference, then, is that Smith
renders universal and natural what for Marx is a social relation pertaining
to a 'definite, historically determined mode of production, viz., the
production of commodities' (1952:33).

It is only by being exchanged that the products of labour acquire, as values,
one uniform social status, distinct from their varied forms of existence as objects
of utility. This division of a product into a useful thing and a value becomes
practically important only when exchange has acquired such an extension
that useful articles are produced for the purpose of being exchanged, and their
character as values has therefore to be taken into account, beforehand, during
production. From this moment the labour of the individual producer acquires
socially a twofold character. One the one hand , it must, as a definite useful
kind of labour, satisfy a definite social want, and thus hold its place as part
and parcel of the collective labour of all, as a branch of a social division of
labour that has sprung up spontaneously. On the other hand, it can satisfy
the manifold wants of the individual producer himself, only in so far as the

mutual exchangeability of all kinds of useful private labour is an established social fact and, therefore, the private useful labour of each producer ranks on an equality with that of all others. The equalization of the most different kinds of labour can be the result only of an abstraction from their inequalities, or of reducing them to their common denominator, viz., expenditure of human labour power or human labour in the abstract. (1952:32)

Marx's argument rests on the analysis of the dual character of commodities, that of being use values *and* exchange values, and in the confrontation within commodities of concrete and abstract labour. Marx develops this confrontation in the seminal chapter on 'The Fetishism of Commodities'. In it he shows that the commodity form of a product of human labour presents the social relations existing between all producers in a society dominated by exchange as relations between the products, relations between things. As a result, things come to life while human relations of production are objectified and obscured: 'there is a definite social relation between men that assumes, in their eyes, the fantastic form of a relation between things' (1952:31).

In a stimulating discussion of commodity fetishism in South America, Michael Taussig (1980) tries to unravel the historical context of contemporary rituals centring on evil figures in the Andean Highlands and the Cauca Valley in Colombia. He describes contemporary rituals such as pacts with the devil in order to increase productivity in the Cauca plantations; offerings to the spirit owners of the mountain, partially demonised, in order to preserve life in the mines (Nash 1979). Taussig explains these rituals as the expression of a basic contradiction between the use value orientation of the peasant economy and the exchange value orientation of the capitalist plantation or mining economies and, increasingly, commercialisation of peasant agriculture as well. This basic contradiction permeates life in these communities. On the one hand, peasant reciprocal exchanges driven by need and the code of mutual assistance are present. This is opposed, on the other hand, to exchange and alienation practices in the mining sector and in commercial agriculture where equivalences are quantified in the abstract and transactions dissolve all attachment of goods to their previous owner. The contradiction is also expressed in the association of female figures with a reproducing 'system of reciprocity and self-renewal' and of male figures with a non-reproducing 'system of unequal exchange and self-extinction' (Taussig 1980:117–20, 209–11).

The process of demonisation of previously existing propitiatory and protection rites expresses the clash between 'pre-capitalist fetishism' – that is, where things are alive because they embody interpersonal relationships and hence produce and reproduce the social fabric – and 'commodity fetishism' – where things appear to have a life of their own, independent of the relations between people and with nature, dissociated from producers, former users and contexts. It expresses, moreover, that the capitalist logic of accumulation does not yet pervade the local culture but, on the contrary, that encroachment of capitalist relations of production is perceived as evil and destructive. The devil contract mediates between the contradictory fetishisms present in daily experience:

The fate of the peasant who is caught in the commercialization of agriculture, particularly where this involves large agribusiness production, is to bear witness to the clash between these two forms of fetishism. The belief in the proletarian devil contract, as well as other instances of fetishism is the outcome of this clash. The devil is more than a symbol of the new economy: he mediates the opposed meanings and sentiments that the development of this economy engenders. For if the peasant or use-value outlook were superseded by market culture, there would be no basis for fabulations like the devil contract. The emergence of this trope is occasioned by the meaning that a use-value culture ascribes to the tropes generated by the market organization of society, production and exchange. The devil contract registers the human meaning of this type of organization and stamps it as evil and destructive, and not the result of morally neutral forces that are naturally inherent in socially disembodied things. (1980:124–5)

One last crucial aspect of Marx's labour theory of value is his distinction between *labour* and *labour power*, where labour is the creative and useful expenditure of labour power which is the mere potentiality to do so. *Labour power* is a commodity exchanged in the market where the free labourer sells to the owner of the means of production his *power* to labour. 'The value of labour power is determined, as in the case of every other commodity, by the labour time necessary for the production, and consequently also the reproduction, of this special article' (1952:81). This includes 'the means of subsistence necessary for the maintenance of the labourer', 'the means necessary for the labourer's substitutes' and the 'equivalent in commodities' necessary to acquire the required skill (1952:81). But labour power is a peculiar commodity in that a labouring individual's natural wants, such as food, clothing, fuel and housing, vary according to the climatic and other physical conditions of his country. On the other hand, the number and extent of his so-called necessary wants, as also the modes of satisfying them, are themselves the product of historical development, and depend therefore to a great extent on the degree of civilization of a country, more particularly on the conditions under which, and consequently on the habits and degree of comfort in which, the class of free labourers has been formed. (1952:81)

Labour, on the contrary, is not a commodity and therefore does not have exchange value. However it is labour that creates value and: 'It becomes value only in its congealed state, when embodied in the form of some object' (1952:21). This distinction between labour power and labour, the difference between the value paid for the former and the value created by the latter and embodied in the product of labour, is what enables the owner of capital to extract surplus value from the worker.

Marx's approach to value is important for economic anthropology first and foremost because of its *historical* dimension; second, because of the complexity, both *material and ideological*, of his analysis of commodity fetishism; third, because of his inclusion of a relative, 'cultural' as well as historical aspect in the determination of the value of labour power. Marx's labour theory of value refers to a society where production is geared to exchange, where exchange is necessary for obtaining most, if not all, the useful things of life. This condition poses interesting questions to anthropologists working with social groups that may be only partially integrated in global commodity exchange, where working people may be immersed simultaneously in various market and non-market exchange processes, where subsistence production or production for use might consume most labour expenditure, etc.

World-system and neo-Marxian theories of the articulation of different modes of production have tried to tackle this problem by suggesting, respectively, that capitalism develops unevenly and presents complex polymorphous forms, or that the capitalist mode of production is defined by a logic of capital accumulation and 'free', contractual, market labour–capital relations, but might be articulated to other, pre-capitalist modes of production in a complex social formation.

A provocative study of swidden agriculture farmers in the Pachitea Valley in northern Peru tries to deal with these theoretical questions

(Chevalier 1982). Most villagers in Puerto Inca farm land which does not enter market exchange circuits but is simply obtained by direct appropriation. Work on the plot is carried out mostly by family members except when the demographic cycle of the domestic group or specific moments in the agricultural cycle drive farmers to hire wage labour. A large percentage (up to 75 per cent in some cases) of the production is directly consumed by the farmers and their family while the rest is sold in order to buy personal and productive goods in the sphere of market exchange.

The aim of these small farmers is described as maximisation of consumption or 'maximisation in-the-concrete' vs. 'accumulation in-the-abstract'. The theoretical problem raised by the Pachitea Valley example rests on the 'use value' 'exchange value' distinction of commodities and labour, in a context where market exchange does not directly affect a large proportion of farmers' production and consumption and, therefore, such a distinction would not be pertinent. Chevalier contends that these farmers do not pertain to a 'subsistence', non-commoditised sphere of production. Instead he suggests that production for direct consumption, as well as direct appropriation of land and the expenditure of the farmer and his family's labour be treated as 'subsistence commodities' where the abstract 'exchange value' aspect of a commodity is not realised through exchange:

by 'commodity' is meant not those material values that are actually purchased or sold but, more generally, all those that are *exchangeable* for money and that contain a definite quantity of value. The peculiarity of 'subsistence commodities' is that they never enter the sphere of circulation not because they are not exchangeable, but rather because their 'abstract' value can best be realised through direct consumption by the producers themselves. In short, production for household consumption may have nothing to do with the preservation of a 'natural economy'. (Chevalier 1982:118–19)

It is the capitalist context of the economy that sets in train a generalised commodification process in the Pachitea Valley. And relations of production and distribution, however different from wage labour and market exchange relations, must then be understood as a form of capitalist social relations.

Up to this point I have presented the concept of value as it has developed in Western intellectual tradition. In this tradition, the meaning of value stems from a distinction between, on the one hand, 'use value' – the adequacy of a good or a service's function to need –

which is independent of exchange; and, on the other hand, 'exchange value' – a concept tied to the general commodification of the economy. I have shown the development of the labour theory of value and how Marx limited its validity to a fully commodified economy. Moreover, I have pointed out Marx's crucial distinction between labour and labour power and how he acknowledged the specific historical, social and cultural grounds of labour power's value.

In the following sections I will present other forms of value that can be studied by paying attention to the *circulation* of goods among different individuals, different social groups, different polities. This view will help us approach the issues around distribution and exchange from a perspective that necessarily integrates the variation of meaning (attached to goods or processes), the conveyance of power and the forms of expropriation of value(s) along transaction routes. Once again, this will lead us toward social reproduction as a more helpful framework for economic anthropology.

CIRCULATION

Different spheres of circulation; social and economic value of transactions

The concept of *circulation* enables anthropologists to follow goods along *chains of transactions*, sometimes covering wide areas, lasting for years or holding multiple values – social, cultural and economic – in different moments or to the different people involved in the long-term processes (Thomas 1991). Rather than positing the circulation of goods as integrated in a unique sphere of exchange determining value, which is assumed to be the case in a market economy, anthropologists tried to find a theoretical framework for the complex and multivocal processes of circulation they encountered.

Bohannan's *multicentred economy* concept is probably one of the first attempts to theorise the circulation of goods in non-market integrated societies. In his description of the traditional Tiv economy (Nigeria) he presents three different spheres of circulation, each of them marked by different 'moral values'.

In calling these different areas of exchange spheres, we imply that each includes commodities that are not regarded as equivalent to those commodities in the other spheres and are hence in ordinary situations not exchangeable.

Each sphere is a different universe of objects. A different set of moral values and different behaviours are to be found in each sphere. (Bohannan and Bohannan 1968:227–8)

First, there was the sphere where subsistence goods were transferred by barter exchange. Money did not mediate exchange but Bohannan speaks of a 'free market' morality for this sphere. The second sphere was one where 'prestige' goods were transferred in non-market transactions. The circulation of goods was associated with ritual or ceremonial occasions. Brass rods were used as a 'measure of value', a 'medium of exchange' and of payment within the limits of that sphere. The third sphere referred to 'rights in human beings other than slaves, especially dependent women and children. ... Its values are expressed in terms of kinship and marriage' (1968:231) where exchange marriage was the norm. According to Bohannan, the spheres were 'arranged in a hierarchy on the basis of moral values' (1968:233), not practical (that is, material) ones. With marriage exchange, prestige and subsistence ranked in decreasing order. The different spheres, however, were not total isolates. 'Conversions' or 'exchanges of items from one category to another' (1968:234) were a usual if not frequent occurrence and were apparently charged with strong moral qualification. Bohannan's model presents certain ambiguities worth pointing out. First, he speaks of commodities while trying to explain a non-market integrated economy (in Polanyi's terms). Second, in theory he sees 'conversion' as an exception while on the other hand he describes its ubiquity and its social and political importance. Bohannan's confusion in fact points to the central question anthropologists confront when studying the circulation of goods: how to distinguish and gauge the social and economic value of transactions; how to explain complex processes that may partake of multiple meanings for those involved in them (see also Bohannan 1959).

Ceremonial exchange in Melanesia is such a complex process. Malinowski's description of the *kula* exchange of valuables as clearly distinct from other transactions could be understood as an example of a multicentred economy. Indeed, the sphere of prestige – the *kula* – is linked with the circulation of a specific type of valuables (armshells and necklaces) and political power and authority, while the sphere of subsistence responds to barter exchange of basic goods – *gimwali*. However, it is impossible to comprehend the Trobriand system without taking into account, together with *kula* exchange, yam exchange gardens and yam presentations. In particular a father or brother's exchange garden for his married daughter/sister. 'Through the annual presentation of yams made to him by his wife's kinsmen (Malinowski's *urigubu* 1977 [1935]:Ch. 6) a man moves into an adult role. He now controls his own supply of yams, the basic medium of exchange' (Weiner 1976: 197). But many other exchanges must be also taken into account: the construction of alliance networks and the circulation of marriage exchange valuables and yams, the exchanges of yams for valuables, women's accumulation of wealth – banana leaf bundles and pandanus skirts – and its exchange during mortuary ceremonies.

Although exchange is highly formalised in Trobriand it is difficult to apply the concept of *multicentred economy* to the distinct but articulated exchange circuits. First, raw yams appear as a universal medium of exchange: yams are produced for direct subsistence and for exchange purposes; yams are exchanged for *beku* stone axe blades and other valuables in marriage circuits; yams are presented to older men for support and magic. Exchange yam gardens are grown by a married woman's relatives for her; used by her husband in further exchange networks and reciprocated in women's wealth used to reclaim rights for the clan and thus regenerate clan identity. Yams are exchanged for valuables that enter the *kula*. We do not find here different spheres associated with particular goods – subsistence, prestige, people – as in Bohannan's description of the Tiv case. On the contrary, the same goods might enter different exchange circuits at different moments (cf. Weiner's description of the exchange history of a particular stone axe blade, 1976:182).

Second, accumulation and circulation of yams and of valuables, of men's wealth and women's wealth, but also distribution of food in feasts and formal presentations and inter-district exchanges of specialised goods, all of these activities participate in the social reproduction of Trobriand society. Neither yams nor any other good circulating in exchange circuits can be considered solely for their material or 'economic' aspect, as seemed to be the case for Bohannan's subsistence sphere. Rather they must be seen as part of a complex system where 'control over the circulation of goods, over workpower *and* over the final regeneration of persons through social and cosmic time' (Weiner 1976:221) constructs and transforms social relations through exchange.

Other examples of ceremonial exchange in Melanesia, the Melpa *moka* and the Enga *tee* (Feil 1984) also present a very strong social and political rationale *together with* an economic one. A. Strathern's (1971) analysis of the *moka* depicts a process where pigs, shells and other valuables are exchanged formally between individual partners and between groups. The *moka* is an unbalanced exchange of valuables that creates and transforms prestige and power relations. It encompasses both network relations of support centred around an individual, and collective expressions of opposition and alliance among groups. It serves local integration and regional articulation. It is a system with a high political component where big men find an arena to consolidate and expand their influence, where group hostilities are negotiated, and ceremonial exchange substitutes for warfare.

The system however has important social and economic aspects. Marriage exchange valuables, for example, are the usual entry into *moka* ceremonial exchange circuits, but also, wives are the producers of the main local valuable – pigs – and affines are crucial exchange partners (more so for ordinary than for big men) (A. Strathern 1971; M. Strathern 1972). On the other hand, purely material aspects have to be taken into account: cooked pork as well as pigs and other edible (marsupials, cassowaries, salt) and non-edible valuables circulate along ceremonial exchange roads. This circumstance, as Rappaport (1968) has pointed out enables the sufficient provision and wide-range distribution of locally produced utilitarian goods. Moreover, in the Papua New Guinea Highlands context, pork is the main source of high quality protein and therefore a basic subsistence good. In the case of *moka* exchange Strathern (1971:112, 218–19; 1980:52) presents the difficulty of treating subsistence, prestige and marriage as distinct spheres of exchange. Rather he suggests that the particular context and occasion of circulation defines both the value and the meaning of the goods being transferred. Strathern speaks of *moka* as a system of total prestations in Mauss's sense, although he stresses 'political competition between groups and between individual big-men' (1971:218). He points, however, at two significant complexities in the system:

The first is that moka can be made to anyone, a political ally or enemy or a comparative stranger, or also to a groupmate; and the second is that it may be made either in private or publicly and either in concert by a number of men or by a single man. I have so far argued for a single 'meaning' of moka gifts, and have suggested that the meaning is political or at least is concerned with the acquisition of prestige. But the meaning is hardly likely to be exactly the same in all the possible contexts which I have mentioned. (1971:218)

For the case of the Enga *tee*, perhaps the widest ceremonial exchange system in Melanesia, Feil (1984:54–5) observes:

The major *tee* items, pigs and pearlshells, are also the essential valuables in every context of exchange including bridewealth. One cannot distinguish Tombemba spheres of exchange on the simple basis of which items are appropriate to each. For this reason and others, the *tee* is best viewed as an exchange forum encompassing all others. The various types of exchanges can be distinguished according to occasion and range of likely participants, but in the end, all exchanges are connected to the *tee* and particular contexts are only arbitrarily defined.

Networks; solidarity networks

But how does circulation work? How are the relations that open up the ways where transfers are made possible, constructed and maintained? The concept of 'network' in anthropology stems from Barnes's (1990 [1954]) article on social class in a Norwegian parish and from Elizabeth Bott's *Family and Social Network* (1975). The need to make sense and construct models of flexible, personal, non-group interaction gave rise to a number of definitions and theoretical constructs (Barnes 1972; Mitchell 1969; Boissevain 1968; Whitten Jr and Wolfe 1973). As Barnes (1972) has postulated, 'the attraction of the idea of a social network has been that it provides a way of *also* looking at those parts of social life where groups do not always form' (1972:4; 1990:72–3). Without entering into the technical terms and concepts that have been defined and discussed in reference to network studies (Mitchell 1969; Barnes 1969, 1972), 'the two fundamental properties of networks' are 'multiple interconnections and chain reactions' (Barnes 1972:3). Moreover it is interesting to note two ideas that accompany the network concept: strategies and transactional social relations. Thus

The study of networks is not tied closely to any particular view of social action but can be used with any theory that sees social behaviour as the outcome of a multiplicity of partly conflicting social pressures on units that have interests of their own and are able to choose among alternative courses of action. ... networks seem to fit well with an exchange theory of social relations ... (Barnes 1972:25)

Social exchange theory (Blau 1982 [1964]), however, is highly problematic because of its economistic nature. Social relations – perceived as mere social interaction – are treated as a market exchange of extrinsic 'social' utilities within a marginalist framework. Complex human social relations are commodified when methodological concepts such as 'benefits', 'risk', 'investment', 'opportunity costs' and 'marginal utility' are applied in a straightforward manner. The question of whether, in a society dominated by market exchange, relations between persons are mystified as an exchange of things, would be a matter for research. Taking it for granted and constructing it as a universal human action theory seems methodologically flawed. Networks, then, are a convenient matrix for studying individual action; they appear as a useful *technique* or analytical instrument for economic anthropology, especially when abstracted from social exchange theory.

The interest of the network concept is obvious in cases such as ceremonial exchange in Melanesia or the study of marketplace interaction but it is also extremely useful for understanding the circulation of goods, services and information in Western industrial societies. With increasing attention paid to the 'informal economy', forms of circulation established at the margins or in the interstices of free, voluntary, contractual market transactions are coming to the fore. In a pathbreaking study, Pahl (1984) presented self-provisioning and informal exchanges of work among neighbours and relatives in the Isle of Sheppey as a form of enhancing levels of consumption. One of his findings was that the unemployed had fewer opportunities to engage in informal exchanges of work – paid or unpaid – although their dependence on the resources that were made available through these non-market channels was greater. By contrast, households with employed members also engaged more frequently in other inter-household work exchanges. This seemingly paradoxical fact could be explained because informal work depended on 'advice and information provided by friends and relatives' (Pahl 1984:333), in other words, on the circulation of information through personal networks. Using the household as the reference unit it could be said that networks of households with employed members provided a higher number and a more diverse range of connections and thus multiplied work opportunities. Social networks have proven to be crucial in the circulation of information concerning employment and more generally work – whether formal or informal – and in establishing specific work relations. Studying post-redundancy histories of steel workers in Port Talbot, near Swansea, Harris et al. have described differentiation in the population of a local labour market (conceived as a social institution):

... not only in terms of *whether* its members are *buyers or sellers* of labour power, but also in terms of the *type of labour power* which is bought and sold and the *characteristics of labourers* (sellers), and in terms of the *geographical location* of buyers and sellers. It is also differentiated in terms of the relation of market members to the *means of labour marketing*.

These means are of two kinds: formal and informal. The *formal* means are state-owned employment/labour exchanges (job centres), private employment agencies and public advertisement. The *informal* means are person-to-person contacts, or chains and networks thereof, which may be facilitated by institutions entirely unconnected with the buying and selling of labour power at the formal level. (1985:156)

By taking into account this complex field of forces, households are seen as differentially located within a local social structure which affects 'both the chances of their members obtaining any employment and of their obtaining particular types of employment' (1985:157). In a context where a contractor system has replaced in-firm departments, 'informal means of labour marketing', that is, social networks, are crucial. Moreover, the character of the social network, whether it is 'collective' or 'individualistic', will affect the redundant employees' chances of re-employment. The 'moral' character of *collective* social-activity patterns and network interconnectedness seems to increase the opportunity of obtaining fixed-term jobs, while '*individualistic* social-activity patterns' seem to confer 'a relatively unfavourable labour-market situation' (1985:161). In fact, post-redundancy labour histories appear to depend on the character of individual social networks and these, in turn, are at least partially a result of people's previous labour-market histories and those of other household members.

The study of social networks can help towards an understanding of how the information leading to the effective constitution of a labour market circulates. Access to and support from particularly well-connected individuals in a social network is a differentiating element of labour markets, but also of financial and product markets. Therefore, the means by which links with such individuals are reached, controlled and activated, but also the ways in which such links are created and maintained, that is, how a person gets to know many people and 'keeps in touch', will give us a closer picture of the social processes at work. These processes have been studied for the business elite (Bourdieu 1988; Marceau 1989; McDonogh 1989; Griffen and Griffen 1977) and for the working class (Lamphere 1987; Cameron 1985; Phizacklea 1983). And feminist anthropologists have stressed the centrality of women in the active upkeeping of networks (DiLeonardo 1987).

In a classic paper, Kapferer (1969) used network analysis to study the mobilisation of support in a dispute confronting two co-workers about ratebusting in a Zambian mine. Indeed, analysis of support-providing processes through personal links has illuminated interesting aspects of working people's strategies when confronted with general hardship or particular crises. Support might include the circulation of goods such as food, clothes, shelter; of services such as looking after children, old people and disabled people, cooking, shopping, home maintenance; of information about jobs or, more generally, livelihood opportunities and also of emotional support. Most of these aspects will be considered in greater detail in the chapters on consumption and social reproduction. Here, however, I want to stress the relevance of female links in effecting these multiplex 'support' relations and, moreover, the relevance of women's networks in the construction of a collective and solidary framework enabling the crystallisation of working-class consciousness and action.

Labour historians have pointed to the differences between male and female patterns of activism. While men's consciousness was rooted in workplace experience, skill defence and male after-work leisure activities (Thompson 1966; Hobsbawm 1984; Rule 1987; Sewell 1980; McClelland 1987), women's consciousness took shape in the shared experience of wage work but also around the day-to-day effort to make ends meet. Women's reproductive tasks in the working-class neighbourhoods of industrial towns created a support network that served to organise women workers' collective action but also to maintain strike discipline and sustain particular struggles. During the Lawrence strike of 1912, the close-knit, female-centred networks built around daily mutual assistance and exchange of information about wages and prices was essential to the construction of a working community that could act with cohesion and solidarity. Women's networks were important in that they helped bridge gender, age and ethnic cleavages within the working class (Cameron 1985). Through female networks, women who had an individual history of discontinuous employment shared their experience of different problems confronted at different stages of their life cycle. Speaking about women collar laundresses in Troy, New York, in the second half of the nineteenth century, Turbin suggests 'that group awareness was continuous and not limited to sporadic periods. A combination of close family ties and shared experiences as workers and activists suggests that collar women were conscious of shared interests as workers' (1987:57). The perspective on female-centred networks 'contributes to recent arguments that class consciousness does not stem solely from work-related factors and the type of labour force participation experienced by men' (1987:66). Moreover, in trying to overcome the gendered dichotomy present in the conceptual frameworks of labour historians Turbin points out that

we should look not only at important minorities such as skilled women but also to men who were less skilled and did not organise. We should question not only the assumption that women's work was temporary but also the generalisation that men's work was permanent. (1987:66)

Network analysis therefore might help us explore forms of constructing a shared awareness of collective interests and of mobilising and sustaining action, which are interstitial to more bounded and structured institutions such as unions. Social networks, however, may also hamper organised protest in the workplace, especially when personal links have been the means to obtain employment in the context of a closely knit community, where the content of relationships is multiplex (Phizacklea 1983; Anthias 1983: 84–5).

Movements of capital and labour; the globalisation of economy

Migration can be seen as the circulation of people in their capacity to be the carriers of labour power (whether fully commodified or not). Moreover, mobility of people conceived as labourers addresses the issue of the distinct values in the costs of reproduction present across different social and political contexts, and of how these variable reproduction costs are materially and ideologically conveyed on to the costs of production. This crucial process sets the grounds for the social construction of labour force segmentation often justified on national, ethnic or racial character and, subsequently, for differential exploitation.

Network analysis has specially benefited studies of migration processes. Previous migrants' knowledge of the receiving area and their willingness to provide information and material support have proved to be a crucial variable in the organisation of migration patterns (Mazumdar 1987; Roberts 1978; Ballard 1987; G. Smith 1989:96–112). Migration, however, must be viewed within the wider framework of circulation of capital and labour in the context of the uneven development of a world capitalist economy. Questions such as the effects of migration on income (re)distribution on a national or international level are important. On this subject, for example, Mazumdar indicates that 'private gains through migration do not necessarily imply a more equal distribution of income either across regions or households' (1987:1117). In my view, however, the two processes tied to migration described below seem to hold more interest.

In the first place, I want to stress the construction of a segmented labour force, and as a corollary the creation of race and ethnic minorities as an ideological barrier to the formation of class. In this regard, I will show how the argument is tied to the area of 'production' that I presented in Chapter 1.

In the second place I shall present a brief account of the use of mobility as a means towards obtaining a livelihood in the context of multiple, interconnected, individual and household strategies. This preoccupation, in turn, will act as a prelude to a more thorough discussion of these matters that will follow in Chapter 3, on 'consumption'.

Both points are articulated in that the differential *reproduction costs of labour* is an essential element in the material *and* ideological construction of a segmented labour market.

Labour migration is only one aspect of the *spatial organisation of production* in capitalist social formations and must not be confused with movements of people (migration) – whether individuals or groups – in other sociohistorical contexts. Labour migration acquires its meaning within the general context of the objectification and commodification of the means (or factors) of production: land, capital and labour. Both labour and capital are mobile while land and primary resources located in it are the only fixed assets of production. Space, on the other hand, is a political arena where struggles for power and their crystallisation in law through history draw a specific field of forces within which movements of capital and labour have to be understood. *Control of mobility*, then, whether through the regulation of immigration or exemption from taxes for certain industries in certain areas, is a crucial element in the organisation of production. It is one, moreover, where the interests of capitalists and those of the state, although not always coincident, are necessarily intertwined and partially expressed through institutional politics. Systems of *migrant labour* are perhaps the best examples of this.

Burawoy (1976) defines *migrant labour* as a system where maintenance and renewal of the labour force are differentiated and physically separated. This form of reproduction of the labour force 'is enforced through specific legal and political mechanisms which regulate geographical mobility and impose restrictions on the occupational mobility of migrants' (1976:1050). The case of South Africa's institutionalisation of a system of migrant labour is expressed in the historical construction and implementation of apartheid. From 1880 to 1926 the mines in South Africa, Southern Rhodesia (Zimbabwe) and Northern Rhodesia (Zambia) were opened. This created a constant rising demand for labour and therefore an upward pressure on wages. To prevent rising labour costs in a labour-intensive industry, employer associations and government colluded and granted a quasi-monopsony over labour supplies to centralised recruiting agencies such as the Witwatersrand Native Labour Association, formed in 1900 by the South Africa Chamber of Mines, the Rhodesian Native Labour Bureau, formed in 1903, and the Northern Rhodesia Native Labour Association, formed in 1929 (Stichter 1985:101–2). On the other hand, 'the fact that the recruiting agencies did not supply all the labour to the mines created a distinction between "recruited" and "voluntary" labour' (Stichter 1985:103). Through coercion and deception, by misleading workers, and frequently backed by the direct force of state agents (Stichter 1985:108; cf. also Fitzpatrick 1987:103 for Papua New Guinea), recruiting agencies managed to increase and control the larger supply of labour while maintaining or reducing wages. Agencies hampered competition for labour among employers as well as territorial competition between relatively high-wage and lower-wage areas. As Stichter remarks:

the final and very critical function of labor recruitment systems was to serve as an effective method of control over African workers. In particular they frustrated the mobility of workers in the labor market, the very mobility which was the chief strategy open to migrant workers for defending themselves. (1985:108, also 102–16)

Control of workers' mobility with the formal *support of the state* is, then, the basic factor in the construction of a migrant labour system.

Through colonial taxation, discriminatory policies favouring European farmers' produce in the market, land expropriation and forced or coerced wage labour, Africans were driven to depend on a capitalist economy. On the other hand, 'traditional' relations were actively 'preserved', by government policies within specially delimited areas with the aim of providing subsistence to those not directly engaged in wage work. Strict regulation of circulation between the areas of employment and the areas of 'traditional' organisation was legally enforced through restriction of residence in urban areas for the unemployed. The articulation and enforcement of a double dependence: on wage work and on 'traditional' subsistence work, located in spatially distinct areas, characterised the system of migrant labour (Burawoy 1976). It enabled the reduction of labour costs. Renewal costs of the labour force were externalised and wages appeared as a supplement to the 'traditional' economy, in fact barely covering maintenance. The system also had political benefits because it externalised unemployment, general social unrest and vindictive political action (Burawoy 1976).

The reproduction of this system of migrant labour, however, depended on the restriction on occupational mobility through the colour bar preventing blacks from occupying other than unskilled positions, and therefore rendering black labour highly homogeneous and exchangeable. This system, then, reduced labour costs and differentiated the labour force on the grounds of race through the pretence of preserving 'traditional' ways of livelihood. In fact, life in the Bantustans was highly dependent on remittances of wage workers, and more recently on the direct wage obtained by women working in industries located in the rural homelands or in border areas (Stichter 1985:161–2; Eades 1987:8). These women were paid extremely low wages because these appeared – wrongly – as doubly accessory: being a supplement to 'traditional' agriculture and a supplement to male workers' remittances. We must bear in mind, then, that the 'subsistence economy' in the Bantustans was not 'traditional' and income was not equally distributed either (Sharp 1987).

The South African migrant labour example is not such an extreme case. Post-Second World War European democracies (such as West Germany, Switzerland, France, Netherlands) organised a system of 'guest workers' which reproduced many of the same elements:

(a)   separation of maintenance and renewal of the labour force;
(b)   externalisation of renewal costs;
(c)   regulation of workers' movements through official recruiting agencies and strict limitation of residence permits;
(d)   restriction of job mobility; and
(e)   the denial of political and civil rights to immigrants (Castles et al. 1987).

Settlement of worker immigrants and family reunification have become a reality promoted by capitalists' need over the years to stabilise a skilled and trained workforce. Also, paradoxically, the ban on non-EEC immigration after 1973 in most countries encouraged settlement. Settled immigrants, however, still suffer from institutional discrimination that denies them most political rights. They are often on the fringes of legality and socially segregated through access to low-quality housing, education and health, mostly living thanks to cheap goods and services which their peers provide in the 'informal sector' economy. Their vulnerability situates them at the bottom of a segmented labour market. The discriminatory measures of Western democracies defining certain workers as different – illegal, alien – with added implicit or explicit reference to racial or ethnic criteria, result in the creation of a highly competitive segment of the labour force for unskilled or semi-skilled jobs. The further public demonisation by governments and the media of these 'competitive' alien groups in a context of high unemployment triggers increased 'racialised' explanations and 'solutions' to economic problems (Castles et al. 1987:38; Burawoy 1976:1083). The effect of these ideologies is to forge profound cleavages within the working class and to impede the formation of class consciousness and organisation. In this context, however, settlement and the socialising effect of women and children weaving networks of everyday relations is usually an important step towards the construction of a shared working-class identity that bridges ethnic and racial differences (Lamphere 1987; Stichter 1985:137, 166).

Not all migrants, however, fall into the category of 'migrant labourers' with its highly institutionalised and strict control of workers' movements between an area of employment and an area of renewal of the labour force. Most labour migration is internal and takes place within a nation-state and frequently within a region (Mazumdar 1987; Roberts 1978). In this case too, migration should be understood as something other than an *individual* response to push–pull regional economic factors and the individual's decision-making capacities to optimise income opportunities. Here too, migration could not be explained only by network theory. Migration should be viewed as a *social* process linked with the historical unfolding of worldwide capitalism and the struggles of people trying to make a living in the context of different forms of commodification. Roberts points out, for example, that it is *rural differentiation*, a result of small commodity production that triggers rural–urban migration in Latin America. Peasants who are able to accumulate some capital and to expand their network of contacts are those more likely to migrate. Indeed, most studies indicate that 'poverty appears to hinder out-migration' (Mazumdar 1987:1108, 1118; Roberts 1978:96–108).

On the other hand, when thinking about the uses of migration for obtaining a livelihood we must look beyond individual strategising. We should pay attention to the complex set of relationships linking migrants and non-migrants through the articulation of households and to how the transformation of these relations through time both influence and are dependent on individual migratory decisions. A telling example is that of the Huasicanchinos of the Central Andes (Peru) described by Gavin Smith (1989). The people of Huasicancha exhibited a certain degree of inter-household specialisation in herding, farming and trade by the beginning of the twentieth century. Households, however, were linked in a network of labour exchanges organising relations of production through communal institutions and reciprocal prestations. This situation was progressively eroded by the expansion on to communal pasture and subsequent rationalisation of livestock production of a neighbouring *hacienda*. This led to repeated confrontation of highland pastoralists with the *hacienda*'s owners. By the 1930s the commodification of labour exchanges with the *hacienda* was barring herders the use of *hacienda* pasture on *huachillero* terms (the right to bring in a designated number of the herder's sheep to be shepherded together with the *hacienda's* flock as a reciprocate return of labour prestation). This, as a consequence, hampered the use of *huachilla* (exchange of labour for animals) and *michipa* (exchange of herding services for other goods and services) between households (see also Martínez Alier 1973).

Together with the regional and national economic expansion, this situation opened 'formal' and 'informal' work opportunities and encouraged out-migration in search of alternative means of livelihood.

A first wave of migration took place in the 1950s and involved pastoralists who could finance migration through the sale of livestock and could count on personal contacts to get started. A second wave of poorer Huasicanchinos in the 1960s came from a mixed but basically farming background. Generally migration was to Huancayo and Lima where petty multioccupational enterprises were established. What is extremely interesting in Smith's account of Huasicanchino migration is the dense network of credit and partnership relations that spread the search for livelihood between residents in Huasicancha and out-migrants in different places, creating what he calls 'confederations of households'. Although not all migrants were integrated in 'confederations of households', this seems to have been the most frequent pattern (up to 53 per cent). It affected individual members' decisions to migrate temporarily (that is, to provide labour for the petty fruit enterprises in Lima during the strawberry season) or more permanently; or to stay in Huasicancha (to take care of the farming and herding ventures of ex-residents), etc. In this case, then, migration is not a definite and isolable individual decision of movement from an economic environment *to* another, breaking economic and social attachments with the 'sending' community. Rather, it appears as an aspect in a complex of fluid inter-household linkages bridging space and geared towards making a living (G. Smith 1989:77–117; see also Ballard 1987:29 for Pakistani migration to Britain).

On the other hand, labour migration cannot be understood apart from the geographical movements of capital with the aim of reducing costs: energy costs, labour costs, political costs, distribution costs. At different historical moments of the expansion and uneven development of capitalism around the world, cost-reducing priorities have been different locally. In Third World countries, for instance, production and market expansion in a context of limited availability of capital might have geared investments towards production, leaving distribution to a highly labour-intensive, informalised service sector (Bauer and Yamey 1968; Roberts 1978). Generally, labour-intensive industries or production processes within an industry will try to cut on labour costs and on political costs through labour market segmentation and relocation to politically repressive national regimes, while capital-intensive industries or production processes will try to cut political costs through stabilisation and the creation of an internal highly protected labour market. Movements of capital and the political, social and economic differentiation of space are therefore crucial to capitalism. The international division of labour concept stems from the organisation of production within an industrial process or firm according to spatial differentiation of labour (Fröbel et al. 1980; Nash and Fernández-Kelly 1983; Grossman 1979; Sassen-Koob 1981). This spatial differentiation as to labour's characteristics is produced and reproduced by the differential use of space in the expansion of a capitalist worldwide system (Dear and Wolch 1989; Harvey 1989).

MARKET CULTURE OR MARKET SYSTEM?

The specificity of the labour market: the necessary 'embeddedness'

Production is interaction of man and nature; if this process is to be organized through a self-regulating mechanism of barter and exchange, then man and nature must be brought into its orbit; they must be subject to supply and demand; that is, be dealt with as commodities, as goods produced for sale.

Such precisely was the arrangement under a market system. Man under the name of labor, nature under the name of land, were made available for sale; ... the fiction that labor and land were produced for sale was consistently upheld. (Polanyi 1971 [1944]:130–1)

The paradox that Polanyi highlights is that a market system requires that all factors of production 'be dealt with as commodities, as goods produced for sale' but neither labour nor land are produced for sale. For both nature and people, then, the commodity aspect is a fiction. Moreover, it is precisely because they are *and* are not commodities that they can be exploited. It is therefore necessary to preserve the dual character of land and labour for the capitalist organisation of production to continue.

In Polanyi's description of the different forms of institutionalisation of the economy, only the market economy appears as a sphere separated from other social institutions, and even then the self-regulating, autonomous market sphere is a utopia: because its full realisation would mean the annihilation of humans and nature, of society, and therefore also the destruction of the market system. In non-market-dominated societies, the economy is *embedded* in the social organisation, but in market-dominated societies too, the strong drive towards autonomy and self-regulating market mechanisms is countered by moves towards the 'self-protection of society' (Polanyi 1971:130) This, according to Polanyi who traces the historical process for Britain, is effected by state interventionism as a response to different pressure groups (landed gentry, working people, industrial capitalists) (1971:131–77). Protective labour legislation both hampers and enables the commodification of labour. It sets the limits within which free market transactions may take place without destroying the human commodity.

Actually, the labor market was allowed to retain its main function only on condition that wages and conditions of work, standards and regulations, should be such as would safeguard the human character of the alleged commodity, labor. (1971:177)

If we follow Polanyi's insight, then, the labour market is necessarily embedded in social institutions other than the market. Polanyi's emphasis is on state regulation through legislation but other institutions have to be considered for the embeddedness of the labour market. Among them are public welfare institutions providing education, health, unemployment coverage, public housing, together with more directly labour-linked social organisations such as unions, and family, kinship, community or ethnic identity associations.

The most important factor of embeddedness hinges on the reproduction – maintenance and renewal – of the labour force. As Marx and other classical economists before him had observed, the costs of obtaining a livelihood are not homogeneous for all working people. Differences may depend on local market variations for subsistence goods, but also on out-market resources obtained through more or less institutionalised channels. Resources comprise goods, services, information. They might be reached through personal networks anchored in ongoing processes of reciprocal prestations, through state organisations such as social security and public education systems, through unions, through neighbourhood, religious or community associations. This social fabric produces differentiation. Labour supply is thus structured in segments as a result of the complex interaction of social relations which *also* harbour (although not exclusively) economic functions.

Take, for example, the family and its provision of non-wage reproductive work. Differences in the structure of domestic group organisation and also in family ideology will affect the position of specific members in the labour market and their bargaining power. Generally, cleavages resulting from family reproductive processes are very strongly linked to gender and age differences. It is interesting to note that the 'family', in its material presence as a group – both conflictual and solidary – in search of a livelihood, and as an ideological construct, is historically entrenched in the constitution of a labour market both on the 'supply' and on the 'demand' side. The 'family wage' resulted in wage discrimination according to gender and age criteria (May 1982:418), but also was used as a working-class argument for better male wages on the grounds of non-waged dependants supposedly improving overall family income (Humphries 1977). Women workers on the other hand have relied heavily on family morality rather than skill ownership arguments in their struggles with employers (Kessler-Harris 1985).

State social provisioning is also crucial in the structuring of the labour market. Generally, the extension of welfare will benefit those segments with the least bargaining power in the labour market. For instance, a strong commitment to extensive, good quality public education will counter privatised transfer of knowledge and skills, although credentials may be more difficult to extend. Citizens, however, have differential access rights to social security benefits (that is, women; claimants to non-contributory social security benefits) (Craig et al. 1985:110–11). Besides, certain groups of labourers such as immigrants are deprived of civil and social rights altogether, and must rely to a larger extent on informal support networks.

The labour market, then, is necessarily embedded in the social relations that constitute labourers as concrete human beings. And these social relations both produce and are reproduced by a hierarchically segmented labour structure.

Thus the labour force in each economy is stratified by class, race, nationality, religions, sex and many other factors. These divisions are created and reinforced by discrimination, differential access to education and training, professional associations, trade unions, employers' associations and ratified by social beliefs and conventions. The resulting inequalities are partially offset by the welfare state but in other respects the state reinforces divisions in the labour market. Supply-side structuring has its demand-side counterpart in the hiring rules adopted by firms which rest on signals transmitted by social characteristics (age, sex, race, educational qualifications, etc.) which are only partially objectively based but which are taken to measure the relative worth of job applicants. ... The important features of segmented labour markets are that relative wages are no guide to relative skills or productivity and that workers of equal skill or potential ability are employed at widely different wage levels. (Craig et al. 1985:113–14)

Another interesting approach to the embeddedness of the labour market comes from the critique of its crucial characteristic: the principle of *freedom of contract*. As Durkheim (1933) already pointed out, in addition to contractual agreements between individuals other binding social forces are at play. Indeed, contracts are intrinsically imperfect because of the uncertainty of future outcomes and contracting parties have to rely on customary practices and on the 'other's good will'. 'The non-contractual features of exchange agreements are central and functional to any economic system based on trade' (Hodgson 1988:159). Far from being 'free' from non-contractual relations, all contracts in a market system rely heavily on *trust*. Labour contracts are an interesting case because the contractual relation rests on the assumption that the labour power will be put to use in a certain manner. And, although technical constrictions (such as Taylorisation) or different degrees of supervision and force might be applied by employers in order to exact what they consider labour dues, in the end the will of the worker has to be forthcoming. Labour contracts are a reward/penalty framework to be applied subsequently rather than a clear description of the *contents* of the employer/employee exchange. Contents are often unexplicit, non-contractual, informal work and management practices and relations, tightly linked to local, branch or even firm-specific custom and to ideas about what is 'fair'. Therefore, 'all employment contracts involve an element of trust which cannot be obtained or expressed simply in contractual terms' (Hodgson 1988:165). Verbal labour deals in the informal sector, for example, are the extreme expression of a necessary hypertrophy of 'trust', increasing the vulnerability of the weaker side: labour.

Granovetter's argument on 'embeddedness' (1985) rests almost exclusively on the production of trust in transactions. In contrast to what he terms an 'oversocialised' conception of economic action which endows individuals with interiorised social norms and institutions and a 'generalised morality', Granovetter's argument 'stresses the role of concrete personal relations and structures (or "networks") of such relations in generating trust and discouraging malfeasance' (1985:490). He uses network analysis as a theory of social relations, one where personal, concrete economic and social transactions build trustful relations between individuals:

Standard economic analysis neglects the identity and past relations of individual transactors, but rational individuals know better, relying on their knowledge of these relations. They are less interested in *general* reputations than in whether a particular other may be expected to deal honestly with *them* – mainly a function of whether they or their own contacts have had satisfactory past dealings with the other. (1985:491)

From this point of view, economic action is embedded in an articulated network of personal social transactions. Social relations are transactional experience and economic action would involve choice between alternative partners in order to maximise the unwritten 'trust' element of contracts. It is, in fact, a formalist version of 'embeddedness'.

A more interesting approach is based on the concept of *habitus* which Bourdieu defines as: 'The circumstances associated with a particular class of conditions of existence produce *habitus*, durable and transposable systems of dispositions, structured structures able to function as structuring structures' (Bourdieu 1980:88). The *habitus* is an ideological environment which is produced by history and produces practices. Within these structures that previous history has established, however, there is an 'infinite capacity of generation', albeit 'strictly limited' (1980:91–2). We will expand on the concept of *habitus* in Chapter 4, but the following perspective regarding the labour market seems an interesting elaboration of Bourdieu's concept.

De Gaudemar (1987) tries to go beyond the idea that the supply of labour merely *adapts* to a demand for labour determined by production needs and set mainly by technological constraints. Instead of distinguishing between the two processes of supply and demand of labour, he suggests 'there is only one single process to be considered' which he terms 'mobilization'. Relying heavily on Bourdieu's concept of *habitus* he tries to develop 'a socioeconomic theory of mobilization that would analyse the reciprocal processes that determine the behaviour of both categories of protagonists and which would thus jointly take into account their social realities' (1987:109). His hypothesis of a 'mobilization network' (MN) tries to transcend the concept of a 'labour market' and emphasises the specificity of an 'exchange' which is in fact the creation of a 'relationship of subordination, availability and mobilization' (1987:113). His MN is the dialectical confrontation between the employer's and the worker's *habitus* in their search, respectively, for labour and a means of livelihood. The MN borrows the character of the *habitus* as both a 'structured structure' and a 'structuring structure' and therefore it may be also interiorised (1987:113–14).

The way, then, in which labour and capital stand in a certain relation to each other is obviously embedded in other than 'economic' social relations. These, on the other hand, may be seen as an essential component of relations of production and in that sense 'economic'. We might think of the heterogeneity of the labour market on 'technical', 'social' and 'cultural' grounds as a process brought about, historically, by the development of capitalism, and of a dialectical nature (Wolf 1982:379). There is a necessary and dialectical embeddedness of the labour market that must be dealt with.

The uniqueness of the natural resources market

Polanyi also perceived there was a paradox in the idea of land entering a self-regulating market as a factor of production: 'What we call land is an element of nature inextricably interwoven with man's institutions. To isolate it and form a market out of it was perhaps the weirdest of all undertakings of our ancestors' (1971:178). He describes:

... stages in the subordination of the surface of the planet to the needs of an industrial society. The first stage was the commercialization of the soil, mobilizing the feudal revenue of the land. The second was the forcing up of the production of food and organic raw materials to serve the needs of a rapidly growing industrial population on a national scale. The third was the extension of such a system of surplus production to overseas and colonial territories. With this last step land and its produce were finally fitted into the scheme of a self-regulating world market. (1971:179)

Although Polanyi was thinking primarily of land and the creation of a real-estate market, his remarks can be extended to all natural resources including sunlight, air, water, flora and fauna. Here, as for the labour market, the main problems he underlines are, first, that nature is interwoven with human institutions and, second, the utopian character of a market economy that requires the transformation of nature into a commodity.

Radical ecological economists (Martinez Alier 1992, 1993; Naredo 1987) have discussed some very interesting aspects of the use of natural resources. Some basic problems are the unequal allocation and exploitation of natural resources across political boundaries and across generations, and the unmeasurable character of natural resources.

The critique of the concept of 'carrying capacity' as it has been used by technocratic environmentalists in international forums is particularly interesting. Generally, carrying capacity has been conceived as a relation between population and environment mediated by technology. This has defined Western experts' theories and internationally sponsored policies that emphasise the negative effects of demographic pressure and of 'traditional' techniques such as slash and burn agriculture that deplete natural resources. However, carrying capacity must be understood in a global, historical and political, context. First, the effects of pressure over natural resources in 'developed' countries are exported to other Third World, dependent countries. Take for example the depletion and exportation of *guano* in Peru (1840–80), used for soil enrichment that permitted increased productivity in European and US agriculture. Moreover, pressure over natural resources in Third World countries is not only a result of local demographic increase. It is also a consequence of production increase induced by capitalist development. Take for instance the plantation, the *hacienda*, or the small commodity producing peasants that generate agricultural produce for export in Latin America (that is, sugar, coffee, cattle, cereals, etc.). The pressure of production, then, encroaches on local subsistence practices (Martinez Alier 1992:76–7, 84). Demographic pressure, on the other hand, is not a 'natural' phenomenon but is tied to political control over population movements. Think of the contradictory and perverse policies of Western democracies that demand strict population control for Third World countries on the grounds of population pressure over world resources, while banning immigration and sponsoring natalist campaigns at home.

Another major problem pointed out by ecological economists is the differential allocation of natural resources across generations. The depletion or destruction of non-renewable resources will affect mostly future generations. These, however, will always be under-represented in political forums and decision-making institutions (if only because the majority are yet to be born!). Although we might allow for the discovery and harnessing of presently unknown resources, and for technological innovation (including genetic engineering) as a means to increase the efficient use of energy, it is nonetheless a fact that present generations transform the environment in ways that will significantly affect the material well-being of future generations. Water, air and soil pollution will have consequences as to production, health and political costs. The impoverishment of the ecosystem's diversity is a necessary condition for its exploitation in terms of energy appropriation. The more an ecosystem is rejuvenated, simplified, disorganised and unstable, the more exploitable it is, but the more dependent and vulnerable it becomes to exterior variation (Parra 1993:14–16). This is an increasingly present reality conditioning future patterns of exploitation and distribution of scarce natural resources. As a result, highly conflictual relations of access to vital resources are exported into the future together with their social, political and economic costs. None of these are seriously being accounted for in the statistics measuring 'economic growth'.

The problem of measuring in market terms environment-related factors such as natural resources depletion, pollution and waste accumulation, is being increasingly addressed by environmentally conscious national governments and international agencies. They face the interlocked issues of value and incommensurability. The French National Accounting System, for example, has devised a dual accounting procedure for the environment. There is a physical account of quantity and quality of available resources together with a parallel valuation in monetary terms (Weber 1993). Those working in this direction are conscious, however, of two crucial problems; first, that 'The valuation of the economy/environment relations can be neither exclusively economic (the availability of resources), nor exclusively ecologic (the state of the ecosystem), but must integrate as well the socio-cultural dimension' (Weber 1993:92); and, second, that environmental phenomena are often not bounded or structured within political-administrative territorial divisions (Weber 1993:112; see also Swift 1993:278–91). Thus, even while speaking of natural resources 'capital', 'stocks' and 'flows', environmental accountants are incapable of evaluating in market terms these 'external' elements of production which increasingly affect the reproduction of the economic system.

Nature, then, is economically incommensurable in market terms.

As there is no economic commensurability we could be tempted to base the decisions on an ecological – instead of an economic – rationality in terms of the concept of carrying capacity. However, the political territorial units on which this ecological politics would be applied do not have any ecological logic, they are products of human history. (Martínez Alier 1993:50–1)

Nature, therefore, is embedded in human society and history. The differential allocation of natural resources across space and time is a political economic process. Taking into account environmental factors means understanding them from the broader framework of an all-inclusive 'moral economy', without overlooking, however, the impact of the uneven world development of capitalism on the formation and transformation of local and worldwide, hegemonic and counter-hegemonic, 'moral' values.

Meaning in history and the development of capitalist economic relations

Talking about the embeddedness of nature and human labour in present-day market economies brings up some crucial questions. Is capitalist society a market *system* or a market *culture*? Is commodification of all factors of production a 'material' reality or an 'ideal' reality? Is capitalism a sequential process progressing from 'formal' to 'real' subsumption of labour to capital, or an opportunist process combining various forms of exploitation, adapting to and transforming existing local relations of social reproduction? At stake is a methodological breakthrough transcending narrow culturalist and materialist perspectives (Roseberry 1989). What we want to know is *how* capitalism differs, if it does, from other systems of exploitation; how the social identities of people both shape and are shaped by the positions they occupy in the process of capitalist accumulation and in the process of producing their livelihood. Meaning in history appears as the hinge between subjective experience and objective positions in the structure of production; as the bridge, also, between crystallised assumptions and negotiated memories of life and work.

   In an insightful account of French industrialisation, M. Reddy (1987) confronts the fact that the labour market was and remained embedded in multiplex social relations. Following Gudeman's (1986) idea of the importance of cultural models as scripts for economic processes, Reddy argues that a 'market culture' was actively resisted by workers as a model for rationalising their forms of securing a livelihood.

   To the nineteenth-century textile workers the embeddedness of their worklife was a constant reminder that their labour was *not* a commodity and *did not* respond to the laws of market exchange, that is, to quantitative equivalences of value (Reddy 1987:186–7, 225, 323, 329–34). Women's and children's labour, for instance, was systematically undervalued because of cultural assumptions about the male breadwinner and the complementary nature of dependants' incomes. Although demand for dependants' labour was high, prices did not follow (Reddy 1987: 8, 162). It is interesting to note, also, that employers used family power relations and ideology to get access and control over dependants' labour (Hareven 1977b; Tilly and Scott 1978; Reddy 1987). On the other hand, workers used family 'morality' to secure higher overall household income through higher male wages (Humphries 1977; McClelland 1987). And, finally, that the meaning of 'family' and its material consequences as to the unequal distribution of resources and power within and beyond the household, was part of the struggle between those trying to obtain a livelihood and those trying to accumulate capital or power.

For Reddy, indeed, all the labour struggles during the nineteenth-century industrialisation of the textile trade in France can be explained by two linked processes: first, workers' resistance to losing control of the labour process, that is, their independence at work, and, second, workers' resistance to a 'market culture' interpretation of their relations with employers, which, according to Reddy, were embedded in family, community and skill-related relationships, with little variation for more than a century. One could sum up these articulated processes as simply expressing workers' resistance to commodification, when the commodity form is seen as both a cultural and a material fact. But Reddy is ambiguous about it because he wants so much to distance himself from materialist accounts of industrialisation, which he sees as thoroughly contaminated by the 'market culture' hegemony.

The whole history of the industrial revolution ought to be treated in the first instance as a cultural crisis that yielded cultural change.

This is not to say that material conditions played no role in the outcome of the struggle. ... [But] there is very little dependable knowledge of what the actual material conditions then were. Nor will such information become available until the whole accretion of pseudo-knowledge of economic conditions couched in the misused and misleading categories of market culture has been jettisoned. (Reddy 1987:15)

He concludes, however, with the following argument:

Something like a moral economy is bound to surface anywhere that industrial capitalism spreads. It arises directly out of the impact of entrepreneurial cost cutting on work routines and the inability of the commodity concept of labour to render employer–employee relations coherent. (Reddy 1987:334)

Reddy's ideas are interesting but the problem remains: how are we to deal both with the fact that labour (and nature) are not produced for sale and are not separated from a multiplicity of non-marketable relations, and the fact that they *are* commodities in capitalist economies. Reddy insists that, for labour, commodification is only the result of a 'cultural' transformation: a market *language* about relations between employer and employee little by little overcomes workers' resistance to its hegemony. But social relations of production were changing and workers were fighting for their independence. Here independence meant the right to retain *in the workplace* social ties *other* than those 'freely' contracted with the employer; social responsibilities transcending those 'voluntarily' acquired with the employer. Workers tried to retain control over the labour process through their defence of skill, of the primacy of quality in production, of apprenticeship regulations. The language of trade organisations and regulations enabled new forms of collective action, where more homogeneous workers' unions struggled for new regulations, attuned to the changing relations of production, and in that process the language of work was also transformed (Sewell 1980). Workers tried to better their income through the use of 'moral' arguments such as the male family wage or a 'fair day's wage' (McClelland 1987), but also through the creation of barriers to the access of the labour market on the grounds of skill, gender, locality, etc. Employers also tried to secure willingness and good work through the use of family or community social ties or the creation of paternalistic and moralistic arguments about the employer–employee relationship; but were ready to adopt a different language and different strategies to secure and control labour if the context changed (Hareven 1977b). Employers also benefited from the creation of an heterogeneous and fragmented labour force where different segments of labour competed against each other, driving prices down and diverting conflict away from capital.

What is remarkable, then, is that both a 'market culture' and a non-market, 'moral' culture were at work in the forging of capitalist relations of production (McClelland 1987:187–202). I would argue, also, that this situation was *not* the result of 'traditional', 'past' values of commonalty resisting the encroachment of new commodified ideas about work. Rather, 'moral' ideas about the economy were being formed as relations of production were transformed and both 'moral' and 'commodified' meanings of work were shaping the path of capitalist transformation. The feeling that a certain type of embeddedness – material and cultural – is necessary to the construction of capitalist relations of production was, I think, Polanyi's point. For Marx, the discussion on 'formal' vs. 'real' subsumption of labour to capital reveals, in my opinion, the same sort of difficulty. Embeddedness was something lagging over from previous social forms of organising production, that would disappear with 'real' capitalist, fully commodified, relations of production. However, 'formal' subsumption *was* capitalism and was in fact perceived as a necessary stage for the reorganisation of social relations in a capitalist framework. Embeddedness is a reality in what seem to be, nowadays, capitalist market economies. Maybe real subsumption is only the expression of a particular form of formal subsumption. The forms of embeddedness, however, are not the same, long-lasting, residual relations from a past mode of life, but different, specifically capitalist forms of embeddedness, which are, moreover, extremely sensitive to *locality*. The need for *trust* to generate relations in 'free' contractual agreements is a case in point.

The opposition, then, of 'market culture' and 'market system' appears as a false dilemma. Rather, what we perceive is a paradox closer to Polanyi's idea of the *utopia* of a self-regulating market, and to Marx's *commodity fetishism*. People can become commodities *because* they are not things severed from the social relations that produce them. Moreover, because social relations – material and symbolic – constitute people's identities through life, these cannot be separated, in market societies, from the constitution of persons as commodities. As commodities, though, people appear to be detached from social relations other than the exchange relation, and they appear to acquire, through the generalised process of exchange, an abstract, quantifiable value. This is not only a 'cultural' phenomenon. It is a fundamental dialectic process where meanings are part of material forces which are formed by, and in turn transform, social relations of production and reproduction. In that process, power relations and the differential capacities of people in their search for a livelihood change. In his argument about the materialism of culture, William Roseberry points out:

among the material conditions under which they [real individuals] live is included a set of ideas, or sets of ideas, themselves historical products, that serve as material forces. (1989:41)

And he concludes:

Real individuals and groups act in situations conditioned by their relationships with other individuals and groups, their jobs or their access to wealth and property, the power of the state, and their ideas – and the ideas of their fellows – about those relationships. Certain actions and certain consequences of those actions, are possible while most other actions and consequences are impossible. (1989:54)

3   CONSUMPTION

The principal focus of this chapter is the process of consumption. It contributes a basic argument to the central thesis of the book on the need to adopt a framework that takes into consideration social reproduction as a whole when trying to explain material, life-sustaining processes.

I will begin by working on a definition of 'consumption' that adequately covers different aspects of a complex process. The next section will present a thorough analysis of the domestic group, which is probably the most ubiquitous social framework of consumption. In this section, Chayanov's theory of the 'labour–consumer balance' which has had a very strong impact on anthropologists' studies of peasant households, will be discussed. This will lead me to the study of the social relations that are constructed around consumption, both within the domestic group and beyond it, showing how power is related to personal identity issues through the consumption process. The last section in this chapter, 'producing while consuming' will complete the circle started in the chapter on 'production' by forcing us, once again, to break down the conceptually bounded region of 'consumption' in an attempt to work toward the analysis of articulated economic realities. This chapter then opens on to the following chapter on 'social reproduction'.

DEFINING CONSUMPTION

The place of consumption in the economic process

What is consumption? Where does it fit in the economic process? Generally, the economic is defined by three functions: production, distribution and consumption of material goods. Of these, consumption is seldom the object of empirical research or theoretical analysis: it appears as an epiphenomenon of production and distribution. Consumption is approached from two distinct perspectives.

The first approach considers consumption in the form of 'demand' as the prime motivation for production. The economic process, then, is set in motion by the need to 'satisfy human wants'. Goods are 'all desirable things' and 'All wealth consists of things that satisfy wants' (Marshall 1964 [1892]:34). Consumers' demand is at the origin of production but, more important, through the market mechanism it regulates the entire economy. The theory of the 'marginal utility' of goods is a consumption theory based on the psychological assumption that desire is a quantitative expression. In Marshall's words:

Utility is taken to be correlative to Desire or Want: and we have just seen that each several want is limited, and that with every increase in the amount of a thing which a man has, the eagerness of his desire to obtain more diminishes; until it yields place to the desire for some other thing, of which perhaps he hardly thought so long as his more urgent wants were still unsatisfied. ... In other words, the additional benefit which a person derives from a given increase of his stock of anything, diminishes with the growth of the stock that he already has. This statement of a fundamental tendency of the human nature may be called the *law of satiable wants* or *of diminishing utility*. (Marshall 1964:61–2)

And he adds:

We may call that part of the commodity which a person is only just induced to purchase his *marginal purchase*; because he is on the margin of doubt whether it is worth his while to incur the outlay required to obtain it. And the utility of his marginal purchase may be called the *marginal utility* of the commodity to him. (1964:62–3)

Within this framework the 'elasticity of demand' describes the greater or lesser 'extension of the desire to purchase' induced by a rise or a fall in the price of a commodity. If demand is very sensitive to the slightest variation in prices of a commodity, then there is a great elasticity of demand; and vice versa (Marshall 1964:69–74).

This neoclassical analysis of consumption is based in a particular idea of *human nature*: that 'desire' has a quantitative expression, that equivalences can be reached and exchange can satisfy desire by producing the amount required. Moreover, the context is that of generalised quantitative equivalences, that is, the market system. The dangers of transforming into a 'natural' and 'universal' law such historically grounded and ideologically charged hypothesis of human action is obvious and anthropologists have pointed to it repeatedly (Godelier 1974; Dumont 1977; Gudeman 1986). It is interesting to note, however, that for marginalist economists, consumption *explains* the economic process but itself depends totally on the mediation of the market's regulatory laws acting upon a 'fundamental tendency of human nature'. Consumption therefore is a given of nature and the market – which is also natural – and is never approached as a *social* (as opposed to a psychological) process.

In a critique of the 'economic' (marginalist) theory of consumption Fine and Leopold (1993) present several interesting objections.

First, the theory of demand is a 'horizontal' theory of consumption. That is, the factors that condition demand are presumed to apply in the same way for all commodities and across society as a whole. On the one hand, then, differences in the processes and social relations of production of distinct goods are assumed to be irrelevant. On the other hand, differences in the social and historical context of consumers are also taken as irrelevant to the process of decision making.

Second, the theory of demand focuses on aggregate consumption. That is, the individual and his marginalist behaviour is an abstract and independent entity whose value is significant only in quantitative terms as total 'demand' for every commodity. Variations in individual behaviour affecting 'demand' are mechanical expressions of the 'utility maximisation' idea. And aggregate demand is tantamount to social demand or, better, the demand of 'society'. Relations between individuals in a historically grounded context of production and reproduction is irrelevant to consumption in the theory of demand.

And third:

There is also a deficiency in conceptually distinguishing the theory of consumption (treated as demand) from the theory of production (treated as supply). For between the two, there is an exact parallel; the demand theory is essentially identical to the axiomatic theory of supply. The maximisation of utility subject to price and income constraints creates an identical mathematical problem to the minimisation of cost subject to output constraints and factor input prices. Conceptually, individual consumers can be interpreted as if they were entrepreneurs producing utility, rather than output, as efficiently as possible. (Fine and Leopold 1993:51)

As an alternative approach to consumption Fine and Leopold suggest taking into account the 'systems of provisions' of commodities, that is the social relations obtaining in production, distribution and consumption processes that contribute to the *material* differentiation of commodities and the social relations relevant in the *ideological* construction of perceived needs and of the possible ways of satisfying them.

This perspective, however, does not address consumption of non-commodified goods and services, nor, for that matter, the relations between commodified and non-commodified consumptions and the transfers between one form and the other. The role of the state and its policies of taxation and welfare are important factors directing the transfers between commodified and non-commodified consumption patterns. The articulation of commodified and non-commodified consumption is relevant to the way in which particular societies reproduce their basic structures and 'systems of differentiation' and in that process transform them. It is also relevant to the way in which particular societies produce and negotiate meaning in the process of consumption.

Take for example, the celebration of Thanksgiving in the US. There, national union of its citizens – purportedly homogeneous, natural and universal – is expressed through the consumption by individual families of a particular wholesome, plentiful meal. The foods consumed ideally refer to primeval and indigenous products of the land – turkey, potato, corn, pecan, pumpkin squash, etc. – and are processed in the 'natural economy' way of the fist colonial settlers, that is, by women in the home. Although the actual foods consumed are brand products bought in supermarkets and therefore set in a framework of specific market-mediated relations of production and consumption, there is a conscious process of de-commodification so as to meet cultural assumptions about the proper Thanksgiving meal. Thus, through material processes and relations of consumption the ideological 'union' of the nation, obscuring differentiation and conflict, is expressed in a culture that constructs the abundance of material consumption as the backbone of harmony and togetherness. In this context the articulation between commodified and non-commodified relations of production and consumption seems relevant to the social and political reproduction of a capitalist society such as the US (Wallendorf and Arnould 1991).

The second most common approach to consumption is one where consumption is perceived as the final part of the economic process.

Consumption is at the same time the *objective* of the economic process and its *completion*. This is a highly ambivalent and slightly tautological definition of consumption but one that is frequently used, often implicitly. It is based on a means/ends approach where the economic process could be outlined in the following way. Needs must be taken care of, this is done through production, and the goods or services produced must be distributed in order to be used by those in need. Then they are consumed. From this perspective consumption is the motivation and the termination of the economic process which, in fact, appears as the *means* toward an objective that remains somewhat outside or at the margins of it. While production and distribution are perceived as complex social processes, consumption is perceived as a simple natural process occurring almost beyond the constraints of society. Personal consumption is the fulfilment of the economic process but it is as if this happened *outside* the economy and *outside* society. This idea of consumption can be found in the concepts of 'natural economy', 'family economy', 'peasant economy' or 'domestic mode of production' where the economic process is defined as production *for* consumption (as opposed to production for exchange). Distribution here is absent or only marginally economic because deeply inserted in non-economic institutions. Consumption, in this perspective, is generally reduced to an enumeration of necessities unproblematically satisfied when the corresponding goods or services are forthcoming. Consumption is rarely analysed as part of a social process. Rather, it is assumed to take place at the outcome of a social process in a self-evident, 'natural', manner.

Another related aspect is the description of consumption as the *annihilation* of goods or services in the act of using them, that is, literally consuming them. Marshall mentions this element when he says that:

consumption may be regarded as negative production. Just as man can produce only 'utilities', so he can consume nothing more ... as his production of material products is really nothing more than a rearrangement of matter which gives it new utilities; so his consumption of them is nothing more than a disarrangement of matter, which lessens or destroys its utilities. (Marshall 1964:42)

In this sense even more so, consumption appears as the end, the termination of the economic process. If we think in terms of an economy geared toward the maximisation of profit through market exchange and producing for exchange, it is obvious that the consumption of a commodity takes it out of circulation and is the end of the realisation of exchange value in that commodity. It is then no longer a 'commodity' but a good, a use value, and when this too is realised in the final act of personal consumption there is nothing left. A new process must begin.

My approach to consumption tries to question this way of conceiving the economic process as autonomous production/distribution/ consumption chains articulated only at the levels of production, distribution and productive consumption (but not personal consumption) because it obscures the understanding of social reproduction as a necessary articulation of both commodified and non-commodified social relations. The articulation of personal consumption and production processes has been taken into account by classical economists when approaching the reproduction of the labour force through wages. However, this articulation is basically understood either as costs incurred by capital, that is, as a form of productive consumption, or as rent derived by the worker from participation in production. On these grounds, labour and human livelihood which are the two aspects at the core of economic social relations, have been approached, then, as peculiarities of the economic structure, somewhat anomalous and annoying, – difficult to quantify – economic realities. I will try to explore these 'annoying' economic realities through detailed analysis of personal consumption and the social relations that are created in that process. My aim is to show how relations of consumption and, more generally, the way in which people organise their livelihood cannot be separated from the way in which production relations and distribution differences are generated.

Personal consumption as means of livelihood; multiple resources and their social value

Consumption is related to the use of goods and services. When these are used in the process of producing other goods or services we speak of *productive consumption*. When use is for maintaining and reproducing human life it is referred to as *personal consumption*. Personal consumption can be thought of also as productive consumption when human life is thought of as labour. This has been one of the main points in the domestic labour debate as we will see below. Personal consumption, however, is an ambivalent concept which can loosely be defined as the *use of resources* in the process of making a living. In market economies we might refer to the realisation of the use value of commodities in an 'unproductive' manner. Marx, for instance, considers all labour related to personal consumption 'unproductive' labour. We will deal with personal consumption in this chapter.

When defining consumption as the use of resources we are subsuming under one label several things which should be distinguished at the analytical level. First, the 'use' of resources comprises at least two distinct processes: (1) the *labour* necessary to transform 'raw goods' into consumable objects, this includes what we call domestic labour but also different sorts of self-help and self-provisioning activities as well as the attitude of attention and disposition to the consumption needs of others that might be labelled 'care' (De Vault 1991); and (2) the *activity of consuming proper*, that is, of realising the utility of a specific good or service. Different societies organise these activities – labour and consumption – in different ways. Processing labour will express power relations within the domestic group. This in turn will depend on the larger political and economic structure and the position of a particular domestic unit and its members within it. *Who does what* kind of processing labour is an important question to bear in mind. *And why* this is so will bring us once more to the dialectical – material/cultural – aspect of human societies. Reference to 'traditional' gendered activities or to a self-evident sexual division of labour, explains nothing. Moreover, it is often the grounds for projecting ethnocentric realities and ideologies. Rather, one must try to understand the historical process by which a set of relations concerning processing activities, come to be organised as they are and how they are reproduced.

Consumption proper is often treated as an intimate, personal, individualised activity, except when it is treated as a 'total prestation' in ceremonial or festive banquets or as an exchange relation when eating is included in work-party deals. Everyday maintenance consumption, however, is generally perceived as unproblematic and self-evident even when differential processing labour relations are acknowledged. Nevertheless, consumption proper is also the ground for conflict and differentiation.

Who consumes *what*, *when* and *how*, and *why* this is so, are revealing questions. Patterns of nutrition, within and between households, for example, are significant at many levels. On the one hand, differential protein and calorie intake express the power of household members to get hold of more or less valuable nutrients. But this power is part of the social relations of production and reproduction of a given society as a whole. Moreover the larger context of the unequal economic and political relations of local societies within the capitalist world-system should be taken into account.

On the other hand, consumption can be considered meaningful from a semiological perspective: as a system of information about social relations (Barthes 1967; Douglas and Isherwood 1978; Baudrillard 1969, 1974; Appadurai 1986). From this perspective, 'commodities are good to think' with and consumption is the means by which cultural categories are expressed. Recurring acts of consumption in a social arena produce a system of information where goods and services are the visible signs of social relations.

In this context, Baudrillard's approach tries to develop a 'critique of the political economy of the sign'. His main point is that, in the study of consumption, the concept of 'need' has been considered as the universal functional principle of the object by marginalist economists, political economists and Marxists alike. In his view, this separation of primary (that is, 'natural') vs. secondary (that is, 'social') needs is ideological and essentialist (1974:77). Rather, the main value of objects is their 'sign-exchange value': the meaning that objects express in the context of a code that enables discrimination. 'Need', basic subsistence requirements appear then as residual to the social process of signification (1974:77–8). The point is that all societies present an articulation of 'subsistence' and 'excedent' consumption and, to Baudrillard, precedence should be given to the latter, 'social' aspect of consumption, the other aspect being a questionable ideological construction of the capitalist system (1974:78–81, 100–1). It is interesting to note, however, that Baudrillard preserves the distinction between different 'domains' – economy, culture – where different 'values' obtain: use value, exchange value and sign-exchange value. Moreover these values are to be distinguished from 'symbolic value' where the object is not autonomous from the *concrete* social relations it creates and incorporates within a 'logic of ambivalence' (1974:54–7). The sign-object, on the contrary, 'is owned and manipulated by the individual subjects, as a sign, that is, as coded difference. It is the object of consumption and it remains an abolished, reified social relation, signified in a code' (1974:55). For

Baudrillard, within the contemporary capitalist system use value and exchange value converge in sign-exchange value, because goods are not only immediately produced for exchange as commodities but for encoded signification as signs:

> The object of this political economy [of the sign], that is, its simplest element, its nuclear element – what the commodity was for Marx – and which is no more, today, either fully commodity nor sign, but inseparably both *and where both have been abolished as specific determinations, but not as forms*, this object is maybe just the object, the *form*/object, where, in a complex mode that describes the more general form of political economy, converge the use value, the exchange value and the sign-exchange value. (1974:173)

Thus it is the social production of sign values, the control and manipulation of the signifying process, monopolisation of the sign code, which are paramount in the domination process. Baudrillard sees this logic in evolutionary terms as an 'ulterior stage' of domination, substituting for the logic of class defined by ownership of the means of production (1974:126–7). It appears as the ultimate metamorphosis of economic and political power.

Baudrillard's analysis presents interesting points, namely his critique of 'need' and 'use value' as constitutive of a universalist and essentialist finality of goods should be taken into account. His approach, however, is an attempt to substitute the cultural expression and production of political differentiation and domination for the economic process of differentiation and political domination based on people's position within social relations of production. The problem with this view is that production relations are wholly subsumed into exchange relations which, in turn, are subsumed into coded signifying relationships of exchange. The result is that the *cultural* aspect of consumption, presented as the totalising logic of the political economy of capitalist systems, obscures the process of construction of signifying codes as part of social reproduction, where distributive politics are both the result and the continuation of production relations and emerge in historical (both *material* and *cultural*) contexts. In other words, political domination cannot be reduced (or abstracted) to the production and control of a code of signs.

Within the semiological perspective, some attempts at understanding the sign-exchange value across cultures and societies, within a world market economy, have proved more interesting than Baudrillard's theoretical discourse. Spooner (1986) in a study of the 'authenticity' value of oriental carpets in European culture, shows how the production of its distinguishing sign value cannot be abstracted from history. Spooner considers together, first, the production relations and cultural meanings objectified in the carpet; second, the process of commercialisation and the production of a transactional meaning between local and foreign merchants; and, finally, the European consumption process producing a sign of 'authenticity' that signifies distinction. Moreover, all these processes are interlocked and are constantly being transformed by their interaction and their relation to wider economic and political contexts (for example the Soviet state's control of Turkmenistan). This, I think, is a much richer analysis of the production of meaning in consumption processes.

The idea that consumption is related to the process of producing *distinction*, not only as a function of differential allocation of material resources but also of symbolic resources, has been expressed in the work of anthropologists such as Bourdieu (1988 [1979]), Appadurai (1986) and Miller (1987, 1995). Consumption in this view is strongly related to identity construction. Appadurai, for example, is concerned with the changing cultural contexts of commodities circulating among a worldwide range of societies. The case study by Spooner, above, seems to me one of the best illustrations of this perspective.

For Miller, the process of consumption is treated in a very philosophical way. It is presented as part of a process of 'objectification', that is, the creative construction of humanity through the double process of 'externalisation' and 'reappropriation' of 'particular form'. Form did not exist prior to the initial creative act and is not eliminated by the latter re-incorporation act (Miller 1987:28). Miller sees consumption, in the context of global present-day capitalism, as the only remaining domain that enables people to forge a meaningful relationship with the world. Consumption, then, appears as a mutually constitutive process of culture and identity creation (Miller 1995:17, 31, 34). Increasingly, consumption becomes the only arena of political agency.

Miller's views are provocative and they appear to present several advantages over previous 'antiquated' (!) 'production' theories. The first advantage is the 'progressive' potential of consumption: that is, when consumption practices may become the key to the transformation of processes of production and distribution. The second advantage is that 'an emphasis upon consumption is an acknowledgement of the potential and creative power of diverse human groups to make of their resources what they will' (Miller 1995:41), referring to the 'relatively autonomous and plural process of cultural self-construction' and 'based on respect of consumption as empowerment' (1995:41). And last, but not least, consumption allows for a 'morality of egalitarianism' based on the empowerment attained through the self-construction of people as consumers:

> People have found that an identity constructed through consumption is far more empowering and controllable than that which is dependent upon their placement within ever larger systems of production over which they have little control. ... There is a clear preference for consumers to be able autonomously to employ their resources for the self-construction of their individual and social identity, rendering their place in work as no more than a necessary constraint created by their obligation to earn a living. It is therefore equality at the point of access to resources for the self-construction of consumers that becomes the proper point of arbitration of egalitarian moralities. (1995:42)

The big problem with Miller's perspective stems from his Hegelian point of departure: the idealism present in the 'objectification' process where a creative, seemingly autonomous, act of human will – 'externalisation' – is at the origin of 'particular form'. As a completing movement, moreover, another relatively autonomous, creative, act of human will – 'reappropriation' – effects cultural and personal self-construction. His consumption theory rests on this idealist self-construction process that enables him to speak of autonomous, creative, empowering acts of consumption as opposed to dependent, alienated, uncontrollable acts of production.

Several questions can be raised to confront this theory. Are people really so submissive and uncreative in their working lives? Also, is the experience of work so completely detached from the experience of consumption? How does an identity constructed through consumption become 'empowering' if it neither aims, nor has the power to transform that 'necessary constraint created by their obligation to earn a living' in which most people in the world spend most of the waking hours of their lives? How can egalitarian moralities be related only – or even preferably or autonomously – to access to resources at the point of consumption, when the availability of goods and services is dependent on processes of production and distribution, and on the differentiated social relations that people create all along these processes?

Several examples question Miller's optimistic bid for a consumption-centred social and political theory. Think only of 'Mad Cow Disease', of its economic and political causes expressed in the resistance of a conservative government, under pressure from the powerful farmers' lobby, to acknowledge the danger of BSE-infected cows for human consumers. This should be taken into account as well as the cultural value of meat in the British diet as a sign of what a 'proper meal' is, together with the expanding availability of meat and other cow products as production costs lowered due to more intensive farming and the substitution of pasture by other feeds. There are no proper epidemiological studies as yet that would enable us to link consumption habits with other professional, class or cultural specificities of infected people, yet we can already clearly perceive that a consumption crisis of such a magnitude can hardly be understood by applying Miller's theory. For an analogous case of massive food poisoning in Spain during the 1980s, that of the 'Toxic Oil Syndrome', there is sufficient epidemiological information to attempt a brief analysis. In this case, thousands of poor urban and rural people died or were severely crippled for life when a few businessmen decided to produce and sell at very low prices oil that was not fit for human consumption. Obviously this happened in a context where *oil* (preferably olive oil, which was what the toxic product was fraudulently sold for) is one of the basic staples in Spanish food culture, where its expansion as the main cooking medium all over Spain is linked to the Francoist regulation of agriculture after the Spanish Civil War (1936–9). But also very important was the context of non-enforcement of regulations about or control over food industries and food distribution channels by the government. Last, but not least, was the fact that those who were to benefit from the production of cheap toxic oil were situated in a very different position in the structure of production from those who were to be the main consumers and victims of the fraud. In the light of these examples, it is hard to see how it would be possible to speak of 'empowerment' through consumption without taking into account in a major way the rest of the social relations of exploitation and domination in a given society.

In my view, Miller's theory suffers from its idealist base, from its overemphasis on consumption as an *autonomous* realm and from its incapacity to firmly ground agency in history. As all of these seem to me to be important shortcomings for a theory of consumption I shall try to present an alternative perspective in the following sections of this chapter.

Bourdieu's approach to consumption is closer to the view I want to offer for consideration, one that opens the way to a theory of social reproduction. Through his concept of 'habitus' (structured and structuring dispositions) Bourdieu tries to ground the process of cultural 'distinction' in the 'objective conditions of existence' that produce class differences. The 'habitus' is a structure of reproduction: produced by 'objective conditions', it in turn produces a scheme of perception generating practices that produce class distinctions and reproduce class positions through the very *material* consequences of 'culture' when considered as 'capital'. Thus, 'lifestyles', as perceived in consumption processes, are treated as the practical expression of the habitus generated by each particular 'configuration of capital' (economic), of 'objective conditions of existence'. But it is also the system whereby personal and collective identities are negotiated in *practice*; where the attribution of identity contributes to reproduce, through a system of representation, the objective mechanisms of class distribution (1988 [1979]).

With all its dense and suggestive theorising and his punctilious study of 'distinction' processes in France, Bourdieu does not offer an account of the differential production of 'habitus'. All the attention focuses on this mediating concept which is supposed to bridge the gap between 'objective conditions' and 'subjective identities', but in the end, we never see it happen. In Bourdieu it remains mostly, still, wishful thinking of a very attractive kind.

All these perspectives (even Bourdieu's) seem to forget that commodities cannot be abstracted from the social relations that produce them. Things have meaning and can express social relations and power struggles *because* social relations and power struggles are crystallised in things. Meaning as the cultural aspect of a dialectical social process should be taken into account, but not as a separate or ultimate dominion of power relations. In fact we should try to put Bourdieu's wishes into practice.

I shall give an example of a perspective that, I think, gets close to this aim. In *Sweetness and Power* (1986) Sydney Mintz studies sugar from a political economic perspective. He traces the consumption of sugar in Europe and links it with the development and expansion of capitalism. For a long time sugar was the preserve of the powerful classes.

Its expansion as a substitute nutrient (together with tea and coffee) among the working classes during the eighteenth and nineteenth centuries 'sharply reduced the overall cost of creating and reproducing the metropolitan proletariat' (1986:180). This depended, in turn, on the development of the plantation system in the West Indies. In the new context the meaning of sugar, also, was transformed. 'Tobacco, sugar and tea were the first objects within capitalism that conveyed with their use the complex idea that one could *become* different by *consuming* differently' (1986:185). Therefore, both material and ideological consumption and production relations at the centre and at the periphery must be treated as part of the overall reproduction process of the world capitalist system.

Although the definition of personal consumption is centred around the *use* of resources, often the *resources* in themselves (not yet their use) are highlighted in the concept of consumption.

When resources are equated to commodities acquired in the market, consumption is easily perceived as 'demand'. Household or personal *expenses*, then, are conceived as the *measure* of consumption. Even in a market economy, however, expenses are an inaccurate measure of goods and services consumed (or obtained for use): some goods and services are provided with public funds in 'welfare states'; others, such as domestic work or all sorts of 'help', are obtained through non-market transfers of work between people linked by kinship, friendship and other multiplex relationships.

Sometimes resources are commodities, or they might be commodities for some time, and as such they should be studied in terms of 'demand', affecting the structure of markets and therefore production. Some resources are never commodities and there is always much more than exchange value even to consumption commodities, because use value is an immediately present, though swiftly vanishing aspect of them.

Personal consumption resources, then, embrace a wide range of commodified and non-commodified goods and services. *Objects* such as food, clothing, shelter; *services* such as public infrastructure – sewage, roads, education, health care, etc. – domestic work, care; *labour* such as child or adult disposition within and between households; and *information*. Many resources might be present both in market and non-market forms and access to one or the other – or complete exclusion – will be conditioned by (and in turn condition) the position of individuals and groups within the political and economic field of forces.

Consumption as a process: access, distribution, processing of resources and final consumption

An attempt to define consumption should embrace the complex set of relationships outlined above. Relationships centred around access to different sorts of resources; relationships that shape and are shaped by the distribution of resources within and between households; relationships concerning the processing of resources and, finally, relationships being produced and reproduced upon the realisation of consumption proper. Consumption, then, is best conceived as a *process*; a process within a process for it cannot be separated from production and distribution. The process of consumption, that is, the complex set of relationships which emerge from it, will not be the same for a *hacienda* owner's family in present-day South America as for a industrial worker in nineteenth-century Birmingham. Global, local, class, gender and age factors, among others, will affect the way people get hold of resources, distribute them between family, kin, friends or neighbours, and in the end, use them. Positions of power and wealth which are partially constructed in production, in the articulation of different forms of production into a worldwide capitalist system, condition people's capabilities to organise consumption and 'signify' through consumption. In turn, all that is consumed – possessed or used – conveys certain amounts of power over other people. Both the *manner of consumption*, as a sign in a social arena where a web of meaning is constantly being re-created and defined, and the *content of consumption* as the incorporation of useful things resulting in the control of a greater amount of energy, or labour, or information into one's life, produce wealth and power, and place each person in a specific field of opportunities regarding production and distribution processes.

Take, for example, recurring commensality among Western societies' upper classes: the fact of dining out a lot, with different people, of attending all sorts of parties, charities, of inviting people often, etc. is a sign of power but *also* it is a means of creating, maintaining and activating networks which are crucial to the circulation of information – on business deals, or competitors' moves on the financial market, on government policies and available strategies, etc.; to access to the means of production through marriage settlements, or the informal negotiation of deals; to enhanced control over the production process through gaining influence with the owners of capital, or consolidating authority within a firm's department, etc. On the other hand, recurring commensality, in the modest sense of sharing food where it is available between poor households is not only a way of incorporating much needed nourishment, but also a means of maintaining networks under stress situations. In turn these networks are crucial to the circulation of information about employment, odd jobs, market bargains, public aid or even edible food waste that homeless people get from the garbage. It is interesting to note that food and information generally circulate in the same networks and often together. Also, food and more generally basic necessities such as clothes and shelter are the locus of the ultimate power/wealth force in most societies. The lack of any other means of access to subsistence resources pushes people into the proletarian labour/capital relation, in Marxian analyses. Historically, enclosures and the New Poor Laws contributed greatly in breaking the access of working people to non-commodified life support networks in England, structuring capitalist relations of production. What we have defined as a process of consumption is, therefore, at the heart of relations of production.

Finally, the process of consuming, of getting hold of and incorporating resources, is a *social* (not a natural) process. As such, conflict, negotiation and differentiation emerge at every stage of consumption and design the field of forces for the next stage. Access, distribution, processing and using resources constitute social arenas where power and wealth, control and possession are constantly at play – arenas, moreover, where meaning is produced that affects the entire economic process and beyond, because it directly constructs people's identities and bodies. Struggle and also solidarity are constant elements in a process which is both private and public, individual and collective, centripetal and centrifugal, homogenising and differentiating.

THE CONSUMPTION UNIT

The social framework of consumption: the domestic group and the domestic cycle

Personal consumption occurs in a social framework often based on kinship relationships. Generally, the household is considered the locus where personal consumption is realised. The household, in turn, is defined as the place of consumption *and* the space occupied by a group of close kin (Bender 1967; Wilk and Netting 1984). This slightly tautological definition is nevertheless useful as a start. It highlights, for most processes of consumption, a set of relationships – kin – and a core space – the household. This is often expressed through the concept of family. When speaking of the household, it is important to distinguish between morphology and function, between what a domestic group *is* and what it *does* (Wilk and Netting 1984). Morphology is a material and cultural concept because – if it is to be defined apart from function, which seems basically an analytical device – spatial boundaries must be defined and binding links between people must be discriminated in advance.

Function, on the other hand, is often perceived as the result of recurring agency among morphologically defined household members. The main household function is purported to be consumption. There is an element of organisation and coordination of activities which appears as important, and leads to a presumption of consensus. Morphology and function, however, are tightly related. What is done to organise consumption produces relations of power and differentiation within the household, while relations of power and wealth produced elsewhere are expressed in the consumption process of the household. Also, morphology and function change through time in what is called the domestic cycle, and relationships between members of the household are continually being re-negotiated along two basic categories – gender and age – which in turn are social and cultural products.

Several questions must be raised. If we take the household as the basic – spatial – element in the definition of consumption, we see that household members are mainly kin but that other people share the same space and are linked by other than kinship relationships (real or fictive). Mostly these are people related to some member of the household by wage relations, that is, servants or lodgers. Often, then, relationships between household members are ambiguous. Moreover they are transformed over time, as the household structure and the personal life histories of connected members evolve. Take, for instance, the peasant household in rural Catalonia (Spain) where single brothers and sisters of the heir (*hereu*) to the farm were often treated as kin-servants working as field labourers and domestic servants for the *hereu* with little reward other than basic maintenance.

A similar situation is described by Nelson (1987) for Kenya, where rural–urban child fostering is frequent. Poor rural peasants send their child to the household of elite urban kin relying in an ideology of kinship solidarity as a strategy to enhance their child's opportunities. However, poor rural kin children often become free household labour for their wealthy urban relatives in a relationship that Nelson calls 'kin-servant'. In turn, the free labour provided by the kin-servant mainly in child care responsibilities enables educated elite women 'to work at well-paid jobs to earn the money necessary to maintain their elite life style' (Nelson 1987:195). Kinship relations therefore can be exploitative and also be the means toward differential consumption among household members. On the other hand, kinship is generally the idiom of relationships within the household and the means of being placed in a specific position in the consumption process, but also in relations of production more generally. Often, members originally ascribed to the household through wages are transformed in the long run into real or fictive kin.

In rural Catalonia, for example, a long-time agricultural servant became 'as a son' (which seems quite logical if we remember that non-inheriting single sons were somewhat 'as servants'); the female domestic servant of a widower became very often his wife and an informally adopted distant younger relative was 'like a son/daughter' and became the prospective heir/heiress of a barren couple. Similar cases are widely documented for European peasantries historically (Mitterauer and Sieder 1979; Plakans 1984). Kinship relationships therefore are dialectically linked with the economic process as a whole. Through the consumption process kinship relations are created and reproduced. At the same time authority based on kinship legitimises differentiation in consumption positions (and, more generally, access to resources – productive and reproductive) which then becomes easily obscured in an idiom of 'naturalness' and 'mutuality'.

As a spatial congregation of people, the household is not the only group regularly enmeshed in a consumption process. Other institutional frameworks of consumption include religious congregations, boarding schools, military barracks, charity networks. But also non-institutionalised networks such as those created by the homeless people must be taken into account. The household, however, has been traditionally defined in most studies as the consumption unit, *par excellence*. How much of this is an ethnocentric extrapolation of a

Western European, middle-class ideology is difficult to assert, but certainly as I will try to show in this chapter, the idea of a small, closed, centripetal, permanent and stable unit of consumption has obscured many consumption process and a large part of consumption relations.

The concept of 'family' as an ideological construct

The concept of 'family' has often been used in the social sciences as synonymous with 'household'. It is, in fact, quite distinct. The 'family', with the core meaning of nuclear family – a couple and their children – has been used as both an ahistorical and universal concept. The reason for this uncritical use of the term is that it is a highly naturalised concept. This problem stems from the idea that procreation and, growing from it, socialisation, are the main functions of the family. As biological reproduction is generally perceived as 'natural', although feminist studies have proved this is not so (Tabet 1985; MacCormack 1982b; McLaren 1984; Rubin 1975), then the social institution where it takes place must also be 'natural' and thus 'universal', although a 'natural' and 'universal' *social* institution seems to be a contradiction in terms.

The 'family' is a Western concept that evolves historically and up to the eighteenth century has the meaning of household: a group of people united by kinship or other links sharing a space and organising consumption, distribution and production processes (Flandrin 1976; Berkner 1972, 1973, 1976; Anderson 1980). During the nineteenth century the idea of the family as strictly limited to close kinship relations and functionally geared toward procreation and socialisation progressively takes hold in the bourgeoisie. Within bourgeois households, still full of non-kin members – servants, lodgers – an idea of 'privacy' linked with the nuclear family expands (Löfgren 1984). At the same time production processes are increasingly distinct from a household endeavour either because labour processes have expanded into requiring many hands or because people must sell their labour force in order to obtain the means of livelihood. Although small independent producers as well as family farms are numerous and even expanding, the family ideology seems to be tied to industrialisation, commodification of labour and the rise of an urban bourgeoisie.

In any case, a double movement seems to shape the family ideology during the nineteenth century: one separating the realms of production and reproduction (procreation, socialisation, maintenance), the other naturalising and privatising the nuclear family. Both movements contribute to the idea of the family as a non-economic, highly emotional set of relationships and naturally gendered responsibilities that should be respected so that the natural moral order prevails. The morality of the bourgeois idea of the family is set against the 'immoral' life conditions of the working class: lack of privacy ('promiscuity'), lack of respect for the 'natural' responsibilities of women (they worked instead of attending to their procreative, socialising and maintenance duties) and for the 'natural' responsibilities of men, that is, to bring home their wage in order to feed the family (instead of going to the pubs, etc.). Moreover poor people often worked at home relying on the help of children. A moralising crusade is launched during the second half of the century in order to impose the moral benefits of the 'family' ideology to the working classes (Löfgren 1984; Lewis 1984; Scott 1988). At the same time factory laws were set to protect women and child labour; and religious recommendations in the economic realm were intended to defend the moral family and thus protect society from the evils of workers' organisations and socialism (cf. the Papal Encyclical of Leo XIII, 'Rerum Novarum', 1959b [1891]). Regulation and intervention were constructing a normative 'family' ideology that was dialectically linked with the development of capitalism in Western societies. At the same time the working class found that the 'family' ideology was useful as a bargaining device with capital and as a means to rightfully preserve a private space from the state's intrusion (Humphries 1977).

The debate over the origins of the 'family wage' is interesting because it presents different hypotheses. For some (May 1982; Land 1980) the 'family wage' enabled capitalists to stabilise and render the male workforce more vulnerable and dependent. It was also a means of segmenting the labour market according to normative 'family' responsibilities. Henceforth women would *always* be dependent on a male family wage, at least in theory, and thus their labour power would be systematically undervalued. The 'family wage' has also been explained as a move on the part of unionised male workers to eliminate female competition in the labour market, by materially reinforcing the ideology of distinct gendered family responsibilities. Often feminists see the family wage as an alliance of male capitalists and workers against women, where men traded class solidarity for the benefits of monopolising the power to control female labour in the household (Hartmann 1981). Still another hypothesis presents the 'family wage' as a working-class – both male and female – strategy in order to obtain higher value for men's labour power and to increase resources by the exclusive dedication of women's work to consumption activities with the overall result of sensibly bettering working households' incomes (Humphries 1977). In any case what is remarkable about all these hypotheses is that they lend support to a multifaceted construction of a hegemonic cultural concept of the 'family' and one, moreover, strongly related to the struggles of the development of capitalist relations of production in Western countries.

The 'family' concept, then, is less useful as a descriptive term than that of 'household', because the links that bind people into families – those of alliance and consanguinity – are highly problematic cultural constructs that depend on social and political relations in every society. Moreover, reproduction, which is the defining function of 'families', is a complex concept covering at least three distinct meanings: biological reproduction; reproduction of the labour force; and social reproduction of the entire social and economic system (Edholm et al. 1977). Generally, an emphasis on procreation tends to naturalise (and often obscure) the other meanings of 'reproduction'. The 'family', then, is best seen as a cultural construct. It appears as a heterogeneous ideology for recruiting people into households, for regulating social relations within and between households and with the social environment. Moreover, it can be seen as a means of securing and obscuring relations of power and exploitation within households (Rapp 1978, 1987). Thinking of discourses around the 'family' as a heterogeneous ideology means taking into account class and the relationship of ideologies to the construction of specific production relations and political structures in capitalist economies (Rebel 1983; Eisenstein 1984; Beechey 1980; J. Smith 1984; Barrett 1980; Beneria and Sen 1982).

Although the 'family' ideology is the product of Western history, it has followed capitalist expansion around the world. As relations of production have developed differently according to historical and environmental, political and economic, local and regional constraints, the articulation of a Western 'family' ideology in different places will also vary according to local ideas about reproduction – procreation, socialisation and maintenance – that probably will not be homogeneous either. Indeed, all 'civilisation', 'colonisation' and 'modernisation' movements have tried to export and impose the adoption of a Western 'family' ideology in order to control households and their members in a specific way and induce them to enter production relations from within a specific ideological framework. Colonial administrations' taxing structures and Western religions' proselytism are probably the best examples of coercion into a Western 'family' ideology pattern with a moralising and rationalising pretence.

A critique of the domestic group/consumption unit concept

It is not surprising, then, that the domestic group has been treated as the consumption unit *par excellence*. However, this has presented many problems. First, the household/consumption unit is generally perceived as a self-centred unit, with firm boundaries, isolated from other similar units. Exchanges are conceived as taking place between an 'inside' household consumption unit and an 'outside' world of 'real' economic processes, that is, production and distribution. Ideologically, the confrontation is set between the moral and the immoral, between heart and heartless, emotional and rational worlds. The household consumption unit concept sets a frontier that divides two completely different spaces both materially and symbolically.

Second, there arises a tendency to *homogenise* the household because it is considered as a *unit* of consumption, not as a bundle of relationships between people brought together in a complex *process* of consumption. Often, the members of the domestic group appear as undifferentiated, integrated in a mass consumption unit. Many analyses are based in the presupposition that there is a 'common income purse' or 'income level' and that resources are homogeneously and equitably redistributed among household members – in fact distribution is often not even mentioned as an intra-household activity. When a common purse is found it should be analysed as a result of power relations and negotiation, rather than being assumed as the 'normal' form of the household consumption unit income. Moreover, the access by different household members to different income sources will presumably affect their control over their allocation to specific expenses or savings.

A third and related problem is the opacity of the domestic unit. This tends to reduce household consumption to what happens at the borders, between the inside and the outside: that is, monetary *income* and consumption *expenses*, thereby reducing consumption to market exchange relations and quantifiable values. In other words consumption is defined as, first, household consumption, that is, terminal transactions between one household unit and the market; and, second, the acquisition of commodities or services in the market. This perspective purportedly allows the measurement on a universal scale of the 'consumption levels' of different societies or groups within a society. It is based, however, on the following false premises: first, that consumption is an exchange relation; second, that the household is a bounded unit; third, that it is a homogeneous and opaque unit and fourth, that circulation ends when a resource crosses the boundary of the self-centred household consumption unit. In order to understand the diverse consumption processes that confront us we should try to unveil power and wealth relations *inside* the domestic unit and then try to go beyond the household unit following the circulation of resources between persons and households through non-market networks.

Because of its pervasive influence in anthropology and history, our critique of the domestic group/consumption unit concept will centre in Chayanov's work. Chayanov's *Peasant Farm Organization* (1986 [1925]) has been an extremely influential work in Peasant Studies. In economic anthropology Sahlins uses Chayanov's consumer/worker ratio as the basic law of his domestic 'mode of production' concept. Thus, Chayanov's theory has pervaded most studies of societies where consumption and production are organised (1) by one and the same social 'unit' (the household); or (2) with none or little market mediation between production and consumption; or (3) more generally where production is perceived as geared by the particular 'private economies' of the worker/consumer unit (that is, income/expenditure family budgets).

Chayanov's work (1986) stems from 'an enormous quantity of empirical material on problems of peasant farm organization' and tries to find a theoretical solution to the 'numerous facts and dependent relationships that did not fit into the framework of the usual conception of the organizational basis of private economic undertakings and that demanded some special interpretation' (1986:38). His methodology is therefore an inductive generalisation from the empirical material, mostly family farm budgets. The problem he faces is how to explain the seemingly irrational (from an entrepreneurial perspective) economic decisions of peasant farms: 'the list of peasant farm violations of entre-preneurial rules' (1986:41). His hypothesis, after detailed analysis of the empirical material, is based on the premise that:

the motivation of the peasant's economic activity [is] not as that of an entrepreneur who as a result of investment of his capital receives the difference between gross income and production overheads, but rather as the motivation of the worker on a peculiar piece-rate system which allows him alone to determine the time and intensity of his work. (1986:42)

His object of study is the:

organizational analysis of peasant family economic activity ... a family that does not hire outside labour, has a certain area of land available to it, has its own means of production, and is sometimes obliged to expend some of its labour force on non-agricultural crafts and trades. (1986:51)

It is 'a farm which has been drawn into commodity circulation' (1986:125), although income in kind may be more or less important. This, however, does not affect the organisational principles of the farm. The emphasis on the 'organisational' aspect of the farm as a particular form of 'private economic undertaking' is crucial in order to understand Chayanov's position and that of his critics. To Chayanov, the 'peasant family labour farm' can be studied ahistorically and apart from its wider economic environment as an 'organisational form' aiming on its own to achieve 'economic equilibrium' (1986:42–3, 49). This is understood as a balance between demand and supply, that is, between consumption and production: the 'labour–consumer balance'. 'If we wish to have a single organisational concept of the peasant labour farm independent of the economic system into which it enters we ought inevitably to base our understanding of its organisational essence on family labour'(1986:42)

The general framework, then, appears as two split economic realms, with two different 'logics', one 'subjective' and one 'objective'. The peasant labour farm's economic activity is based on the analogy of the individual pieceworker. The work motivation of family members, the intensity and productivity of their labour as well as other economic decisions regarding land and capital investment will depend exclusively on the 'subjective labour–consumer balance'. This will be the basic law of motion of the on-farm processes.

Beyond its limits in the sphere of interfarm relations, the peasant farm appears and can only appear, through its objective actions. It is from the mass inter-relations of these actions with those of others composing the system of national economy that the objective social phenomena of price, rent, and so on are formed. (1986:46)

These objective laws are, obviously, the market laws of (presumably) marginalist economists.

It is interesting to note that however distinct the 'subjective' and 'objective' realms may be in Chayanov's theoretical structure of the economy, there is a silent analogy of the demand/supply market regulation theory in the subjective labour–consumer balance. It looks as if, first, the peasant labour farm was a miniature economic market system; second, the 'subjective' labour–consumer balance of the family farm – based on the analogy of the individual pieceworker's economic strategising – was the 'natural' human economic logic; and third, 'subjective' and 'objective' rationalities seem not so far apart then, both geared to the 'equilibrium of economic factors' set in motion by demand. In fact, more than other private economic undertakings where the imbalance between 'gross income' and 'production overheads' is the motivation for economic activity and is understandable only as part of a wider system which is self-regulating and tends toward equilibrium, the family labour farm is a whole system unto itself, self-regulated and balanced, a total economy which mirrors in its specificity some of the main theoretical tenets of the marginalist theory.

What, then, is Chayanov's hypothesis? It is based on the idea that family consumption needs drive family workers' production activities. The total family income, including both agriculture and other crafts and trades, compared with family demands 'gives the basic economic equilibrium' (1986:103). During a family life cycle its composition changes and the proportion of family members able to work in relation to total consumers varies greatly. This changing consumer/worker ratio will directly affect the economic activity of the peasant labour farm.

Thus, *every family*, depending on its age, is in its different phases of development a completely distinct labour machine as regards labour force, intensity of demand, consumer–worker ratio, and the possibility of applying the principles of complex cooperation. (1986:60)

Hence his main hypothesis:

Since the labour family's basic stimulus to economic activity is the necessity to satisfy the demands of its consumers, and its work hands are the chief means for this, we ought first of all to expect the family's *volume of economic activity* to quantitatively correspond more or less to these basic elements in family composition. (1986:60)

This means that 'other things being equal' labour intensity will increase with the pressure of family demands on the peasant workers. 'The volume of the family's activity depends entirely on the number of consumers and not at all on the number of workers' (1986:78). In addition, Chayanov points out that, first, 'energy expenditure is inhibited by the drudgery of the labour itself. The harder the labour is, compared with its pay, the lower the level of well-being at which the peasant family ceases to work' (1986:81). And, second, 'the peasant farm tends, by means of renting land, to bring the area it is exploiting agriculturally into optimal relationship with family size' (1986:111), although this will depend on the market situation of agriculture as compared to that of crafts and trades (1986:113).

We may sum up Chayanov's hypothesis as follows: the ratio of consumers to producers will be directly related to intensity and productivity of labour, although progressively inhibited by drudgery of labour, and inversely related to the extension of 'land farmed'. A consumer-driven rationality for production is presented as a specific theory of the 'family farm' economy with a law of motion of its own, one that can be separated and abstracted from the rest of the economic environment. Built on a particular idea of consumption, this economic theory has been extended to a large number of heterogeneous processes all around the world and has even been reified as a 'mode of production' (Sahlins 1972).

I think, however, that not enough attention has been paid to the central tenet of his hypothesis: *consumption*. Let us closely analyse Chayanov's description of consumption (Chs 1 and 4). Two basic questions are of interest: first, what does he consider consumption to be? and, second, what are the *units* accounting for real persons in the peasant households?

Let us deal with the first question. Chayanov analyses in detail the consumption budget of two farms (one with a low, the other a high monetary expenditure) (1986:122–3) the budgets include unprocessed food produce, clothing wool and hides, soap, lighting and firewood, utensils, spiritual needs and games, and outside processing of agricultural food produce (milling) and of flax (spinning). The consumer budgets are *global household* budgets which include *goods* obtained by the household unit but only exceptionally *services*. Except for milling and spinning the processing of raw produce into edible meals or other domestic work incurred in everyday livelihood does not appear in the budgets. Interestingly 'domestic work' is considered 'work' (that is, production) and is accounted as the main labour expenditure of peasant women and girls (1986:180).

The second step is establishing the individual unit of peasant consumer budget. Chayanov presents a table, borrowed from secondary sources, of the actual consumption rates of various forms of food for different '*guberniyas*' 'in terms of an *annual male consumer*' (1986:129). The table shows important variations above and below the averages in consumption of different food categories according to region. Some regions, such as Olonets, present the highest consumption of 'meat and fish' and 'butter', second highest consumption of 'grain products' and above average consumption of 'milk, sour cream and curds', 'sugar' and 'vegetable oil'. Others, such as Vologda, have below average consumption in all categories except 'sugar' and 'milk, sour cream and curds'.

It would not seem unsound to perceive wide differentiation in protein, vitamins, minerals and generally basic nutrient intake between these regions. Nevertheless, Chayanov's commentary is that 'peasant diet is fairly stable and varies sharply only in produce, which to some extent is a "luxury"' (1986:128). He notes, however, that the annual expenditure in kind and money per consumer ('all expenditures on personal needs' expressed 'in terms of one consumer') varies sharply from one region to the other with Vologda *guberniyas* spending about half of Moscow *guberniyas*' budget (1986:130). He also notes that consumption seems 'constricted by a reduced level of well-being' (1986:128–30). He admits that consumption rates 'fluctuate within very wide limits' and in his explanation of it points at 'increased incomes and the larger budget which follows', and at 'an expansion of the demands themselves due to elements of higher urban culture that penetrate into the countryside' (1986:130). This second, *cultural*, factor affects directly the structure of consumption and, although correlated to commodity farming and areas of crafts and trades (1986:134), it is not theoretically articulated to these socioeconomic processes but merely subsumed under 'cultural', 'urban habits'. It is worth stressing that by substituting the influence of 'urban culture' for that of 'increased incomes' Chayanov and many after him point to culture and ideology while obscuring material social and economic differentiation processes.

In regard to the question as to what Chayanov considers consumption, it is essential to remember his caution about the fact that 'the consumption rates we have quoted are precisely rates of real consumption and by no means a quantitative expression of demands themselves as such'. In addition he admits that demand for any product of personal consumption could only be expressed hypothetically 'in the form of a whole scale of consumption rates which corresponds to the gradual satiation of demand and its extinction' (1986:131).

This marginal remark, however, points to one of the major problems of Chayanov's methodology: he could only observe and take account of actual consumption rates, not consumer *needs*. Therefore his labour–consumer balance theory cannot determine consumer pressure *before* or *apart* from the actual process of trying to make a living in a given historical social and economic context. As Harrison very succinctly puts it: Chayanov's labour–consumer balance 'couldn't grasp the difference between *ex ante* needs and effective demands and the way that society intervenes in the mediation between the two' (1975:413). What he achieved in fact is the ideological consolidation, the reification, of a historically constructed level of demand as the natural abstract factor driving toward a mechanical equilibrium the consumption and production unit of peasant families. And tautologically: if 'subjective' economic equilibrium was achieved for those rates of consumption then the actual levels of production, labour employment and income obtained were adequate (Harrison 1975:411–14).

The second question is related to how the labour–consumer ratio is accounted for, that is, to the *units* quantitatively representing different categories of persons during the family life cycle. Chayanov acknowledges that he adopts 'the rates established in the Vologda budget studies in accounting consumer and worker units, simplifying them somewhat and retaining division by sex only for the parents' (1986:58). The 'units' are the following: male adult = 1; female adult = 0.8. Non-working children below the age of 15 (that is, only as consumers) are divided into three different categories: babies under 1 year of age = 0.1; children from 1 to 8 years = 0.3; children from 9 to 14 years = 0.5. Older, working, children are divided into two different categories: 15 to 19 years old = 0.7; over 19 years old and (presumably) up to their marriage, when they would acquire 'adult' status = 0.9 (this, probably, being the average of young male and female adult equivalences when not taking division by sex into account). Working members of the household are accounted with the same unit as consumers and as workers (i.e. each is presumed to consume the equivalent of what they produce).

These very detailed units of accounting are the ones used mechanically to obtain the consumer/worker ratios and hence the consumption pressure driving the peasant economy toward equilibrium. Further, it is interesting to note that the units chosen as representative of peasant family composition in the abstract are those referring to the Vologda area, one of the poorest regions according to the comparative study of the 'annual male consumer' budgets. One wonders which criteria were chosen in the budget studies to determine the *comparative worth* of household members regarding consumption and production. The possible answers both seem methodologically unsound: whether a fixed categorisation was established in advance and imposed by those doing the statistical survey or whether the categories and 'units' were inductively derived from the empirical – and therefore socially and economically contextualised – observation of a particularly deprived region. In any case we are presented with an *abstract* categorisation that becomes the foundation of the labour–consumer balance analysis and theory. And this is not without consequences.

First it *reifies* relations of consumption and production within the household even while taking into account the family development cycle. Relations become categories and numbers, and can be universally and mechanically quantified. This methodological framework cannot account for, and in fact actively obscures, relations of domination and exploitation between household members which are significant for consumption and production processes.

Second, by creating standard categories it *naturalises* gender and age differentiations and renders them ahistorical, non-negotiable and non-conflictive. The social construction of difference along gender and age lines – both ideological and material – is impossible to grasp within a framework that assumes from the start rigid and set categories.

Last, the metaphor of the family as an individual with its 'biological development' 'starting at birth and finishing at death' (1986:56–7) renders real existing household members mere limbs of an organism which is the family. Consumption, then, is *family consumption* assessed through total household budget. Only *after* is it disaggregated following standard units. The direction of the procedure is significant. While it looks as if detailed consumption distinctions are taken into account for each household member, in fact they are not. Personification of the peasant family appears more bluntly in decision-making about labour allocation. Here a consistent ambiguity blurs the difference between the adult male household head and the 'peasant family'. The combining of different individuals in a unique 'family' personality inhibits analysis of the struggles present in the *negotiation* of agreements within the family, as well as the possibility of open conflict between its members.

Far from presenting an analysis of relations of consumption within domestic groups Chayanov sanctions the opacity of consumption units. Therefore, consumption, which is the most important element in his theory, is a mechanical dissagregation of a global consumption budget for an undifferentiated household unit. This disaggregation, however, becomes the key element in the labour–consumer balance theory.

One of the main critiques addressed to Chayanov by the Marxists focused on his idea that differentiation among peasants was related to the demographic factors of the family life cycle and the consumer/worker ratio. This was not only disproved by statistical data but Chayanov himself admitted that there existed differentiation *and* that it was important in determining both the production and the well-being of the peasant family. To witness: his remark that 'better conditions for the application of labour gave the workers the opportunity to increase their output considerably, and this, with an unchanged consumer/worker ratio, inevitably brought about an increase in family and consumer well-being' (Chayanov 1986:79).

Marxist critics, on the contrary, placed differentiation in the context of the historical development of capitalist relations of production as it affected agriculture and industry (Lenin 1977 [1899]; Harrison 1975, 1977, 1979). Chayanov, however, never developed a theory of how some peasant families had 'better conditions for the application of labour than others' to begin with, while others were extremely constrained in their strategic decision-making options. A second important and related critique can be addressed to his methodology and was already voiced by his contemporaries (cf. Chayanov's Introduction, 1986:43): the idea that the internal organisation of family labour farms can be analysed in isolation without taking into account the surrounding social and economic historical context. I will develop this point in the following sections.

WHAT HAPPENS WITHIN THE CONSUMPTION UNIT?

Consumption relations: conflictive vs. harmonic perspectives

In order to avoid Chayanovian errors we should break through the boundaries of the household consumption unit. We may then try to analyse *the relations of consumption* between the persons sharing the household space. How is the access to consumption resources effected? Who controls the management and distribution of which resources? Who performs which services? How is terminal consumption realised (terminal consumption being the final act of consumption that destroys its object in the performance of its end)? This and other questions will enable a closer understanding of relations of domination within the household, of lines of conflict, processes of negotiation and coalition-building. Even consensual action should be explained against a background of diverse and complex relations between the people in the household and should never be taken for granted.

In relation to lineage societies, French Marxist anthropologists (Meillassoux 1978; Godelier 1974) pointed to the fact that 'the unit of consumption is not an empty social framework for it is ordered by a specific social authority with power to allocate resources' (Godelier 1974:163). Meillassoux builds his domestic mode of production theory on the hypothesis that the temporality of the agricultural cycle creates a dependency of younger generations on the seed produced by older generations. This is expressed in the control that lineage seniors have over agricultural produce for subsistence, produced mainly with the labour of the juniors. 'Thus a circuit is established between the dependants who produce the subsistence goods and the senior who presides over their distribution' (1978:324).

The capacity of juniors to retain control over subsistence products will increase during their life as they get older and expand their social relations through a network of allied and other partners and the attachment of dependants whose labour they can control. Their increasing control over the allocation of agricultural subsistence produce will confer authority on them but will also express their greater authority and control over the production process obtained through their command of dependants' labour (Meillassoux 1978).

Although this hypothesis refers to extended domestic communities or lineage segments, it is of general interest as an approach to the power relations that are built around the control and distribution of food. In addition, it points to the dialectical relationship between relations of production and relations of consumption and the potential for conflict that exists between generations. Conflict is intensified when production and consumption are integrated in one unit: the lineage segment, the household. We are driven to focus on the process of social reproduction as a whole and within it appear relations of consumption which are conflictive and highly significant with regard to the social organisation of the lineage system. This might be termed the 'conflictive' approach to social relations obtaining within consumption units. The particular historical, economic and social context in which consumption units are located will be the determining background against which relations of consumption will have to be viewed. Struggle for the control and allocation of resources within the consumption unit will most certainly be present to some degree, and it is not so much its presence as its particular manifestation that should be explored.

On the other hand, social theorists such as Gershuny (Gershuny 1988; Gershuny and Miles 1985), speaking of Western 'post-industrial' societies have underlined non-conflictive aspects of intra-household consumption relations. Gershuny's analyses of domestic work and self-servicing activities point to transfers – mainly of services – within families. He uses an idea closely related to the concept of 'general reciprocity' to qualify these generalised – that is, implicit, non-quantified, long-term, and often very long-term, indeed often never consummated – economic exchanges taking place between the various members of the household. This is because 'these [intra-household] exchanges are typically between non-quantifiable or incommensurable values' (1988:581). In contrast to the exchanges within households, those between the formal production system and the household are 'explicit, quantified and relatively short term' (1988:581).

Because intra-household exchanges involve 'incommensurable values' equivalences cannot be found and therefore it is impossible to judge if exchange is equal or unequal. In other words the relationship that carries exchange, but also is constructed through exchange, cannot then be analysed either in terms of surplus value appropriation (i.e. exploitation) or in terms of direct constraint to work (i.e. domination) The logic is the following: within the household market exchange equivalences do not apply, therefore generalised exchange is the norm, that is, no other equivalences are possible *and* no system of balanced reciprocity with or without reference to market rates and equivalences can be hypothesised for intra-household transfers.

The household becomes, once again, a black box. The idea of generalised exchange moreover, sets a framework where the recipient's needs and the moral obligation to reciprocate seem sufficient and self-evident qualifications of the relations between people within households. All seems for the better in the realm of the consumption unit. Although he tries to establish and quantify unpaid work within households, Gershuny's interest is in asserting the changes in the 'chains of provisioning' of particular needs (1988), not in understanding intra-household consumption relations. One example would be the shift from the purchase of final service commodities to self-servicing with the aid of consumer durables related to the particular service function that is needed (Gershuny and Miles 1985:34).

Relative increase of the 'domestication' and 'privatisation' of otherwise marketed and public services is undoubtedly an important trend in the chains of provision, and one that affects household consumption as well as the 'formal production system'. However, the actual import of the transformation cannot be fully grasped without a thorough examination of consumption relations including: control of resources, processing of raw goods, cleaning and other home maintenance services, care. The ideological *and* material constraints that force concrete people into expecting and providing specific services and levels of consumption, into fulfilling specific needed work, into deciding for intra-household provisioning against market service consumption, must be studied.

In valuable work on the Isle of Sheppey (Pahl 1984; Pahl and Wallace 1985), Pahl found that 'employment and self-provisioning go together, rather than one being a substitute for another' (1985:377). Households with more income, more adults, higher status 'produce more and consume more, formally and informally' (1985:378). Although Pahl admits that material constraints as well as 'a value system which puts home-centred activities as the central focus of a distinctive lifestyle' (1985:374) may be at play in the decision to self-provision, the cultural factor seems to be paramount in his understanding of 'domestication' and 'privatisation'. He insists repeatedly on the importance of a 'home-centred value orientation':

> However the work is done and to whatever standard, the domestication value which unites many households in self-provisioning sees the house and home as a central defining and determining feature of a lifestyle and as a symbolic and material expression of success in life. (1985:379)

Moreover, material constraints are also perceived as a side effect of feeling 'obliged to keep up to the standards of their local milieu' (1985:380).

Pahl suggests that 'what is "choice" and what is "constraint" under these circumstances is ... hard to disentangle' (1985:380) but his emphasis is on home-making values, lifestyles, etc. Although his interest in *culture* and *choice* as inducers of self-provisioning attitudes is legitimate, it also obscures differentiation within the household because *culture* appears as an homogenising factor, one immediately consensual and self-evident. This may in fact be far from the case in actuality; one may ask whose 'success in life' a determined 'lifestyle' represents, whose 'predetermined standard of domestic comfort and style' (1985:379) is aimed at? And what are the ideological constraints, such as a particular understanding of the 'family', and the material consequences of the work 'responsibilities' attributed to each member, including such intangible activities as attention and care (De Vault 1991)? How do power relations within the family affect consumption 'choices' such as self-provisioning? And how do state policies such as the abandonment of public transportation and health care services not only affect households differently but also affect people within households differently? The shift toward a 'community care' pattern affects mainly lower-income women (Eisenstein 1984; Gershuny and Miles 1985:38). Therefore constraints leading to self-provisioning should be seen as both cultural and material, set in a social, economic and political environment, and differentially affecting household units *and* household members.

Addressing very different societies, both the conflictive and the harmonious approaches may be considered as a starting point in looking into consumer relations within the household.

Control vs. management of everyday resources: gender and age cleavages

Empirical evidence is increasingly available which permits detailed analysis of relations of consumption within households. Feminists' awareness of power relations within families and international and national institutions' preoccupation with nutritional, educational and health standards have been the two main motors in intra-household consumption studies. Poor households in Third World and Western countries have been the focus of most studies. This is because material deprivation, real 'need', gives a sense of urgency and impels researchers toward work that may structure public and private organisations' aid policies. The results, however, are globally relevant.

In a very interesting study on 'sex disparities in the distribution of food within rural households' in Bangladesh, which includes a wide review of related studies, Carloni (1981) shows that sex and age differences must be taken into account when assessing nutritional status. Global household food income does not suffice because 'food is inequitably divided among household members in relation to their nutritional requirements' (1981:3). Carloni finds that male adults' caloric and protein food intake is consistently higher than that of female adults and points to an important disparity in relation to the energy needs of women and men, especially among women of childbearing age. For children the disparity between boys and girls is enormous with girls being comparatively more deprived and malnourished. This is reflected also in the higher incidence of female infant mortality. As Carloni underlines: 'the point is not so much that food is *unequally* divided among household members, but that it is *inequitably* divided in relation to the requirements of males and females of different ages' (1981:4). Moreover, seasonal or chronic scarcity seems to increase inequitable allocation of food within households, depriving still more women and children, mainly girls. Conversely, a positive correlation appears to exist between greater control of food resources or income by women and the nutritional status of *children*.

These studies indicate that several factors are significant in asserting the differential allocation of food between household members. The first factor is *control and management* of food, that is, who obtains (has access to) the staples either by producing them or by buying them? Who cooks them? Who distributes them at meal times? Second is *terminal consumption processes* or meal habits. For example, sheer physical dexterity or force enhances food intake probabilities in a competitive situation such as that created when everybody eats at the same bowl. Nibbling while processing food might substantially increase food intakes for women who cook (1981:6). The third factor is *cultural criteria* with regard to perceived nutritional needs of different household members, building upon considerations of energy expenditure in work, pregnancy and lactation, growth, retirement, as well as on perceived human investment strategies for the long-term sustainability of the household (for example, girls leave home at marriage, boys stay and work bringing income to the household) (Carloni 1981; Pala 1979; Stavrakis and Marshall 1978). This last point brings to the fore an important question that should be carefully addressed by policy makers: 'How does the unequal distribution of food relate to the survival strategies used by households among the rural poor in allocating scarce resources?' (Carloni 1981:5)

For the United Kingdom excellent studies (Graham 1987; McKee 1987; Wilson 1987; Charles and Kerr 1987) show the importance of gender and age cleavages in resource distribution within families. Family income, for example, is not as crucial as resource distribution between family members when trying to assess women's well-being. In a survey of poor white families, both two-parent and female-headed one-parent families, Graham (1987) found that lone mothers felt better off than when they were married although they had less money. The main analytical distinction that seems relevant to resource distribution concerns *control* and *management* of income sources (mainly money).

The control of money is more likely to be a male than a female domain. It involves making key decisions about how much money individuals within the family will have and what items of expenditure they will take responsibility for. The *management* of money is more typically the women's job. It involves implementing the financial decisions of the individual or individuals who control the money: organising the budget, shopping, paying bills and finding ways of economising when income and expenditure are out of line. (1987:62)

In relation to control it is important also to take into account the sources of income entering the household as well as the relative quantitative and qualitative value of the various incoming resources. For example, a woman earning a small wage from homework, although exploited and poorly paid, will generally be able to *control* it and decide on its allocation. On the contrary, households fully dependent on a male breadwinner will presumably have him in strong control. Generally speaking the more the income sources are distributed among different family members the less concentration of control in one hands. The fact that control and management of income are the responsibility of different household members – the 'breadwinner' and his wife – generates *conflict* in the context of scarce resources.

An example of the conflict-raising issue related to the separation of control and management for a productive/reproductive endeavour in a rural context, is very present in the area where I did fieldwork in southwestern Catalonia, Spain. There, heirs to medium-sized and large farms gain management responsibilities little by little. Final decisions concerning investment in farm and home improvement remain, however, under the control of the predecessor. It is interesting to note that here control is not always linked to full ownership of property. It depends more strictly on possession or use-rights which are kept by the predecessors even when they transfer property rights to the heir at marriage. In this case, separation of control and management of resources creates recurring conflict between predecessor and heir (Narotzky 1990).

Material constraints on differential access to resources; ideological constraints

The totality of resources necessary for household consumption seldom adopt the unique form of a single money income pay packet. More often, there will be some resources in money while others will be in kind, either goods, services or information. Money resources may come from an only 'breadwinner' or from various members of the household contributing different amounts from their pay packet. In-kind resources are provided from an even larger set of sources. Prominent among these are those obtained through kin, friends and neighbours and are generally related to housing, food, clothing, child care, home maintenance and repair. We should bear in mind that the position of each household member in the web of income resource provisioning will affect differentially his/her power to control and manage particular resources. This is what Carloni (1981) has termed the 'household food path' in relation to food distribution, but it is also significant for all other household resources. For example, the ability of some women to create and expand a network of acquainted mothers (whether kin, friends or neighbours) may give them access to child care services, child-related information, child clothing and child appliances. These resources, then, will be controlled and allocated directly by her. Obtaining food, whether raw or cooked, from kin will enhance control over it, including the possibility of secret allocation. Access to information will not only concern management, as when a thrifty housewife knows how to shop around and look for sales, but may also improve *control* over unaccounted savings, nest-eggs. This (filch) is important to keep in mind, for it frequently concerns not only women but children and elderly members of households as well, and is often related to the act of shopping and running errands.

Material constraints of relations of consumption are not free from ideological assumptions. In fact, *who* has access to which resources and how to establish a hierarchy of priorities in allocating final consumption, is mediated by ideologies about family responsibilities, about gendered capabilities to compete in the labour market, about energy requirements, about identity representation, etc. It is difficult here, as elsewhere, to disentangle material from ideological constraints for they are dialectically constructed. An interesting study is that of Charles and Kerr (1987) on family food consumption in the UK, based on households obtaining their main income from the male head's pay packet. They found that women adapted meals to the food preferences of their husbands or, in their absence, to their children's. Significant differences existed in the quality of food between adults and children and in the quantity of food portions between women and men. On the other hand foods seemed to be ranked hierarchically 'red meat is the most highly valued food followed by poultry, fish, eggs, cheese, fruit, leaf vegetables, root vegetables and cereals in that order' (1987:161) with men, then women, then children in that order getting access to the higher-status food. The idea of providing a 'proper meal' for the male breadwinner seems to be a cultural expectation of men as well as women. 'Men are felt to deserve a proper meal on return from work, and its preparation demands that women spend a significant amount of time in the kitchen prior to men's homecoming; fresh ingredients should be cooked from scratch' (1987:159).

Thus, cooking and more generally servicing are part of the relations of power that structure final food intake. On the other hand it is the ideology of the male 'breadwinner', irrespective of what his real-material energy requirements are *in relation to* those of the other family members, that seems to give priority access to food – quality and quantity – to male adults (think of the energy and nutrient requirements of a part-time working, pregnant, housewife vs. her bank clerk husband). An interesting finding seems to indicate that employment is the main power asset of men within the family in relation to differential food access.

A good many families of manual unskilled workers existed on a low income. Yet it would appear that women in these families limit the meat they give to themselves and their children to ensure that men receive a disproportionate share of what is available. In the families of the unemployed, by contrast, a limited amount of meat seems to be shared more equally. (Charles and Kerr 1987:171)

In contrast to this, lone mothers exercised greater control (not just management) over the family diet, which led them to put children's preferences first (Graham 1987:68–9). Poverty was the basic material constraint with motherhood the fundamental ideological constraint. In a poverty context 'the bills' come first (1987:66–8); fixed expenses tend to be met before 'flexible' expenses such as food: 'because of its place in the family economy, as a large item over which the parents can exercise some control, it is through their diet that low income families confront and try to contain their poverty' (1987:68). Yet, because of the priority given to growing children's nutrition, this often means that mothers cut down on their own food intake. Thus, although direct control over income gave lone mothers the possibility to cook what they preferred, the material constraints of poverty together with the ideological constraints of motherhood resulted in their radical cutting – in terms of quality as well as quantity – of their personal food intake. Here, empowerment of women in the household often led them to increased nutritional deficiencies to the benefit of children (1987:68–74). This should remind us that power relations within households are *always* related to power relations in the society as a whole; and that, as Carloni (1981) stressed, we must try to uncover not so much unequal but *inequitable* distribution of resources which, in relation to food, means trying to assert the differences between the nutritional needs and the respective food intake of the different members of the family.

BEYOND THE DOMESTIC GROUP BOUNDARIES

Formal and informal resource circulation: salaries, social benefits, help

Consumption units, then, must not be conceived as predefined, closed units, getting a homogeneous income in money that enables the purchase of commodities to be used in final consumption and distributed homogeneously among the unit's members. Consumption units are not bounded. Their limits are porous and often consumption networks give a more accurate description of ongoing, complex, recurrent processes of personal consumption. Income is heterogeneous and very seldom is it limited to the male head of the household's pay packet. Generally income or resources for personal consumption have many forms and different people have access to them through different strategies. Resources can be in money. Money can come from formal employment or informal (some of them illegal) occupations, money can be transferred by welfare institutions to people complying with specific requirements (lone mothers without employment, retired people having had formal employment for a number of years); money can be got on credit, through pawning or lending; it can come as a present or through charity.

In-kind resources include housing, all sorts of objects needed in the home such as appliances, furniture, clothing, food and day-to-day necessities; but also virtual goods such as information. Services include child care, care of the elderly, help with activities such as shopping, cooking, cleaning, ironing and sewing on a regular or exceptional basis; repair and maintenance jobs, etc.

Household members have different possibilities of access to the varied resources that combine into making a living. These differential possibilities are strongly related to the political and economic structure enabling some people but not others to get hold of specific resources. The structure of the labour market, for instance, favours males for certain jobs, females for others; it highly values credentials in certain contexts or finds them 'overqualifications'. Age and experience can be an asset, or it may be youth and the possibility of 'forming the person into the job'; unskilled women may stand better chances of finding informal service jobs as domestics, while unskilled males may stand better chances in construction.

Welfare is not supposed to reach everybody and those it benefits are under tight control from the authorities to make sure that they comply with the requirements and there is no fraud. Old age pensions, women with children, disability payments, unemployment benefits depend on very strictly determined causes and are easily lost even when the recipients' life circumstances have not substantially changed. The mere structure of the household (whether housing an able adult male or not) might be determinant in order to benefit from aid to women with dependent children (Stack 1975).

On the other hand, the social structure more generally, and in particular kinship, friendship and neighbourhood networks, are crucial in determining the individual's capacity to obtain resources. Parents, siblings, sons and daughters as well as distant kin can be helpful in many ways and to different degrees. Expectations over their 'help' depends on many factors: emotional closeness, financial capacity, special skills, spatial proximity.

Resources for consumption, then, are obtained from many sources and in many forms. Money that gives access to commodities is just a variable portion of the means to accomplish personal consumption. Understanding relations of consumption means following the path of provisioning of goods and services and analysing the factors influencing key decisions – of production, of allocation – along the path. Along the path general decisions will have to be taken within particular social-economic and political contexts, probably by different people. As we get closer to the locus of final consumption, issues of power and differential access to resources will involve people recurrently connected through the consumption process. These are the people whose interaction generates consumption relations, but not all are members of one household. Rather, they belong to different households although their membership in a particular household may be the significant criterion establishing the personal link crucial to the consumption process. If households are the units pooling and internally allocating resources we may think of relations of consumption as growing around the circulation of resources between different households, between households and the state, between households and the market. But households are not stable and are more accurately described as bundles of relations – of consumption, production, reproduction – that are constantly being negotiated in a wider economic context.

Moreover, households may not be meaningful units of consumption at all. Carol Stack's (1975) analysis of a black community in the United States clearly shows how consumption relations are scattered between different homes: people eat at one place, sleep at another, borrow clothes, move frequently. Here the idea of 'domestic network' seems to better describe consumption relations. Even more so, homeless people don't generally constitute 'households'; nevertheless they consume and establish relations of consumption along their paths of provisioning (Hill and Stamey 1990). Social networks, therefore, constitute a meaningful way of approaching consumption.

Social networks and consumption; circulation of goods and people

Resources, therefore, circulate among individuals through links based on kinship, friendship and neighbourhood. Individuals might distribute and share resources within an institutionalised framework such as the household/family, or through other more flexible arrangements.

In her account of life in The Flats, 'the poorest section of a black community' in a Midwestern city of the US, Carol Stack (1975) gives a detailed account of 'swapping', a constant round of borrowing and trading with those participating in a domestic network as a means of getting by, day after day.

As people swap, the limited supply of finished material goods in the community is perpetually redistributed among networks of kinsmen and throughout the community.

The resources, possessions and services exchanged between individuals residing in The Flats are intricately interwoven. People exchange various objects generously: new things, treasured items, furniture, cars, goods that are perishable, and services which are exchanged for child care, residence, or shared meals. Individuals enlarge their web of social relations through repetitive and seemingly habitual instances of swapping. ... Degrees of entanglement among kinsmen and friends involved in networks of exchange differ in kind from casual swapping. Those actively involved in domestic networks swap goods and services on a daily, practically an hourly basis. (1975:34–5)

The description of swapping brings us back to the discussion about 'reciprocity', in particular generalised reciprocity. This is a situation where gifts often 'can be reclaimed by the initiator of the swap' (1975:34). The perception of those involved is that 'you are not really getting ahead of nobody, you just get better things as they go back and forth' (1975:34) and 'you ain't really giving nothing away because everything that goes round comes round' (1975:42). A situation where 'value of an object given away is based upon its retaining power over the receiver' (1975:42). Here, the process of consumption entails the continuous circulation of goods and services. In their movement these serve to fulfil daily needs in a context of very scarce and variable resources but also constantly regenerate the social fabric and the ideological framework of The Flats community. For Stack 'The cooperative life style and the bonds created by the vast mass of moment-to-moment exchanges constitute an underlying element of black identity in The Flats' (1975:43).

This 'cooperative life style', however, is not without conflict, and the constant claims from the social network are often tense and perceived as exploitative (1975:38–9). In the context of scarce resources there seems to be no option to privately control and allocate resources. Incoming resources are immediately and widely publicised in the domestic network and claims readily ensue. This situation inhibits the privatisation, the closing of nuclear family/household units. Because there is no long-term security of regular employment (on the part of males), the ideology of the male 'breadwinner' cannot be materially sustained. 'Women come to realize that welfare benefits and ties within kin networks provide greater security for them and their children' (1975:113).

The precarious situation of black males in the labour market means they will not be able to keep up the family unit 'breadwinner' hegemonic model of consumption organisation for a long time and both members of a conjugal pair will eventually revert to their domestic networks. Therefore, privatising and closing the family/household unit when income becomes temporarily regular is a high-risk strategy. Privatising consumption means effectively reducing the domestic network's resources and is strongly opposed. 'Participants in the network try to break up such relationships in order to maximize their potential resources and the services they hope to exchange' (1975:115). Those who break away from the rounds of swapping are effectively compromising their position in a domestic network (Stack 1975:77) and thus their future access to consumption resources. The concept of domestic network emerges from consumption processes which include the circulation not only of material resources but particularly of services and 'help'. Caring for children is the central element of a domestic network and is the responsibility of women of several generations resident in various households. Children circulate among women of the domestic network and children articulate matrilateral and patrilateral networks (Stack 1975:62–105). In their movement children not only share in the resources of a particular group of women who assume parental responsibilities; they also provide services – babysitting, running errands, doing some housework – and income through their welfare assignation. This underlines the relational and complex web of consumption and the way it is permanently transformed. It also stresses:

(1) the importance of women in structuring social networks that might support personal consumption processes;
(2) the importance of the global economic context where consumption processes are embedded, such as the labour market; informal, including illegal, income opportunities, etc;
(3) The importance of the state in the configuration of domestic networks through the regulations of welfare provisioning (non-marriage; circulating children; fluctuating residence patterns) (Valentine 1978: 124–5);
(4) the conflicting aspects of material constraints and the hegemonic values of the society (i.e. nuclear family provided for by the male 'breadwinner') (Valentine 1978: 126).

The example of The Flats might give a passive picture, where people adapt to extreme poverty by continuously channelling resources through domestic networks. But we might want to look at the active struggle of self-employed women in India. In order to transform their position in the labour market and to gain bargaining strength women have organised into cooperative movements, women's unions and associations. This example is relevant because it links women's responsibilities in the day-to-day management of household members', mainly children's, basic subsistence consumption; the inability to get sufficient resources through male household members' employment (if any); the need to get some income; the difficulty of finding regular employment, the recourse to casualised work, often homework; and the struggle to organise self-help groups and unions. These not only aim at increasing wages and obtaining 'employee' rights and recognition, but also very specifically have the aim of securing changes in the social structure which involves traditional constraints on women's control over resources and affects power relations within the household. Also, creating consumers' cooperatives in order to reduce the prices of goods is an important objective. Networks of solidary action referring to consumption are created, structured and institutionalised.

Here the consumption process can be grasped fully in its multiplex constraints, in its economic, political and social dimensions, and it can be seen as a process which is actively transformed by its participants. Consumption processes involve struggles that are political. And those deprived can become active agents of change. Networks are created and become a web of commonalty leading to solidary action and persisting through time. As Swasti Mitter (1994:36) comments:

The visible success of some of the women's unions may mark a change in the future direction of union traditions. The bidi and tobacco workers' union in Nipani, Karnataba, India, in this context, deserves a special mention. ... it is a home-based bidi workers' union of a novel kind. It is basically a women's union with actions that go far beyond wage negotiation. Since its formation in 1980, its members have fought successfully for economic rights such as minimum wages and provident funds; they have fought equally powerfully on issues such as dowry, divorce and male alcoholism. Around the struggle against social and communal injustice, several supportive measures have been taken. A multipurpose cooperative has been set up to provide grains, kerosene and cooking oil to women at a cheap rate; there is now a small savings scheme to advance loans to women members at a reasonable rate and a home for *devadasi* (temple prostitutes) and other women needing refuge.

Consumption appears here, then, as part of a wider struggle for economic, social and political rights.

The production and reproduction of power relations within, between and beyond domestic groups

Consumption processes, then, are intertwined with relations of power which are forged and reproduced in the daily struggle to make a living. The position of individuals regarding the formal and institutional means of access to resources is determinant in the production and reproduction of power relations affecting consumption. Informal exchanges of resources are also important in this regard.

An interesting example is that of the Catalan village where I did fieldwork. There, access to land, house, maintenance money, food produce, child care, care of the elderly and agricultural day labour are in an important degree linked to informal exchanges between households. Up to the 1950s, most landed households (*casa*) instituted the devolution of inheritance of the main property assets to an only heir at the time of his marriage. The marriage contract established the duty of the heir to 'work for the *casa*' and usually required co-residence with the predecessor couple. However, in order to minimise conflict between predecessor and successor couples while both were active, data shows that the younger couple usually rented a small apartment during the initial 10 or 15 years, later moving back to the older couple's residence. Although property rights were transferred to the heir at marriage, use-rights were retained by the predecessor couple until the death of both spouses. The marriage contract served to institutionalise power relations between different household members around productive and reproductive activities. The predecessors' property was exchanged against the successors' work but control was retained by the older generation. Access to maintenance was obtained against work, while care of the elderly couple overdetermined final access to property. In fact one of the heir's main responsibilities was to assume care of his/her predecessors in old age.

More recent practices must be understood against the background of this very institutionalised process. Nowadays marriage contracts are not drawn up. The exchange relationships that were ingrained in them are still the backbone of relations of consumption and of production, however. While a certain 'tradition' still seems to give precedence to a firstborn male child in the access to the greater portion of patrimony, informal exchanges of work, maintenance, food and care seem to be much more significant in structuring and completing final property transfer. Thus, a firstborn son will work his parents' land under some sharecropping arrangement, and his young wife will help in the olive harvest. She will also get produce from her in-laws' vegetable garden. Often she will count on her mother-in-law for help in caring for her baby, while she takes in homework. Later, she will be increasingly responsible for the care of her husband's ageing parents. At this point the younger couple will usually move in with the older couple, getting closer in order to help, generally also in order to increase their management responsibilities regarding household budget and eventually their control over various resources (including old age pensions). As the death of the propertied parent approaches a notarised donation *inter vivos* will probably transfer the main property assets to the younger couple, reserving use-rights to both parents until their death, in order to make sure that they will receive proper care. This pattern is extremely frequent and although it resembles, and is ideologically sustained by the 'tradition' of the marriage contract arrangements, it enables a greater flexibility. In fact it gives *any* son/daughter who recurrently enters into certain informal exchange relationship with the predecessor couple the possibility of effectively becoming the successor couple. As both households' development cycles progress, and as different income-earning opportunities are made available (full-time employment in the city; emigration; earlier opportunities of gaining access to a predecessor couple's assets, etc.) individuals produce, reproduce and transform the power and dependency relations that enable them to earn a livelihood.

Care of the elderly predecessor couple is, in the last instance, the factor determining the transfer of property assets to the next generation. This is extremely interesting with regard to our discussion of the consumption process. Taking care of the elderly is a consumption-related service that becomes the responsibility of the woman in the younger couple. However, as one informant remarked, she took care of her mother-in-law until she died but it was her husband who inherited, implying that she herself did not get anything in return, nothing that she could *control*. The reverse situation, when the heiress is the woman in a couple, after her husband has worked his parents-in-law's land for years, is less blatantly unequal. First, there will have been a sharecropping arrangement between son-in-law and father-in-law which means that some of the returns on the young man's farm work will represent direct income for him. Second, when the woman has the property she generally transfers management *and* control of it to her husband. Thus, although not fully formalised, the male prospective successor's transfers of labour are reciprocated partly by market-mediated equivalences and partly by implicit expectations of future material rewards. On the contrary, the female prospective successor's transfers of labour-care, although extremely significant, may never be directly reciprocated.

But if, instead of looking at this complex bundle of relationships with property inheritance in mind (that is, ownership of land, house and other means of *production*), we choose to look at them from the point of view of *consumption* processes, we can give a slightly different emphasis to the analysis. The varied resources necessary to make a livelihood on these medium-sized olive producing farms include labour on the farm, care of the children and the elderly, housework, food produce from the vegetable garden, income from day labour, income from homework, income from temporary employment *and* access to house, land, membership rights to the oil processing cooperative, agricultural machinery and other inputs. At least *two* households – although they might eventually merge into one – are strongly committed to the endeavour of consumption and generally members of other households are also recurrently involved in the exchange networks that help getting by: other sons/daughters, brothers/sisters, uncles/aunts, nephews/nieces, friends, neighbours, etc. However, this commitment to consumption constrains the younger couple into dependent, sometimes exploitative relations with an older couple in exchange for a sharecropping income and other resources such as shelter, babysitting or food produce donations. As time goes by, consumption relations strengthen claims over material assets such as property, and, moreover, consumption needs of those enmeshed in a consumption process change. The increasing priority of care as opposed to farm labour for the elderly couple, transforms the power balance between younger and older couple, although property ownership is the definitive sanction to the transfer of *control* between generations. And the transfer is not completed until both spouses in the older couple die.

The picture that is drawn here is one where consumption relations are structured around transfers between households. These transfers reproduce power cleavages between older and younger generation couples, between those siblings able to strengthen claims to future inheritance and those unable or unwilling to do so (because single, emigrant, dissenting), between men generally gaining with time *management* and *control* rights regarding farm (productive) assets and income, and women owning less *control* power regarding farm income, although occasionally more regarding alternative income and services. The picture is also one where consumption relations strengthen gendered ideologies of access to resources: men generating income through farming, women obtaining, exchanging and producing services; men working 'outside' in the world of market prices for labour and products – although market equivalences might not always be formally assumed, they clearly set an exchange value for priced commodities – women working 'inside', trading services on a reciprocal help basis, with no apparent exchange value but highly charged with intangible *moral* value. And last, it is a picture where consumption processes and relations are absolutely intertwined with production processes and relations; not only with the 'family farm' production process but also with agribusiness and food retailing industries and also with the garment industry and the tourist industry to name but a few. There is an extremely complex relationship between the different capabilities of individuals to access resources, their position within the productive process, their power in regard to consumption processes, and the cultural contexts where these relationships take place.

PRODUCING WHILE CONSUMING

The domestic labour debate

As we try to analyse the process of consumption we are drawn increasingly to the awareness that consumption cannot be easily separated from production, distribution and circulation processes. Ironically, it is domestic labour, at the heart of consumption, that has provided the strongest evidence for a need to link consumption and production in a simultaneous expression of economic activity.

Domestic labour is probably the most debated aspect of 'consumption'. Domestic labour includes the production of goods and services. The 'goods' that are produced, for example, meals or Do-It-Yourself (DIY) provisioning, are often immediately consumed and tend to be assimilated to 'services'. Services are not 'goods' but activities which are consumed as they are produced such as cleaning, caring for the young and old, and socialising children. Another aspect of domestic labour is *care* not as a concrete material service (as when taking care of a child's needs) but a general overall state of awareness, of disposition to household members' needs (De Vault 1991). This care is described by women as time- and energy-consuming, it is the most 'invisible' sort of work. Work such as planning, managing a meal (that is, having everybody participate and enjoy it), gathering information, screening and sorting products when shopping, keeping track of supplies, and more generally monitoring household members' needs. As one woman explained: 'The antennae are always out' (De Vault 1991:55–7). A starting definition of domestic labour is the production of goods and services in the household, and care in its general sense.

A first conceptual problem appears when trying to make a clear distinction between domestic production and personal consumption. Should we consider domestic production activities as 'production' when the products are meant to be used by other members of the household and as 'consumption' when they are produced for the producer's own use? How can we distinguish, for example, how much of the time spent in preparing a meal is 'production' and how much 'consumption'? Rather than trying to make sense of the production/consumption divide, which addresses the individual producer's final *relation with the object* or service produced, a better approach tries to unveil the relationships *between the people* involved in the domestic production of goods and services and those realising their personal consumption needs.

This approach leads to two alternative perspectives on domestic labour: one that can be defined as 'reproductive' and another that can be defined as 'productive'. The 'reproductive' definition of domestic labour is well represented by Walker (1978) who includes as domestic production *all* the activities – waged and non-waged – of *all* the household members that create goods and services *which enable the household to be reproduced as a unit*. These include income generated through employment and used for household consumption *and* the activities of household members such as the children and the old who might otherwise be discarded as marginal to domestic production. The 'productive' definition of domestic labour is presented by Reid (1934, 1968) and considers domestic production as *non-waged activities* undertaken by and for members of the household and *which could be replaced by products and services existing in the market*. This second definition implies that it is the incorporation into the household and decommodification of goods and services with market equivalences that makes them 'production'. When market equivalences do not exist domestic labour is considered 'consumption' and therefore rewarded *in its realisation*.

The domestic labour debate centres around whether the activities of providing goods and services by and for the household members can be considered 'productive' or not. The central issues of the debate can be summarised in four points. First, in Marxian terms, is the question of whether the production of use values – goods and services – is 'productive' or 'unproductive' work (that is, whether it is 'social' or 'private' work), whether domestic work should be thought of as producing 'exchange value' (that is, the commodity labour power) instead of just 'use value'. The second question is whether non-commodified labour can produce surplus value incorporated in the commodity labour power – that of household members who do enter the labour market. That is, can labour power be indirectly commodified, for example, through the family wage? The third question is whether the basic character of labour power is precisely that it has *not* been *produced* in the capitalist realm of social relations of production, for this enables the worker to be the *owner* of his own labour power and thus able to sell it, entering *then* into a capitalist relationship; or whether certain members of the household use their labour power as 'capital' and force other members of the household to enter into a work relation similar to that between labour and capital in the market. Fourth, what are the terms of transfers of goods and services between the members of the domestic group? Is the relation one of 'generalised reciprocity' or one of 'exchange'? Are the transfers equitable or do they generate differentiation among household members? Is it possible to 'think' of a process of 'accumulation' by certain members of the household (husband, children) with the labour resources of other members (wife, mother)?

All these questions, in turn, reveal the need to quantify domestic labour and find its 'exchange value' while at the same time it becomes increasingly clear that these activities cannot be reduced to a monetary equivalent. This paradox, present in the domestic labour debate, has opened an altogether alternative way of viewing labour (including wage labour): that is, to consider it from the reproductive side, from the means of livelihood perspective. In a way that recalls Chayanov's theory of the peasant economy and 'petty commodity production' theorists, what becomes central here is *use value*, whether it is mediated by a market circuit or not.

However, the main emphasis in women's studies has been that of trying to assert the 'market equivalent', the exchange value of non-market, domestic production of use values. Interestingly, this view originates with the 'domestic science' of 'home economics' which was a turn-of-the-century bourgeois project. It intended to create a professional space for college-educated women; enhance the social value of domestic labour in order to control middle-class women's discontent; and transfer responsibility for the quality of life to women (Ehrenreich and English 1979:141–82). Domestic science should be understood in the context of Taylor's 'scientific management' studies to increase productivity through the separation of management and execution in labour process. In the realm of home economics, management, in turn, was divided into 'high' management – advice of 'experts' on hygiene, nutrition, budget-keeping – and 'everyday' management – organising housework in a 'rational' way. Thus women were deprived of their knowledge because they had to follow the experts' advice, but they were burdened with the responsibility of creating a rational and 'efficient' labour process out of housework activities. However, the efficiency that could be gained by 'scientific management' of housework as with all tasks that require a high proportion of 'manipulation', was small.

> For the homemaker, household scientific management turned out to mean *new* work – the new managerial tasks of analyzing one's chores in detail, planning, record-keeping, etc. ... First, each task had to be studied and timed. ... Only then could precise weekly and daily schedules be devised. Then there was the massive clerical work of maintaining a family filing system for household accounts, financial records, medical records, 'house-hints', birthdays of friends and relatives and (for what use we are not told) a special file for 'jokes, quotations, etc.' – not to mention the recipe files and an inventory file giving the location and condition of each item of clothing possessed by the family. (Ehrenreich and English 1979: 163)

Instead of being 'globally qualified' for their work – knowing, thinking and doing – in an aggregate process, housewives had to do twice the job, first as planners and after as labourers, while 'knowledge' was expropriated and substituted by experts' advice. Domestic science meant that domestic labour was in effect considered as 'productive labour' on a par with industrial labour and therefore was subject to rational organisation in order to increase efficiency. If domestic labour could be analysed and quantified through time and motion studies (as it was) then monetary equivalents and market value could be established for housework. Efficiency rates could be devised and housework could be compared socially, through time–budget studies and equivalent market values. It is interesting to note, however, that what was measured and given an equivalent market value was the *execution* of housework, not its management. Housewives, then, had management responsibilities but were valued as blue-collar workers.

When trying to quantify the 'productive' value of domestic labour, women's studies were set to find equivalent market values and had to rely on the time–budget methods devised in the Home Economics departments. Several problems can be raised regarding the attempt to measure domestic labour and find its 'exchange value'. First there is the general technical difficulty of measuring management time and energy expenditure, when much of it is materially 'invisible' and might take place simultaneously with other execution tasks. Second, a decision has to be made as to what will be the market equivalent selected to 'value' the work. Here three different possibilities are available, each of which presents particular problems. First, domestic labour can be valued by considering the *'opportunity cost'* of the labour power used in housework. That is, what 'exchange value' is the labour invested in housework forgoing in the labour market? Or, put in another way, what exchange value could *that* labour power fetch if it entered the market? The difficulties of measuring such an hypothetical circumstance are obvious. Nevertheless, this 'value' should somehow be taken into consideration when gauging the market value of domestic labour.

Second, domestic labour can be valued by considering the price paid in the market for the *labour power that produces* domestic services. In this case management work is not taken into account because in the market, domestic service labour power is not supposed to assume planning of housework (this is left to the housewife or to management) but only execution. Third, domestic labour can be valued by considering the equivalent *market price* of the *goods and services* produced in the household. This obscures the value of non-commodified goods and services – those that cannot be obtained in the market. On the other hand, market equivalents both for labour power or goods and services highlight one of the main methodological problems raised by the domestic labour debate: giving an exchange value equivalent means that domestic work is *impersonal*, social work that becomes pooled by exchange, and can be referred to a 'socially necessary time' of realisation. Domestic labour becomes abstract labour through the market movement toward equalisation of values that are exchangeable and indifferent as to their concrete personal carriers.

However, domestic labour, carried out by members of a household outside the market is *not* exchangeable and impersonal. Women are generally bound to housework through a highly personalised, emotionally charged, family relationship. The specific concrete qualities of the relationship make it possible that goods and services produced for household members should not be paid for, and that housewives' domestic labour power does not compete in the market. One-way 'altruistic' transfers of goods and services take place under the labels of 'love' and 'sacrifice' and are hardly comparable. The second term of the housewife's domestic 'contract' implies, first, that inefficient homemakers will not be expelled from their job and eventually from a spurious 'domestic labour market' and, second, that the 'commodity' produced by domestic labour, the labour power of household members that do enter the labour market, does not follow market laws, that is, it is *not* more costly if the housewife that produced it is *less* efficient. Rather the reverse tends to be true. Much as the quantification of domestic labour through the search of market equivalences is a telling device to gauge the value of domestic work, one must bear in mind that domestic labour *is not* abstract labour because its value *is not* equalised through the market. However it is obviously *social* in some sense: not all societies organise domestic work in the same way and Western capitalist societies have actively sought to produce a particular way of structuring domestic work within a household/family material and ideological construct (Wallerstein et al. 1982). This has been effected through volunteer proselytism of bourgeois women among the working classes; through state-sponsored social workers; through the 'family wage' (Lewis 1986; Ehrenreich and English 1979:170–8; May 1982).

The need to get at the social through the concrete qualities of domestic labour has led to a fourth, 'reproductive', attempt at finding a measure of value: *subjective evaluation*, that is the value that domestic work has for those that benefit from it. This perspective tries to measure the adequacy of domestic labour supply to the demand for it. Two different approaches are possible within this demand geared framework. One referring to *use value*; the other referring to *marginal utility*. The demand for a concrete use value and its adequacy is very difficult to measure. The specific quality and quantity demanded is almost impossible to determine and there is generally a flexible range of possible domestic labour adequacies that will fulfil it. Moreover, use value equivalences are not 'universal' but 'particular', subjective values. Thus, transfers of 'use value' goods and services between the members of a household may not be congruent, that is, equivalences satisfactory to both parts may not be reached, although the transfer takes place: notions of 'sacrifice' or 'taking advantage of the situation' reveal that use value transfers are prone to conflictive evaluation (Boulding 1978). The concept of generalised reciprocity that has often been used to explain use value transfers within the household, obscures the fact that power relations and a strong ideological framework are necessary to sustain long-term inequitable transfers. Therefore, trying to measure aggregate demand for the use values produced by domestic labour is extremely difficult.

On the other hand demand for domestic goods and services can be referred to marginal utility and follow its logic: the more the initial need is satisfied by the required good or service the less an additional unit adds to its satisfaction. Although this perspective seems easier to quantify, it is highly questionable in its 'objective' determination of 'needs' and falls prey to the subjective character of demand for non-commodified domestic labour use values.

For all its quantification flaws, the 'reproductive' use value approach points to the 'means of livelihood' objective of domestic labour but also of the other income-producing activities of household members. Domestic labour is accounted as income, as non-monetary resources necessary to make a living. Thinking of work in use value terms for a 'reproductive' unit such as the household highlights the fact that all people enter into specific work relations in order to live, but within these relations, some are able to exploit others' labour, that is, the resources for life are not equitably distributed. The reproductive perspective, sees 'consumption', the quality of life resulting from combined strategies of work, as the remuneration of household *units*. Thus, it tends to assume homogeneity of resource redistribution among household members. The main problem of this approach is its centripetal focus on the household, that separates its 'logic' from the general 'logic' of a capitalist system.

The 'productive' approach to domestic labour also presents methodological and quantification problems. It has the advantage of clearly linking domestic labour to the global economic context of 'production' and 'accumulation'. If domestic labour is conceived of as having not only use value but also exchange value (although not realised) it can be seen as creating surplus value (above the value of reproducing the labour power) which is incorporated in the 'commodity' produced, that is, labour power. This surplus value would be realised together with, and in addition to, the surplus value extracted from the wage labourer. This approach questionably stretches Marx's theory of value to a realm, that of the production and reproduction of labour power, that was not directly addressed in the development of the original theory. Then, obviously, the concepts of 'exchange value' 'surplus value' 'production' and 'exploitation' should be thought of in this application as *metaphors* that can help us understand the relationships people enter both within and outside of households.

Both 'productive' and 'reproductive' approaches to domestic labour illuminate certain 'values' of work although both create shadows in other respects. Any one-sided view seems to miss important aspects. For the time being, a dialectical tension between the 'reproductive' and the 'productive' perspectives should be encouraged, in order to provoke the sort of intellectual 'disquiet' that can lead to the creation of new concepts and an integrated, social reproduction approach.

Toward the analysis of articulated economic realities: means of livelihood and the accumulation of capital

The domestic labour debate is a good introduction to the conceptual problems that have to be addressed by anthropologists (and other social scientists), when trying to make sense of 'economic' relationships. The main problem that has to be faced is that the production/distribution vs. consumption conceptual divide obscures the complex character of most economic relationships. The domestic labour debate highlighted the fact that work ascribed to the realm of 'consumption' could have clear implications in the realm of 'production'. On the other hand, the example of *bidi* homeworkers and other self-employed women in India (many of them petty traders) shows how these women workers are aware of the crucial interconnection between consumption and production realities. To make even clearer the fact that the conceptual production/consumption divide acts as an ideological instrument from within the 'objective' economic models of policy makers and academia, it is useful to look at activities related to 'consumption' which *directly* (unlike domestic labour) produce surplus value accumulated in capitalist endeavours. The case of self-provisioning, of DIY furniture, has been mentioned previously and is an excellent example of how furniture firms transfer 'productive' labour to the 'consumer' and extract something similar to surplus value from him/her without even entering into a labour/capital relationship. Other cost-cutting advantages that affect the structure of furniture firms as a result of DIY expansion have been mentioned, as well as commercial advantages such as the transfer of 'responsibility' for final quality to the consumer/worker. Here we can see how activities labelled as consumption which are often explained as a means to obtain otherwise unattainable goods in view of enhancing the quality of life – that is, in order to increase the level of consumption – are directly related to the organisation of production and of particular ways of exploitation.

Another telling example is that of network marketing. Tupperware and Avon are well-known cases but a wide range of products are sold in this way. These are mainly products targeted at women either as housekeepers or as attractive companions: household appliances, cleaning products, beauty products. Women are recruited into the sales network through a friend and are paid a small percentage on the sales, although sometimes they are rewarded in kind with a certain amount of the same products they are meant to sell. Generally, there is also a reward for recruiting salespersons – either as a direct bonus or as a percentage of sales accruing. The context where this work takes place is particularly interesting for our discussion. Sales methods are explicitly related to the realm of consumption, of homemaking and women's commensality. Sales take place in the home, where a tea or coffee party has been prepared for the occasion. Prospective clients – friends, neighbours, kin – are 'invited' to share the food and the 'information' about the wonderful products that will make their housewife life easier. The general ambience is relaxed, friendly, gossipy and non-economic. Nevertheless, the objective of the saleswoman is to sell as much as possible, by using a mix of persuasion and of social pressure. The ambivalence of the context and of the relationships present is a basic element of the sales method.

In the first place, marketing makes use of previously existing networks of social relationships. It stimulates and tries to realise directly, and as soon as possible, the word-of-mouth spread of information that creates prospective markets and influences consumption of household goods (Johnson Brown and Reingen 1987). Thus the relation between seller and client is not created by the exchange relation, it was already there, charged with social meaning. It might be transformed by the added mediation of the market, but it has not emerged with the market, for the market. It is ironic that insurance salespersons who make extensive use of personal networks refer to this as the 'natural market' (Mozo 1995).

On the other hand, the physical context of the home and the friendly setting of the gathering, together with the type of products marketed are significant. Also, the personalised, non-commodified, realm of consumption is highlighted with its implicit meanings of non-economic relations and altruistic behaviour; with its objective of family well-being and women's responsibility in accomplishing it. Moreover, in this context the type of products sold appear as real impelling *needs*, not so much an object of choice. Finally, the friendly gathering around some food brings consumption in its most pleasurable aspect into an indistinguishable blend with consumption as crudely mediated by the market: buying and selling. All the paradoxes of 'consumption' can be at once present in these network marketing gatherings: duty and pleasure, altruism and interest, work and leisure, gift and exchange, etc.

This ambiguity of women's marketing networks is an important asset for the firms using their labour power. The 'consumption' context, materially and ideologically, is so strong that it de-economises and obscures the labour/capital relation, as much as it dilutes the commercial relation between the saleswoman and her client. In addition, monetary rewards are low and directly tied to effective sales and network expansion. Bonuses in kind reinforce the housewife/consumer aspect of the saleswoman. What should be emphasised is that women are *specifically exploited* as salespersons in network marketing *because* materially and ideologically they are tied to the 'consumption' realm of household and family. But they are exploited by established firms that pursue blatantly 'economic', profit-making activities through the production and distribution of commodities.

It appears, then, that the production/distribution vs. consumption divide is highly questionable. Arguably different 'logics' of 'production' and 'reproduction' can be seen at work. Accumulation through exchange value in the realm of production and distribution confronts increased personal well-being through access to use values. However, what the above examples make clear is that in real life consumption is part of production, directly affecting its organisation and the labour process. This is so, not only because reproduction of labour power is clearly one of the crucial elements structuring production, and therefore relations of consumption are forces directly shaping the quality and availability of the labour factor, but also because relations of production may surreptitiously penetrate consumption activities and directly create 'surplus value'. The added value created by the self-provisioning consumer/worker, expropriated and accumulated by capitalist firms, is not *properly* surplus value, but is transferred through prices to the firm. Moreover, the ideological framework of 'consumption' and the presumption of non-market, equitable and reciprocal relationships, enable specific forms of labour/capital relations that benefit from a highly ambivalent context.

In order to understand economic relations the tripartite division of production/distribution and consumption might prove useful as an analytical tool. But it must not be mistaken for a faithful image of a fragmented reality under penalty of becoming a mystification. It might be time to look into processes that flow into each other, to risk thinking in an articulated and integrated way about the economic realities where life grows. The 'means of livelihood' approach teaches us that everybody's main objective is to make a living, but this personal quest occurs in a worldwide context where capital accumulation is presented – materially and ideologically – as *the* motor of society. Therefore, the personal quest for a livelihood is historically constrained by today's variable expressions of capitalist economies. People want to live as happily as possible in a society that welcomes them as members, within a cultural environment that they can share and understand. But to get hold of even a distant semblance of this reproductive utopia, they will have to enter into one or many of the specific relationships that in turn produce and reproduce the myriad forms of a capitalist system. In the present, personal reproduction (identity) and social reproduction (society) are inextricably tied to the reproduction of a capitalist system (capital). Theory should be able to address this complex reality in a simple way, and I will demonstrate in the following section how this might be done.

4 SOCIAL REPRODUCTION

The argument which began with the need to break down bounded regions of economic discourse has led to this chapter on social reproduction. Here I will present in the first place some feminist and Marxist approaches that can be seen as the prelude to the perspective I want to propose: a theoretical framework of social reproduction. In the second section I develop this social reproduction framework, trying to show that the articulation of material and ideological realities is part of a materialist tradition focusing on 'experience'. The chapter ends with the example of Catalan nationalism, in an attempt to show how material relations have to be analysed within the larger framework of social reproduction, that is, the movement through which a concrete historical social reality sets the conditions for its continuity, and the way in which the concrete historical reality is embodied in agents through personal and collective identities.

PRODUCTION AND REPRODUCTION

A feminist critique of the dichotomy; a definition of reproduction

As I have tried to show in previous chapters, the attention feminists have paid to domestic labour and to women's work more generally, has been the major challenge to a production-centred view of economic processes. Women's work, even when it is clearly 'production' work as in sweatshops all around the world has suffered from what Mies terms 'housewifisation'. This concept stems from the awareness that:

1. Women are the optimal labour force because they are now being universally defined as 'housewives', not as workers; this means their work, whether in use value or commodity production, is obscured, does not appear as 'free wage-

labour', is defined as 'income-generating *activity*', and can hence be bought at much cheaper price than male labour.

2. Moreover, by defining women universally as housewives, it is possible not only to cheapen their labour, but also to gain political and ideological control over them. Housewives are atomised and isolated, their work organisation makes the awareness of a common work process of production, very difficult. Their horizon remains limited by the family. Trade unions have never taken interest in women as housewives.

3. Due to this interest in women, and particularly in women in the colonies as the optimal labour force, we do not observe a tendency towards the generalisation of the 'free' proletarian as the typical labourer, but of the marginalised, housewifised, unfree labourer, most of them women. (Mies 1986:116)

By focusing on women's work, and bringing it to the foreground, this perspective questions the idea of the dominance of 'free' wage labour in capitalist relations of production. As housewives, women are invisible workers, as employed housewives they are marginalised because they are not considered the main 'breadwinner' in a family. At the same time, housework, consumption work, increases constantly in Western 'overdeveloped' countries, mostly in shopping and self-provisioning (Glazer 1984; Mies 1986:126) which is to be related to cost-cutting strategies by marketing firms. In the realm of production, women's work and employment (part-time workers, workers in the service sector), both formal and informal, have also been increasing. This situation, moreover, is not limited to Third World countries but is a blatant fact of Western 'developed' labour markets. Several studies (Beechey and Perkins 1987; J. Smith 1984) show for the UK and the USA how employment of women rests on the assumption that they are subsidiary workers because their basic job is elsewhere (housework) *and* because their income is not expected to reproduce the labour force (neither present nor future generations), but is a mere 'complement' to a full, male, 'family wage'. Therefore the definition of women as economically dependent on a male wage and as primarily non-wage houseworkers for their family is a fundamental aspect of their being employed in rapidly expanding low-wage sectors of the economy such as services, and in low-paying forms of employment such as part-time jobs. This paradoxical situation is highlighted by Joan Smith:

Therefore, to the extent that the growth and relative importance of these industries are central to the transformations in typical economic practices of the nation, the set of social arrangements characterising women's lives as nonwage workers are incorporated into the very grounds of the economy. These social arrangements are precisely those that support the assumption that women are properly considered a cheaper and more dispensable labour force and are less dependent on their wages than male workers.

In short, women's poverty and continued economic dependency are now the central operating premises of the most rapidly expanding sectors of the US economy today and form the basis for the profound changes that have characterised that economy over the past decade. (1984:309)

Moreover, the present situation in Western democracies, with the financial crisis of the state and the drastic move away from the welfare model, means an additional burden of work for many women. Services such as the daily care of the very young and very old are being transferred by the state to the 'community', either the private individual family or volunteer associations organising 'community work'. In either case, mostly women will be responsible for the additional non-wage caring jobs, increasing their usual load of reproductive, 'domestic' work.

Feminism, then, has taken the lead in questioning the conceptual dichotomy of production/reproduction. Beyond the domestic labour debate, the issue of the inclusion of the reproduction of the labour force (waged and non-waged workers) in the structure of production has emerged as a basic theme to be addressed.

In a pathbreaking article Edholm et al. (1977) argue against the 'uncritical adoption of the term reproduction' and point to the danger of the analytical separation in the capitalist system of an 'economic' productive level and a 'reproductive' level, where different kinds of work are associated with human biological reproduction and assumed to be autonomous from the 'productive' process set in motion directly by capital (1977:103–4). The authors then question the general assumption that 'human reproductive practices will be empirically similar in all modes of production' (1977:104); that control of the reproduction of labour force is identical with control over women, perceived as the key elements in human (biological) reproduction; that sexual division of labour is a natural corollary of human reproduction as an unproblematic, female-centred function.

Therefore, in order to be operationalised the concept of reproduction should be carefully disaggregated into distinct 'reproductions': social reproduction, reproduction of the labour force and biological reproduction. *Social reproduction* would refer to the 'reproduction of the conditions of social production in the totality' (Edholm et al. 1977:105). This in fact is a general expression of Marx's idea of social reproduction of the capitalist mode of production, where productive consumption, personal consumption, circulation, distribution and production are linked in a process that reproduces the material elements of capital, their value, and the social relations existing between capital and labour which is the key to the capitalist character of the production process conceived globally (Marx, *Capital*, Vol. II, 20 and 'Prologue' in the *Contribution to the Critique of Political Economy*, Ch. 2).

Reproduction of the labour force corresponds to the daily maintenance of the labourers and to the 'allocation of agents to positions within the labour process over time' (Edholm et al. 1977:105). These two aspects should be clearly distinct: one can be thought of as including work such as domestic labour or the processing of commodities in order for them to be consumable use values. The other includes at least two slightly different ideas: first, that of socialisation, transfers of knowledge and introduction into social networks; and second, in a more general sense, that of distribution, that is, the differential allocation of resources (material and cultural) in a society as a whole, that positions people in reference to means of production and means of livelihood in a way that sets the field for the relations of production. Socialisation can be seen as part of the process of resource allocation, one which, at least in part, takes place in a realm of relationships often conceived as non-economic: those between kin, neighbours, friends, peers.

Biological reproduction refers to reproduction of human populations. The question of human, biological reproduction is interesting to analyse. Indeed, since Malthus, overpopulation has been one of the more powerful ideas because it was considered a 'natural' phenomenon. Economists have used it uncritically to explain poverty, decreasing wages and generally the worsening conditions of labourers worldwide. Edholm et al. ask whether it is 'correct to assume that the normal condition of human populations is expansion' (1977:102). Other feminist anthropologists (Tabet 1985; MacCormack 1982a) have also argued against the assumption that 'natural' human fertility is high. In fact in human societies no fertility is 'natural' and social practices – forms of marriage, rituals, patterns of food allocation – influence fertility and the demography of human populations. On the other hand, the control of human reproduction should be studied in the context of a society's complex means of controlling the resource of labour power.

This disaggregation of the concept of reproduction is a necessary analytical device and a starting point. The theoretical aim, however, should be to integrate these 'reproductive' processes in the understanding of 'economic' processes. Thus, conflict and consent, material and ideological relations that help create and result from specific relations of production, might become clearer. The aim should be, it seems to me, an integrative framework such as that of social reproduction.

Marxist perspective: the articulation of different economic 'logics'

In order to integrate production and reproduction in a wider framework, an analysis of Marxist approaches to these 'domains' of economic practice should also be undertaken. In Marxist analysis there are two possible economic 'logics': one where the objective of production is the final consumption of needed use values; the other where the objective of production is accumulation. This occurs by means of the appropriation of surplus value created within specific social relations of production and through the realisation of this value in commodity circulation. In short, one stresses the production of use values to be obtained directly – as when a peasant works a subsistence plot – or indirectly as in simple commodity production where exchange is limited, in theory, to the indirect acquisition of needed use values. The other stresses the production of exchange values: commodities that circulate in order to enable the realisation and accumulation of the surplus value embodied in them. While in the first 'logic' exchange can only be a mere medium to the use value motive; in the second 'logic' use value appears as a mere medium to the exchange value and accumulation motive.

However, the degree to which these distinct logics are applicable to an economy as a whole is questionable. More likely, different groups of people in a society will be motivated by different 'logics' according to their capacity to control and act upon resources – means of subsistence, land, instruments, raw material, people, information. In capitalist economies, for example, the labourer and the capitalist are moved by different 'logics'. The worker sells a commodity – labour power – in order to get money that will enable her/him to buy the use values for her/his own and her/his family's livelihood. And this movement of simple commodity circulation in the market is completed by a movement of 'simple commodity production' of the commodity labour power outside the market, within the domestic group. It is, in its most basic form, the sale of a use value that cannot be put to use by its owner but can be exchanged in order to obtain the necessary use values for consumption. To live in order to work in order to live: this chain of circumstances leads to the reproduction of the labour force and globally to social reproduction.

On the other hand, the capitalist is moved by his drive to accumulate, because ownership of capital is what makes him a capitalist, what gives him the power to control resources and results in his commanding position in the social relations of production. This also leads to the reproduction of agents allocated to specific controlling positions within the labour process over time and globally to social reproduction. As Sweezy (1964 [1942]:140) pointed out:

> The difference of behavior and motivation as between capitalist and worker has, of course, nothing to do with 'human nature'. It springs ... from the different objective circumstances in which each is placed. Through failure to make this distinction, orthodox economics has frequently been led into one or the other of two opposite errors: the error of supposing that under capitalism *every one* is driven on by the desire to make profits, or the error of supposing that *every one* is interested only in use values and hence that all saving is to be regarded in the light of a redistribution of income through time.

Moreover, as Cook (1984) has argued, we may find 'different objective circumstances' within apparently 'homogeneous' groups of people, for example within households, following gender, age and status lines: among husband/wife, parent/child, brothers/sisters, married/unmarried, heir/non-heir, etc. Within the broad distinction of workers and capitalists, then, different people will be placed in positions such as to be able to develop different economic 'logics'.

The two 'logics' in capitalist social formations do not represent different 'modes of production', societies or even homogeneous social groups. They appear as different aspects of the dynamics of social reproduction. The element that concentrates this basic paradox of conflicting 'logics' in capitalist social formations is human labour power. The reproduction of the labour force is the knot where different 'logics' come together and surplus value is potentially generated. Because the worker is in a position that makes her/him independently incapable of generating or getting hold of the necessaries of life, he/she must put himself in a dependent position in respect to a different group of people who hold the objective means of everyday maintenance. In the classical model of capitalist social relations of production, the worker sells his labour power in order to survive, but his labour, then, produces exchange value in excess of the equivalent market value of the use values necessary for his reproduction. This surplus value appears to belong to those having acquired the use of labour power. And the use to which they put this acquired value will determine their economic 'logic'. It is precisely because both 'logics' become part of the same movement that something like 'surplus value' can be theoretically (not to say materially!) generated.

The key position of the reproduction of the labour force can also be seen in the main theoretical problems confronted by classical economists such as Ricardo and Malthus. The value of labour power – that is within what 'logic' it is generated – has always produced theoretical uncertainty; paradoxically, this expresses its theoretical significance. When thinking of the value of labour power classical economists came to confront two very simple but basic issues: first, what sort of exchange value could human labouring capacities have, being, as they are, a mere corollary of human life? And, second, how to think theoretically about 'production' of human life?

Ricardo postulated a double approach (as for all commodities): one relating to the production process, the other to the circulation process. The first, natural price, was historically grounded in concrete circumstances in the production of labour power such as, for example, acquired life standards in a specific place and moment, the cost or availability of food and other necessities – market or non-market (Ricardo 1959 [1821]:71–83). This also pointed the way to a political dimension where better standards could be gained by confronting capitalist classes (Picchio 1992). The natural price or value was meant to express the value of the labour power incorporated in its production process, that is in the means of subsistence necessary to reproduce the labour power. There remained always, however, a mysterious and rather tautological aspect that stemmed from the fact that while labour power was postulated as a commodity and as such was presumed to be produced in much the same way as any other commodity, the effective production process was phased out in part (non-commodified housework) while other parts (biological reproduction) became relevant, paradoxically, in relation to the circulation approach to the value of labour power. The second Ricardian approach was linked to the market, circulation and the eventual balance of supply and demand. Both approaches, which were presumed to be articulated – not merged – for all other commodities through competition between producers, thus eventually bringing together market and production processes, were more difficult to link in the case of human labour power.

Here, Malthus's population theory presented a solution simply by postulating:

That the power of population is indefinitely greater than the power in earth to produce subsistence for man. Population, when unchecked, increases in a geometrical ratio. Subsistence increases only in an arithmetical ratio. ... By the law of our nature which makes food necessary to the life of man, the effects of these two unequal powers must be kept equal. This implies a strong and constantly operating check on population from the difficulty of subsistence. (1982 [1798]:71)

Malthus's theory is in fact a theory of distribution of people and food, where two different powers, the law of human generation regulated by the institution of marriage and the law of food production, regulated by the institution of property, are permanently brought into balance by 'the law of our nature which makes food necessary to the life of man'. As soon as property and marriage are instituted in society (conceived as a unique and universal condition) 'inequality of conditions must necessarily follow' (1982:142) in order that, paradoxically, those who suffer from want might claim 'the surplus product of others, as a debt of justice' (1982:143). However:

the number of these claimants would soon exceed the ability of the surplus produce to supply. ... And it seems both natural and just that, except upon particular occasions, their choice should fall upon those who were able, and professed themselves willing, to exert their strength in procuring a further surplus produce; and thus at once benefiting their community, and enabling the proprietors to afford assistance to greater numbers. (1982:143)

Malthus's theory is attractive because of its mechanical simplicity based on natural – therefore unquestionable – laws and quantitative values that are firmly tied in an equation by the axiom of nature that food is necessary to human life. The equation leads to a supply and demand balance which in turn feeds back into the demanders (of food) side (that is, destitute labourers) mechanically influencing the production of people, the reproduction of the labour force. Thus the value (price) of labour power appears to be mechanically set by quantitative variations in the proportions of food and people. However, this theory is strongly dependent on a specific a priori social distribution of property and power: the distribution of food between people concerns only 'surplus food' – that remaining after the owners' own consumption has been met – and 'all who were in want of food'. Moreover, it is obvious to Malthus that 'the owners of surplus produce', who are the ones to distribute it amongst the needy and supernumerary hordes of claimants, will discard 'moral merit' as 'a very difficult distinguishing criterion' and will 'in general seek some more obvious mark of distinction' and thus it is 'natural and just' that they select those willing 'to exert their strength in procuring a further surplus produce' (1982:143). What is important in Malthus and his followers is that they present their views as scientific 'laws of nature' and that they subsume the problem of the nature of labour power to a simplistic supply and demand theory of value formation in an ahistorical context. Where Ricardo tries to deal with the social and historical issues affecting the value of labourpower through the reproduction of the labour force, therefore leaving the door open to the eventual analysis and theoretical integration of the reproduction of the labour force into the labour theory of value, Malthus ignores the problem by rendering a priori and universal the relations of production reproduced in distribution through the existence of groups of suppliers and groups of demanders (of food) and by shifting the attention to a further distribution between 'demanders' of a particular 'fund' of food. This view in fact obscures relations of production *and* relations of distribution.

The reproduction of the labour force is the linchpin between the use value and exchange value 'logics', between life and accumulation. Productive consumption and personal consumption, for example, come together in the reproduction of the labour force: what is personal consumption for labourers is productive consumption for employers: income as costs. On the other hand, in the framework of any labour theory of value (classical or Marxian) living labour is the ultimate use value, that which creates and is incorporated in all other produced use values, that which can be abstracted in a general exchange context and thus can become a universal equivalent for exchange then revealing exchange value.

How people confront need in concrete social and historical contexts, and how they have to spend their physical and intellectual energies in order to live, produce economic social relations. Specific social and political circumstances give some people more control over their own and others' livelihood, further driving people into different positions in their attempt to reproduce life.

Ultimately, the degree to which the maintenance of life is controlled by oneself (as an individual or as a member of a group) affects the degree to which life-producing energy might be conceived a separable, alienable and consumable apart from the self. The attempt to explain how life is produced as labour and how labour can reproduce life is the attempt to understand the particular way a society is reproduced by its members materially and ideologically.

The need for a wider theoretical framework: toward social reproduction

Going back to the standard division of the economic process into production/distribution/circulation/consumption, it is interesting to note the many relations between people that directly affect material livelihood and have consistently been left out of the picture or reintroduced by forcing them to fit into old frameworks. Things get better when the whole movement of production and reproduction of the relations of production is taken into account: to witness, Marx's chapter 2 in the 'Prologue' to the *Contribution to the Critique of Political Economy* (1970b:247–68) where he points to the dialectical relationship between what he sees as different moments of a totality that he terms 'production'. Production in this global sense, however, includes not only production in its restricted sense as a particular moment of the entire process, but also distribution, circulation and consumption as distinct moments of the total process that are tied into reciprocal relationships. In this complex web of dialectical construction of a unit, nevertheless, the relationships between people in the moment of production determine the forms and the reciprocal relationships of the different moments (1970b:267). There is in Marx an idea that production is the expression of the entire economic process. For example: 'consumption as a need is an internal moment of the productive activity, but the latter is the point of departure of its realisation and, therefore, its foremost moment, the act in which the entire process is resolved anew' (1970b:260–1). 'But in society the relationship between the producer and the product, as soon as the latter is finished, is purely external, and the comeback of the product to the individual depends on his relationships with other individuals' (1970b:261). And these relationships are determined by the previous production processes. Social reproduction, for Marx, is the reproduction of the conditions necessary for a particular form of production to take place.

In fact, social reproduction in this sense is close to his concept of distribution (not so much of products but of the means of production and the allocation of people to different positions in production) (1970b:263). This distribution is the basis of the process of production. But it is not a pre-given natural fact: it is the outcome of previous, *historical*, production processes and the transformations within them (1970b:264). Social reproduction is perceived as the replacement of things and people in a particular framework of relationships that enables the production process to continue (*Capital* Vol. II, Ch. 20).

Marx's view is interesting because of his historical formulation of the reproduction process and because he clearly ties the concept to the social relations instituting differential allocation of resources to people. The problem for us, is that Marx studies social reproduction as the necessary movement of value and matter between the sectors of capitalist production (production of means of production and production of means of consumption) in order for the system to be able to continue at the same pace – simple reproduction – or at an increasing pace – enlarged reproduction. Production is very narrowly defined as industrial production where all workers sell their labour power to the owners of the means of production, and where only commodities are taken into account as values and matter being replaced. But this is not the capitalist world, at least not as we can perceive it nowadays.

If 'classical' industrial labour/capital relationships may yet be extrapolated to an ample (maybe dominant) part of the production process, it seems a fundamental flaw to present them as the only relationships to be taken into account (together with capital/capital relations) in capitalist social reproduction processes. We have seen, for example, that many resources do not circulate as commodities but are nonetheless allocated in ways that are significant for the positions of individuals within society. We have also seen, and the case of gender relations and housework is the most salient, that relationships other than the labour/capital one must be explained as fundamental parts of the social reproduction process of capitalist societies. What is now more and more obvious for Western capitalist societies has always been perceived as present (by Marx and others) in pre-capitalist societies and capitalist social formations. It is then the spirit, but not the letter, of Marx's social reproduction concept that I would like to make the starting point of a useful, global, concept of social motion in 'economic' anthropology.

SOCIAL REPRODUCTION

The dialectics of the material and the ideological

In a much quoted paragraph Marx (1970c [1859]:37) states clearly that

the sum total of these relations of production constitute the economic structure of society, the real base, on which rises a legal and political superstructure and to which correspond definite forms of social consciousness. The mode of production of material life, conditions the social, political and intellectual life process in general. It is not the consciousness of men that determines their being, but, on the contrary, their social being that determines their consciousness.

This and other passages of his work have been used to construct the base/superstructure theoretical model, where the economic structure determines consciousness and other social and institutional relations. While this interpretation has been advocated by orthodox Marxists, and, with some qualifications and a theoretical emphasis by Althusser and his school (Althusser 1969, 1974; Balibar 1969; for a critique of these views see E.P. Thompson 1978), a thorough and wide-ranging reading of Marx's work (and that of Engels) puts his words in a different light. In his *Philosophical Writings* of 1844 (Marx 1970a), his letter to Annenkov (1846) and *Theses on Feuerbach* (1845) (all in Marx and Engels 1975), in *The German Ideology* (Marx and Engels 1992 [1845–6]) *The Misery of Philosophy* (Marx 1950 [1846–7]), and in Engels's *Ludwig Feuerbach and the End of Classical German Philosophy* (1886) and his letter to Bloch (1890) (both in Marx and Engels 1975), but also in Marx's more 'mature' *Grundrisse* (1972 [1859]), in the '*Formen*' part (that on pre-capitalist social formations), we find a view that differs

widely from the orthodox rendering. In fact it is in this last work
(*Grundrisse*) where, I think (unlike E.P. Thompson), his idea becomes
clearest, in his discussion about the objective conditions of work and
the subjective social being of the individual where he stresses the
separation of these aspects as a product of history which is only completed
in the relationship between wage labour and capital (1972:351–8). If
we add to this his constant emphasis on approaching *real life* as opposed
to idealist positions (such as that of Proudhon) constructing society in
the image of a previously constructed theoretical model and, foremost,
his refusal to *separate* being and consciousness (although *differentiating*
them) (1970a [1844]:143, 145–7) we get a slightly different picture.
It is Marx's emphasis on the production and reproduction of *real life*
and his struggle against idealist philosophers that we should recall.

In the 1844 manuscripts he presents a broad idea of human work
as 'vital activity': a conscious *and* material process that is the 'practical
production of an objective world' which is 'the assertion of man as a
conscious generic being' (1970a:111–12) and, further, he points out
that it is precisely the alienation of work in capitalist relations that
transforms work into a mere *medium* to satisfy need instead of it being
the direct material *and* spiritual process of need satisfaction
(1970a:109–13).

In the *Grundrisse*, this same problem is discussed in a more elaborate
form in the *Formen* (a section on pre-capitalist social formations),
where the presumed historical process of the 'freeing' of labour from
social and material ties in turn is related to the use value/exchange
value logics and to the dissolution of the social relations bound to use
value production. It is the same problem and the answer is in a similar
way tied to a historical, a real process, of *separation* of the 'objective
conditions' from the 'subjective social being': the separation and
confrontation of the people involved in producing real life
(1972:368–74). We should then, I think, bear in mind that in the
base/superstructure passage quoted at the beginning of this chapter,
several different statements are merged together.

First, Marx advances a theoretical debate against idealism and presents
historical materialism ('the production and reproduction of real life',
Engels 1975 [1890]:520) as the only way to approach human society.

Second, it is asserted that the process of production includes 'social
production' of consciousness and of ideologies such as religion (*Theses
on Feuerbach*, VII). That thought is only real 'in practice' (*Theses on*

Feuerbach, II) and that historical materialism should go beyond 'contemplative materialism', that is, beyond 'a materialism that does not conceive the activity of the senses as practical activity...' (*Theses on Feuerbach*, IX, in Marx and Engels 1975:427–8). Marx's position is 'that human essence is not something abstract inherent to each individual. It is, in its reality, *the sum of social relations*' (*Theses on Feuerbach*, VI, my emphasis, Marx and Engels 1975:427). Social life is *human practice* and our objective is to understand this practice (*Theses on Feuerbach*, VIII).

Third, also, Marx puts forward the idea that in real social practice capitalism operates a *separation* between the subjective being and the objective conditions for the production of life, as well as an *alienation* of consciousness from the process of production of life. Thus the separation of ideal and material appears not as 'natural' or inherent in humanity, but instead as a product of an historical process (*Theses on Feuerbach*, IV; *Grundrisse* 1972:352–6, 368).

Fourth, stemming from this, it is argued that the ideologies of capitalism tend to reify abstract categories whether in political economy or religion, etc. And against this, in his study of a concrete social formation, there is an emphasis on the primacy of real social relations through the focus on the objective conditions for the production of life, now limited to bare material production, industrial production.

In this light, the idea of a correspondence/determination between the production of material life and forms of social consciousness appears as a (clumsy) way to stress the materiality of social life in an abstract model of a concrete capitalist social formation where work has been alienated and social being divided into mere material practices (that is, work for wages as a medium to obtain subsistence) and 'other' spiritual practices necessary for the 'practical production of an objective world'. Although in this famous passage of 1859 a sequence of causation is clearly stated, there is a continuous reference to *social relations* as the locus of movement and transformation, of process, that is, 'real life'. Productive forces are the result of previous social relations and not the autonomous force they appear to be in this passage. And social relations are the practical, real, materialist expression of human activity for the production and reproduction of real life.

Moreover, in an interesting passage of the *Grundrisse* on 'reproduction' (1972:329–30), social relations (and, explicitly, *not* products) appear as the main result of the production and valorisation process, namely in capitalist formations, the relationship between the capitalist and the worker. 'This social relation of production is a more important result of this process than its material fruits' (1972:330, see also 377–8). Marx, in fact, criticises political economists for stressing the 'things produced' as opposed to the relationships produced. He highlights the production of relationships *between people*. That is, *real life*, while the emphasis on things and relations among things appears very clearly defined in the chapter of 'Commodity Fetishism' (*Capital*, Vol. I) as an ideal abstraction of a specific human practice, an abstraction of concrete social relations between real people.

For Marx, then, social relations, the result of practical activity which includes consciousness, are the focus of his analysis. And it is only in capitalism that matter and consciousness are confronted as different aspects of life. Marx is not clear, though, if this is an appearance or a reality, and this is probably because, in his dialectical thinking, mystification is both.

The Marxist tradition and 'economic anthropology': Gramsci, Williams, Thompson, Bourdieu, Godelier

Some writers in the Marxist tradition have tried to develop precisely this strand of Marx's thought: the tension between matter and ideas which is resolved in human practice (material, historical, conscious). Gramsci is perhaps the first to expand his thought in this direction. His preoccupation is always related to history, to political action, to the role of the state as 'educator', 'acting on economic forces, reorganising and developing the apparatus of economic production, creating a new structure' (Gramsci 1987 [1929–35]:247). Although Gramsci maintains the analytical distinction of structure – that is, material forces and relations of production – and superstructure – political, juridical and political forces – his repeated statements are very clear as to the unity of structure and superstructure in history (that is, 'real life'). Time and again he expresses the concept of the 'historical bloc' where material and ideological forces are welded in practice which is always political activity of different sorts: the fight for hegemonies in 'civil society' – cultural, moral, ethical; the struggle of a subaltern group to press claims against the multiple coercions of 'political society' – punitive force, law – (Gramsci 1987:12, 52, 180–3, 242–4). Time and again Gramsci fights mechanicism and monism both materialistic and idealistic, whether he speaks of the 'relations of force' and the various economic and political levels at which relations of force are generated and expressed (1987:180–5) or whether he speaks of the philosophy of praxis 'the identity of contraries in the concrete historical act, that is in human activity (history-spirit) in the concrete, indissolubly connected with a certain organised (historicised) "matter" and with the transformed nature of man' (1987:372). Gramsci's intent is, clearly, to understand 'the real dialectical process' (1987:366) in order to 'justify a particular practical activity, or initiative of will' (1987:185), that is, in order to help in the construction of a self-aware political (subaltern) force: 'the essential task is that of systematically and patiently ensuring that this force is formed, developed, and rendered ever more homogeneous, compact and self-aware' (1987:185), ready for political action when the moment arrives. And, for Gramsci, *culture*, together with historical understanding which can be thought of as a different expression of the same process, is the glue of 'practical (collective) activity' and 'an historical act can only be performed by "collective man" and this presupposes the attainment of a "cultural-social" unity through which a multiplicity of dispersed wills, with heterogeneous aims are welded together with a single aim' operating not only intellectually, but also emotionally (1987:349, cf. also p.413). What is interesting in Gramsci's thought is that it emerges from concrete, practical involvement with Italian politics, that is, with 'real life' and the struggle for change. It is his attempt to understand history from the viewpoint of the practical experience of real politics and present-day strategies for action, that in a sense *forces* him to look at what in effect moves people to action. In this light, material/ideal or structure/superstructure distinctions may be considered analytical tools but can never be constructed, in real life, as a mechanistic projection of an external, abstract, linear, causal direction, but only as a necessary reciprocity in a dialectical process, constantly (re)setting limits and producing pressures from within the dynamics of process (Thompson 1978:159–60).

Following and further developing a certain strand of Marx's and Gramsci's thoughts, R. Williams and E.P. Thompson reintroduce into the academic disciplines of the social sciences and/or the humanities (cultural materialism, history, anthropology) the idea of *real people* as subjects/agents of history as opposed to the Althusserian abstract notion of people as *supports* of functions determined by 'the structure of the relations of production' (Althusser 1969:194; Balibar 1969:226). In Williams and in Thompson human *experience* becomes the focus (as opposed to 'structure' or 'economy'), and within 'experience' the objective and the subjective, matter and consciousness, are indivisible and may obstruct knowledge when they appear as idealist reifications (Thompson 1978:97, 171, 175–6; Williams 1977:75–82). Experience is a material process but one where we must think not only of the material production of maintenance but also of the *material* production of a social and political order and of a cultural order without which the material production of life would be impossible. Experience is a process of forming and transforming social relations in the everyday context of production, of politics, of culture and of the personal, intimate, family environment. Experience is at once an individual process and a social process and both are also indivisible in human societies. For Williams (1984 [1961]:55), communication of descriptions of the relationships between people and with the environment is fundamental for human associative life, that is, life in a community. And this 'effort of learning, description and communication' (1984:54) permeates the whole social process with a creative drive:

Communication is the process of making unique experience into common experience, and it is, above all, the claim to live. For what we basically say, in any kind of communication is: 'I am living in this way because this is my experience' ... . Since our way of seeing things is literally our way of living, the process of communication is in fact the process of community: the sharing of common meanings, and thence common activities and purposes; the offering, reception and comparison of new meanings leading to the tensions and achievements of growth and change. (1984:55)

Consciousness here appears as a material expression of experience – giving meaning to social relations in real life – and as a material force, exerting pressures leading to change.

What is important in this view (and E.P. Thompson insists on it) is that 'ideology', 'values', 'feeling', the realm of social consciousness as well as that of moral consciousness, are not some autonomous creation of the mind, are not imposed upon material, necessary (that is, 'production') social relations, but are themselves materially produced in the various contexts of human life and all of it joins in a 'distinctive class experience' (1978:170–5) which is a fundamental part of the historical processes for reproducing human societies. What Thompson points to (taking up Marx's early writings) is that the separation of 'economic' social relations and processes from the areas of 'culture' and 'morality', more generally of consciousness, as being something pre-existing or preconscious is itself part of bourgeois utilitarian ideology.

The good old utilitarian notion that all facts are quantifiable and measurable (and hence can be ingested by a computer), and that whatever is not measurable is not a fact, is alive and kicking and in possession of a large part of the Marxist tradition. And yet, what cannot be measured has had some very measurable material consequences. ... Values are neither 'thought' nor 'hailed', they are lived, and they arise within the same nexus of material life and material relations as do our ideas. They are the necessary norms, rules, expectations, etc., learned (and 'learned' within feeling) within the '*habitus*' of living; and learned, in the first place within the family, at work, and within the immediate community. Without this learning social life could not be sustained, and all production would cease. (1978:175)

Bourdieu's concept of 'habitus', that Thompson uses, is yet another attempt to understand the production of practice as a result of the pressures and limitations that the structuration of previous experience inflicts upon action. The 'habitus' is an interiorisation in the 'structures of perception' of the exterior objective structures of 'concrete conditions of existence'. It is then an individual but social structure, for it incorporates individually what are social relations of (re)production of material life. As an individual 'scheme of perception' it enables creative practice, but as a social structure it sets limits and exerts pressures to conform to a certain 'logic' inscribed in 'reasonable' action:

A product of history, the 'habitus' produces individual and collective practices, and therefore history in accordance with the schemes engendered by history. The 'habitus' assures the active presence of past experiences that, placed in every organism in the form of schemes of perception, of thought and of action, better than any formal rule or explicit norm, tend to guarantee the conformity of practices and their continuity through time. (Bourdieu 1980:91)

Once again, 'experience', 'practice' and 'process' in human societies call for a dialectical understanding of matter and consciousness, of 'real life'.

But what, then, of the 'economy', of the pertinence of highlighting production from within the reproduction of 'real', material life? In an interesting article Godelier (1978) attempts to free himself from Althusserian structuralism and from vulgar economism (see also

Godelier 1984). He states very clearly that 'the distinction between base and superstructure is not one of levels or instances nor of institutions. ... It is in its principle a distinction of functions' (1978:157). However, there exists a 'hierarchy of functions' of social relations in order to reproduce any society and:

the social relations that are 'determinant in the last instance' are always those that function as relations of production; because they function as relations of production they dominate the reproduction of society and hence the representations that organise and express them also dominate. (1978:169)

Nevertheless, causality, determination, is not linear:

the relation of causality that emerges is that of a *hierarchy between functions that exist simultaneously and presuppose each other...* (1978:167)

In this same article Godelier very nicely detaches 'superstructure' from the connotations of ideal construction and highlights the ideal content of any material social relation and in particular of social relations of production (1978:157, 161–2). But why, then, should the social relations that function to produce objects (and, crucially, to reproduce themselves as a social order of access to means and power) have precedence over those that produce people? In his work, empirical and theoretical, Godelier solves the issue by stating that in most primitive societies kinship social relations have the function of social relations of production (this is close to Marx's view in the *Grundrisse*). The problem is that the analysis of what appears to occur in capitalist social formations – the separation of an economic area of 'production' – becomes reified here as a separate universal 'function' of social relations. They are no longer seen as a 'level' or 'instance' of material substance, for social relations are at once constituted in the material and the ideal, but still as a separate 'function' in theory.

We have seen, however, that in trying to explain 'economic' social relations – of production, distribution, circulation and consumption – we are time and again driven toward power and culture, coercion and hegemony, force and meaning. As Williams puts it, the production of a social, political and cultural order (together with [industrial] production) are 'real practices, elements of a whole material process' (1977:93–4) and hence they keep breaking the 'economic' order *from within*, introducing old issues in a new light, forcing in new questions such as housework and the sexual division of labour, migrations and ethnic identities, shadow work and informal circulation of resources, work vs. employment, etc.

More integrative explanations are then needed in order to drive our attention toward social relations – that is, matter, ideas and communication in between real historical people – that produce and reproduce real life. And in fact 'production' is just one more inroad toward the understanding of the 'whole material social process' constructed in an endless movement of human practice and experience, and the struggle for change, which is history.

When we think, then, of a more integrative and processual model for 'economic anthropology', one that will help us confront what meets our ethnographic experience and our empirical data, a model, moreover that remains resolutely attached to material matters, we think of a concept of social reproduction in its full, complex and interlocking sense.

Space, culture and capitalism: material relations in cultural contexts

In thinking of social reproduction, we must be careful, however, not to imply that the *objective* of a society is to reproduce itself, to maintain a certain order of things, to perpetuate a concrete form of organisation. By personalising society we fall in fact into a functional organicist, harmonious image, where different limbs with different roles serve together a unique purpose decided by the head. In so doing we obscure the possibility of dissent and conflict between groups. By presupposing perpetuation as the aim of the social body we also preclude the viability of rupture, of radical change or the mere construction of alternative ways of life and of thinking within a dominant hegemony. Counter-hegemonies, that is, *cultural constructions* capable of creating cohesion among a large group of (dominated) people and of supporting organised action in order to press claims and confront the hegemonic (dominant) group, appear then as strange bodies that should either be 'assimilated' (that is, digested and incorporated) or destroyed, with 'integration' as a middle term where a group is permitted to keep some non-threatening identity signs as long as it fully submits to the basic hegemonic claims. Nationalism is a case in point, where the cultural construction of a social body has a political aim but is also tied to concrete relations of production. If we take the example of Catalan nationalism we can see how capitalist relations of production relate to space and to cultural contexts in history.

Although in the Catalan area one could trace back cultural, political and economic historical processes that diverged from those of the Castilian hegemonic rule, it would be an anachronism to speak of Catalan nationalism before the nineteenth century. Catalan nationalism is tied in with the surge of the German Romantic movement and the search for roots in popular folklore, in history and in common law (Prats 1988). It appears as the search for a specific 'character' defining Catalan nature and spirit. But Catalan nationalism is also very strongly tied to the Enlightenment version of a nation of citizens, a free society of men all of whom have equal rights within the boundaries of the nation-space they have agreed to share. The idea of a free, voluntary, *contract* with a community of others that will then constitute a political body with power to govern itself is present in most strands of political Catalanism although not with a consistent meaning. There is also a very interesting economic component of the rise of Catalan nationalism, albeit not a simple obvious relationship but a complex one.

The Catalan area emerged as a meaningful political unit with the first inroads gained to the south of the Pyrenees in Islamic Iberia in the ninth century. The territories rescued for Christendom in the name of the Holy Emperor Charlemagne were under the jurisdiction of strong feudal lords, the Counts. Soon the Counts freed themselves from the vassal link to the Frankish king while they consolidated and institutionalised their feudal structure in the *Usatges*, a written code (Valls-Taberner 1954). The following centuries saw the play of dynastic alliances and military expansion that enabled Catalan merchants to control commerce in the Western Mediterranean. At the same time, local political institutions were taking form. In the fifteenth century a dynastic change gave the rule to a Castilian king and henceforth the Catalan polity was under constant pressure from the Castilian monarchs' drive toward political expansion and hegemonic rule. This loss of autonomy was resisted constantly and sometimes violently (1640 War of Secession; 1705–14 War of Succession). Under the Bourbon dynasty (1714 onward) the Catalan region lost most of the particular institutions it still maintained and was intensely Castilianised. Economically, however, this situation opened the interior markets to Catalan products and from 1778 up to the loss of the Spanish colonies in Latin America, the royal privilege given to the port of Barcelona (shared with other

Spanish seaports), enabled Catalan merchants to directly engage in commerce with the American colonies. Catalan industrial products (cotton and wool textiles) and commercial agricultural produce (spirits) gained most from the new market privileges, and capital began to accumulate that was invested in the consolidation of industry (Soldevila 1978; Vilar 1982 [1962]; Nadal 1979). The loss of most of the colonies at the turn of the nineteenth century was a strong blow to the Catalan textile industry which exported around 20 per cent of its production. This focused the interests of industrial capitalists on the national market (Nadal 1979; Vicens Vives 1986). Against the ground of the nineteenth-century political unrest (Napoleonic invasion, War of Independence, Absolutist Restoration, Liberal and Conservative uprisings and constitutions, several Civil Wars, the First Republic, the Restoration, the loss of the last colonies in 1898 ...) the Catalan bourgeoisie tried to further its interests, sometimes in conflicting ways. Generally, during the nineteenth century the aim of the Catalan bourgeoisie was to influence the central Spanish governments in two vital areas: with regard to the resolution of the 'social problem' and to the preservation of the markets (the last colonies, the national market). This is the background of the emergence of nationalist ideologies in Catalonia. Here I will try to show the differences and similarities of the several nationalist ideologies, their bourgeois drive during the nineteenth and early twentieth centuries, their open confrontation with the growing internationalist proletarian ideologies from the 1870s to 1936, and the union of the left and bourgeois nationalist democrats under a Catalan nationalist ideology during Franco's dictatorship.

The first move toward a nationalist cultural awareness was inspired by German Romanticism and addressed the recuperation of the Catalan language, folklore and literature and the construction of a Catalan history. Politically, this first romantic drive seems to have been liberal and constitutionalist but soon it turned toward a conservative historical particularism that stressed the *volkgeist*, the national spirit of the Catalan people (Vicens Vives 1986:171–5). This romantic definition and description of the Catalan 'soul' was institutionalised by the University of Barcelona in its teaching, by several local newspapers printed in Catalan and by the inauguration in 1859 of a Literary Contest of medieval inspiration: the Jocs Florals (Flower Games). None of these movements could be considered 'nationalist' of themselves because there was not yet a clear drive toward a political identity, toward a project of self-government.

The emergence of political nationalism proper in Catalonia is tied to the Spanish political events that led to the fall in 1868 of the reigning monarch, Isabel II, and soon after to the advent of the First Republic. During the first half of the century the Catalan industrial bourgeoisie had wavered between its support for liberal and conservative governments (Balcells 1992). Liberals brought up reforms that were needed for capitalist and industrial development such as the disentailment laws (especially in the 1830s) that broke traditional links between peasants and feudal or ecclesiastic lords, creating a 'free' workforce and privatising jurisdictional, monastic and municipal properties. Conservatives on the other hand, used militarist policies to restore social order, disrupted by the numerous strikes and revolutionary outbursts. Moreover, feudal landlords and the Church in rural Catalonia supported mostly the *ancien régime* with its absolutist, traditionalist hierarchies, but also with its '*fueros*', or local special privileges that regulated the maintenance of agreements, tenancies and leaseholds between peasant and lord for generations, and included a common law regulating social relations of production within the peasant copyholder's household.

Thus, after the economic and subsistence crises that precipitated the advent of the First Republic there were at least three different proto-nationalist currents representing different groups of Catalans, with different strategies regarding Catalonia and the rest of Spain, yet never dissociating them in political action.

First, there was a group of Federalist Republican Democrats in Catalonia. These were liberal intellectuals inspired by democratic federal countries such as the USA or Switzerland and with a real interest in the 'modernisation' of Catalonia but also of Spain more generally. The idea of its main exponent, Almirall, was that of a Catalan state freely choosing to forge a political relationship with other equal states. For him, however, and this was the distinctive element of Catalan Federalism, the state was the significant political unit, as opposed to the disaggregation of multiple free-standing politically equivalent levels of contract such as the municipality or even the individual (Pi i Margall 1854, 1973 [1876]).

In the labour relations domain they present a liberal attitude with full recognition of workers' associations as opposed to the paternalism and author-itarianism that dominated both Catalan bourgeoisie and Spanish conservatism which conceived of inequality as a natural institution by God's will. (Trías 1975:170).

They represented an enlightened bourgeoisie that clamoured for individual liberty as a necessary framework for political and economic transformation. The aim was a bourgeois revolution that could be capable of attracting workers into a project of cooperative, harmonious relations between labour and capital. But the model of workers' associations they had in mind was more that of the *ancien régime* corporations than that of the new post-revolutionary workers' associations (Trías 1975:168; Sewell 1980).

An important faction of the Catalan Federalists became progressively estranged from what they saw as a 'rationalist' institutional concept of the federal state on the part of Spanish Federalists, as opposed to their 'historical' and 'natural' definition of the Catalan state (Almirall in Trías 1975:433–52). By 1882, after the Bourbon restoration and the installation of conservative and liberal alternation in government, Almirall and his followers decided to forgo all participation in 'Madrid' (sic) political parties and to concentrate on 'Catalan politics'. The call for the second Catalanist Congress (1883), organised by Almirall's Centre Català (founded in 1882), declared its aim as 'to give birth to genuine Catalan politics' but this 'politics of identity' was based on the homogenisation of all other possible differences that might express conflict and diversity of interests within Catalonia. The Centre Català seeks to unite 'Catalans of all religious or political ideas, it wants to be formed by all those whose interest is the regeneration of our character and the betterment of our land, whatever their social condition' (Almirall et al. in Trías 1975:323).

In fact, by the 1870s workers in Catalonia were mostly internationalists and revolutionary, and were not interested in participating in the bourgeois political game, which, they argued, did not intend to radically transform their situation. Their aim was to get the workers organised and to make a revolution that would collectivise the means of production. By 1873 internationalist workers were explicitly and strongly opposing the main 'progressive' formula that the democratic bourgeoisie was presenting as the eventual solution to the social problem: production cooperatives. The argument was that cooperatives lured workers into becoming individualists and bourgeois, and distanced them from their real aim – putting an end to capitalist exploitation – and from their real means: a workers' union, 'solidary, federative, international' (Izard 1979:186–7). Workers asserted clearly their aims and means and their estrangement from the Catalan democratic federalist project of 1883 (Trías 1975:453–4).

Second, there was a group of monarchic, conservative, anti-liberal bourgeoisie, mainly concerned with social unrest and very willing to ask for the state's military repression in order to keep Catalonia calm. After the brief revolutionary and republican interlude during the last quarter of the nineteenth century, their main interest was to ban or restrict workers' freedom of association, to enforce law and order, to restrict the privilege of political rights to the bourgeoisie by opposing universal male suffrage. They were also interested in keeping the Catalan civil law that established and regulated social relations of production within the family household (the *casa*), by creating both differentiation and strong ties between the members of a domestic group in relation to the ownership and use of the means of production. The Catalan civil law was the institution that preserved a certain ideological and material fabric of relationships organising the economy in agriculture and in industry (McDonogh 1989; Terradas 1984). Conservatives, but not only them, feared the trend of central governments (especially liberal ones) toward a unified Spanish Civil Code. And last, but not least, they were very strongly protectionist with regard to their industries. They feared and opposed the free trade policies of the Restoration's 'liberal' governments, as they had done before, in 1869, with the introduction of free-trade agreements by the liberal revolutionary governments. The Catalan industrialists, through their two main associations – the *Instituto Industrial de Cataluña* of the large cotton manufacturers and the *Fomento de la Producción Nacional*, smaller semi-artisanal cotton, wool and silk manufacturers – tried to present the argument for 'protection' as a *unified social project* to protect *work* through the protection of industry from foreign competition. In the first massive demonstration organised by the Fomento in 1869 there were men of very different political affiliations (liberal, conservative, republican, even some workers' representatives) (Trías 1975:62–3, 131). In 1881 another set of movements against free trade policies were said to 'unite' *all* Catalans – conservatives, liberals, republicans, industrialists, landlords and workers – in defence of protectionist measures (Termes and Colomines 1992:69–70). It is interesting to note, however, that, on the one hand the conservative bourgeoisie was *very* insistent on presenting its protectionist arguments as beneficial for the *Spanish* economy as a whole (in fact addressing the interests of large estate landowners in the south). In effect, the 'Catalan' protectionist project was to preserve the 'Spanish' national market and the colonies that were left (Cuba and the Philippines) for the Catalan industries. And, on the other hand, as Izard has pointed out 'all Catalans were not protectionists, neither was all of the rest of Spain a free-trade supporter' (1979:97). Moreover, and this seems especially significant, the largest workers' association in 1874 *'Tres Clases de Vapor'*, very clearly stated that they were not interested in the protectionist/free trade debate because 'there is no important difference between workers' situation in the countries with free-trade as compared with those that live where protectionism reigns. Therefore, for the working class, these are not such essential questions as it is pretended' (in Izard 1979:97). In fact, the moderate free trade agreements of 1869 were not detrimental to cotton industrialists. The *Tres Clases de Vapor* in 1874 hints at a possible relationship between capitalists' perpetual lamentation against the wrongs of free trade and their drive to lengthen working hours and withhold pay increases: workers asserted that since the free trade agreements 'the industry has improved and developed a lot' (in Izard 1979:117). Catalan historians such as Vicens Vives (1986) also think that free trade benefited Catalan industry as a whole. The protectionist argument, however, was the main element in the construction of a 'Catalan' economic identity for the conservative bourgeoisie.

Finally, there was a group of extremely traditionalist Catholic absolutists. These were mainly landlords, peasants and the Church. They were strongly anti-liberal: they fought for an authoritarian social structure based on the primeval organic order of the 'family' mediated by the Church and guarded by the King who would protect the 'traditional' order but should not alter it (Millán 1991:19). They fought against individual autonomy, against the idea of an egalitarian basis for a contractual political and economic structure. But they did *not* fight against capitalism, an economic project geared to market production and capital accumulation. Landlords and the Church wanted to retain economic privileges attached to their position in the 'traditional' order. These privileges were threatened mainly by the disentailment policies of the liberal governments, but landlords mostly managed to transform 'privileges' into 'private property' rights. Privileges, however, were never only economic. In the rural areas of inland Catalonia, this traditionalist, Catholic, anti-liberal movement had strong support not only among landowners, farmers, sharecroppers, priests, monks and nuns, but also among landless labourers and putting-out cottagers. This has been explained by the diverse pressures exerted during the nineteenth century by disentailment, subsistence crises, the rise of the factory organisation, increased taxation, and general insecurity brought up not only by economic conjunctures and transformations, but mostly by the liberal disruption (without a clear alternative) of the personal social links and reciprocal moral duties of an order that sustained livelihood. It is important to emphasise, with Terradas (1984:268–9), that the material and the cultural order of the Catalan family farm (*casa*, or *masia*), its institution of an only heir to the patrimony, its creation of a dense and differentiated set of relationships between kin and neighbours and affines can help explain the situation. 'The work relations in the world of *masies* [Catalan family farms] were not perceived as relations between two classes of people clearly differentiated' (1984:269) because the non-inheriting brothers and sisters usually worked as sharecroppers or servants of propertied neighbours or affines:

Agricultural servants lived in peasant houses that had the same interests as that of their own parents and with a way of working where obedience could not be separated from contract nor loyalty from responsibility, nor – and this might be the most important – ingratitude from revolt... (Terradas 1984:268).

This does not mean that conflicts could not and did not materialise, or that landless labourers or cottagers mechanically participated in the 'family farm' culture. It does mean, however, that conflicts and confrontations were never perceived as strictly economic. For the Catholic traditionalist elites, then, the ideology of a 'Catalan family' presented as a natural, organic structure that could harmonise hierarchy and differentiation and contain economic relationships within a filial cast, became the essence of a regionalist identity. Regionalism was here related with the ideological construction and the material enforcement of a certain social order expressed in the idealised world of the family farm (*casa*, or *masia*). Its political expression (once the dynastic civil wars were over and Catholic fundamentalism was losing ground) was the fight for a Catalan civil law as opposed to a unitarian Spanish Civil Code. In fact regionalists were not only reviving or preserving but actively creating an institutional framework for social relations through the Catalan Family Law (Roigé 1989). This ideal model did not correspond to the full expression of material relations in the areas where it could be easily found. But, more interesting, it was difficult to find it in large areas of southern Catalonia (*Catalunya Nova*) (Prat 1989). The Church adjusted its traditional fundamentalism to fit a conservative form: it presented regionalism as a natural unit as opposed to the anti-natural liberal state that pretended to impose itself on domestic, religious and communal life. The liberal centralising state, with its uniformist trend, was seen as the first step towards egalitarianism and socialism, the worst menace. The idea was to reinstall or preserve the Catholic values of an organic hierarchy, duty, resignation and charity in civil life, not only in the rural areas where this movement had originated, but also in the industrialised centres where the social problem was getting out of hand and workers were successfully organising confrontation in terms of clear-cut, economic, international class distinctions.

Torras i Bages, perhaps the main exponent of the Church's regionalist programme, said among other things that 'to defend property and industry, today under menace, to light the flame of discreet charity that soothes the rough relations between owners and workers ... this is the straight and secure road to regionalism' (in Termes and Colomines 1992:126). This, in fact was a regionalised strategy in line with the official 'Social Doctrine' of the Church that Leo XIII proposed from 1878 onwards in several Papal Encyclicals. 'Socialism, communism, nihilism' were a 'mortal cancer' that was putting society in mortal danger. It had to be stopped. Re-instilling the Catholic doctrine was the only real solution that the liberal constitutional states had sinfully rejected. As opposed to the idea that 'all men are by nature equal':

the Evangelic teachings have it that equality between men consists in that having the same nature, they are all called to the same eminent dignity of Sons of God ... . However, there exists an inequality of right and authority, that derives from the Author of nature himself ... . The Church constantly instills in the people the precept of the Apostle: *There is* ... no authority except by God, and that which exists has been ordered by God, so that those who resist authority, resist God's disposition, and those who resist it bring *condemnation upon themselves*. This precept also orders that subjects *abide necessarily*, not only by fear of punishment but by *conscience* ... (Leo XIII 1959a [1878]:184)

The family, firmly held by the religious sacrament of wedlock expressed patriarchal authority in the image of God: 'Because, following Catholic doctrine, the authority of fathers and owners derives from

the authority of the Father and Heavenly Lord' (Leo XIII 1959a
[1878]:187). Catalan Catholic conservatism, then, was regionalising
universal doctrine as a tactic and a charter of nature confronting the
liberal central state. This was done through all sorts of juridical,
historical and cultural reconstructions while territorialising Catalan faith
through the reconstruction and glorification of local shrines (Figuerola
1991, 1994). But the Catalan regionalist project was in fact part of a
universal Catholic strategy for the submission of the working class.

These different nationalist ideologies merged at the turn of the
century in a clearly nationalist (but no 'separatist') political party:
Unió Catalana. It was this party that wrote in 1892 the founding
document for a 'Catalan Constitution', the *Bases de Manresa*. The
document, it should be noted, gave voting rights to the family heads
organised in three 'classes': 'manual workers', 'professionals' and
'landowners, industrialists and merchants'. In 1904 the same party
organised a meeting to debate the following issue: 'Catalanism and the
Social Problem'. It will not come as a surprise to find the conservative,
organic corporativist ideology expounded as a material reality and as
the only solution to the social problem. The document states the need
for Catalonia to be an 'organic body with differentiated organs, unified
in the national function by affective links and the moral cont[r]act of
each with the other' (Unió Catalanista 1993 [1904]:51).

Catalanism has to work with the help and cooperation of *all* Catalans; and
those that with mean spirit, because of differences of opinion over what is
incidental, would want to destroy the unitary outlook ... [they] are not
Catalan nationalists, they are defective elements that can do more harm than
good to the cause of Catalunya. (1993:61)

To counter the menace to Catalan integrity brought up by the social
problem the document warns against two mistaken ways, first, workers'
internationalism and strikes (Unió Catalanista 1993:70, 84, 120–2) and,
second, the state's intervention (conceived as 'socialism') perceived as
an 'artificial' as opposed to the 'natural' force of Catalan society
(1993:96, 113). The proposal stated in the document is that the
Catalan way is in the first place, *paternalism*. Addressing capitalists the
document states 'you will be responsible for them as a sacred trust. As
the proletariat gives you all it has, through you he should get all that
he lacks: healthy food, decent housing, instruction and culture of the
soul' (1993:77, 83, 93). Second, the Catalan way is *corporativism*.
Associations of interests should not be:

closed unto themselves, because in themselves it is impossible that they fulfil life's objectives, therefore associations should be always in mutual communication, as well as classes, seeing each other always, sharing ideas, sentiments and affections, because with this communication is how these societies progress, not only in the particular function of work, but in the integral functions of life. (Unió Catalanista 1993:113)

Finally, the Catalan way is *workers' cooperatives*: 'believe us, workers: *cooperation* is your redemption' (1993:84).

In short, nationalism appears here as a bourgeois conservative programme, the heir to anti-liberal conservative and traditionalist regionalisms. Catalan nationalism, like other nationalisms (Anderson 1991; Eriksen 1993), wants to create an 'imagined community', but what is particularly revealing is that, clearly, the main objective is creating an 'imagined community' in *social relations of production*, an ideology of harmony between capital and labour through national identity. Also revealing is that the democratic, republican, federalist group of proto-nationalists lost all its force and did not resurface until after the Primo de Rivera dictatorship (1923–9) which, in fact, was well received by a large part of the bourgeoisie (Roig i Rosich 1993:62). With the advent of the Second Republic (1931) the republican nationalist trend organised in a party, the Esquerra Republicana de Catalunya (ERC) (Republican Left of Catalonia), that won the first democratic elections in Catalonia. The 'left' was represented by a group of liberal republican intellectuals, some small unions (especially the shop assistants' association) and a group of extreme nationalist groups (Estat Català), particularly virulent in its juvenile branch. It was an odd mixture that included sincere republican democrats together with a proto-fascist movement that engaged in organised violent actions against anarchist workers (Cullá 1977:162–3, 168, 296). It is not surprising that the main working-class organisations in Catalonia (BOC, CNT) did not see in the nationalist 'left' of ERC the defence of their interests (Cullá 1977: 199–200). The working class of Catalonia was resolutely 'internationalist'. Interestingly, this has been explained away by some Catalan historians by the fact that they were *not* 'Catalan' but 'immigrants' (Vicens Vives 1986:128–9, 148–9; Giralt 1986:vii). In any case, the nationalist left's ideas in relation to the social problem were essentially the same as those of the bourgeois conservatives (Pi i Sunyer 1983 [1927]:221, 291, 318, 319) and they obviously did not appeal to workers. Only with the advent of a right-wing anti-democratic central government in 1934 did the democratic republicans within the ERC, then in power in the autonomous Catalan government, explicitly present themselves as the preservers of democracy within the Spanish Republic (Cullá:301–2). Just before and after the start of the Spanish Civil War two working-class parties were formed in Catalunya, the POUM (Partido Obrero de Unificación Marxista) and the PSUC (Partit Socialiste Unificat de Catalunya), neither with a 'nationalist' programme. It was not until after the Spanish Civil War and the Social Revolution of 1936–9, that the working-class organisations, mainly the communist PSUC, took up the nationalist democratic discourse against the Franco regime. This should be understood in the general context of European post-Second World War reconstruction and economic expansion, of the weakening of the 'internationalist' spirit of working-class solidarity, of a 'nation-alisation' of workers' organisations in Western contexts; but also in the context of a unified fight for democracy against a repressive regime. For the communist party in Catalonia, the PSUC, the cultural identity symbols of nationalist resistance, for example the Catalan Church's sacred places – the shrine of Montserrat – the Catalan language, the Catalan flag, were useful as rallying points in order to get the support of the intellectual and democratic bourgeoisie in the struggle against Franco. There was, too, a vague notion that all those that suffered from Francoist repression *must* have something in common and be solidary in their fight. And there was the increasing feeling that the right's centralism and militarism were worse than nationalist civilian conservatism for the working class. After Franco's death (1975) nationalism again divided into different strands. Workers' organisations could now retain a certain nationalist nuance because bourgeois nationalism had adopted a more liberal, less organicist ideology of the nation and workers' unions and parties had adopted a more corporativist ideological dynamic of understanding capitalist economy as 'best for all'.

The example of Catalan nationalism seems to me pertinent in that it shows how the rise of a counter-hegemonic cultural process (Catalan nationalism) against the hegemonic cultural power (Castilian centralism) appears as the attempt of a conservative bourgeoisie to maintain a cultural hegemony (corporativist organicism) against a rising counter-hegemony (liberalism) in the context of the development of capitalist relations of production. Because:

Capitalism required important political aspects of the absolutist state and ideas of ascribed *status*. ... the capitalist transformation of Spanish society did not

require a profound change of the political society. The liberal transformations of the state were not useful for a liberal society, they were utopian. In
fact, liberal society required a non-liberal state, full of absolutist characters.
(Terradas 1984:256–7)

In the same vein and more generally, speaking of the traditionalist
reaction that permeated the whole of Spain during the nineteenth
century, J. Millán writes:

Some alternatives for the development of a bourgeois society do not require
a liberal configuration ... of politics. ... Liberalism furnished a utopian horizon
... that only in part and under specific conditions agreed with the aspirations
of the bourgeois groups. (1991:18)

By focusing on the development of the different strands of nationalism
as they relate to the development of social relations of production, the
construction of meanings and the structuring of agency in Catalonia,
we have been able to get a nuanced picture of material relations in a
local context. If we wanted to understand the whole movement of
social reproduction, however, we would necessarily have to take into
account, for any historical period, a much wider set of related issues.
These would include, for the above example, the participation of Catalan
merchants in the slave trade and in the plantation economy in the
colonies, the social relations and transformations occurring in cotton
plantations in America, the worldwide market for textiles and the social
relations of production obtaining in different producing countries
(England, India ...), social relations of production in agriculture and
industry in other parts of Spain, processes of migration, etc. It would
also include the diverse worldwide local constructions of consciousness
grounded in experience and generating agency, because all of it relates
to the local Catalan experience. There is obviously no space in this
book to undertake such a project, but Wolf's *Europe and the People without
History* (1982) is a magnificent example of what can be done in this
vein. I want clearly to warn, however, of the dangers of an uncritical
use of the idea of 'local culture' theories when they become central
tenets in economic models. In the last, concluding, chapter I will try
to distinguish the social reproduction approach from other overly
simplistic ersatz versions.

5 CONCLUSION: LOCAL CULTURE AND ECONOMIC MODELS

The example of Catalan nationalism brings us to the conclusion of the journey with a clear position stating that social relations of production should be analysed both in their material and cultural aspects within the integrative framework of social reproduction. I have tried to show how material relations are interlocked with local cultural contexts within a framework of wide-ranging capitalist forces but also of global hegemonic cultures such as Christianity, while stating the need for an even wider agenda of research.

There is, however, one more area to explore which is important because it exposes serious methodological flaws in recent 'economic models' that make liberal use of concepts such as 'local culture' and 'community identity', as central to the reorganisation of the social relations of production, pretending to 'anthropologise' economic analyses. Because this concerns anthropology in its relation to economic questions, and because it is becoming somewhat of a 'hegemonic' trend, I consider it relevant to make a critique. Moreover, the critique, organised around the case study of the Catalan area where I did fieldwork, brings together in a practical and contemporary example much of what has been presented so far. I will stress, from a methodological point of view, the impossible separation of material relations from their representation (both 'popular' and 'academic').

I will start by exploring present-day labour/capital relations and how they are embedded in local cultures. The argument will concentrate on a wide range of relations of production in a capitalist economy which *do not* correspond to the classical core definition of a capitalist labour/capital social relation, and which I have broadly categorised as 'independent producer figures' (IPFs). This immediately poses the question of a non-homogeneous working-class experience, not only objectively (different forms of labour/capital relations), but subjectively rooted in local cultures.

By putting together these strands of analysis and meta-analysis I wish to show how the 'structure of exploitation' is established around the diversification of labour/capital relations and the segmentation of the labour markets on 'cultural' grounds, and how this influences the construction of working people's social identity and their power to transform reality.

The point of departure is a case study of the various working experiences that can be found in Les Garrigues, Catalonia. This brings us to the appreciation of three interesting factors: first, the various forms of labour/capital relations and the predominance of non-wage ('employee') relations; second, the material importance of the local cultural concept of '*casa*' and its transformation in the construction of specific relations of production and reproduction; and third, the historical context of the development of certain local 'communal' economic structures such as the cooperative.

THE CASE STUDY: LOCAL PROCESSES IN THE CONSTRUCTION OF LABOUR/CAPITAL RELATIONS

Means of livelihood

Catalonia is one of Spain's autonomous regions. It has a strong national identity which has been constructed and reconstructed as culturally hegemonic in the area throughout the last century. Catalonia was also the first and most successful industrialising area in Spain following a 'classical' English model based on textile manufacturing production. Rural industry in the 'proto-industrial' putting-out form was widespread in many areas. Factory villages (*colonies industrials*) following the Llobregat River course and other energy-providing water courses were an important element in the industrialisation process during the nineteenth and early twentieth centuries (Terradas 1995). Moreover, as we have seen, the consolidation of a modern form of nationalism during the nineteenth century cannot be separated from the structuring of a local industrial bourgeoisie.

The area where I did fieldwork, however, was not linked directly to the rural textile industry. The *comarca* of Les Garrigues in inland

Catalonia is a dryland farming area specialising in the production of olive oil. Specialised agriculture is a characteristic feature of this area at least from the eighteenth century onwards, at first producing for the domestic market and, since the beginning of the twentieth century, for the international market, mainly Italy which had become the largest trader. Small and medium property (5–20 ha) is presently the main form of access to the means of production, that is, land and membership in the agricultural cooperative. During the nineteenth century, however, large numbers of day labourers (up to 50 per cent) and a substantial number of sharecroppers constituted the productive structure, although the size of properties was on average similar. Private oil mills were then the only means available for transforming the crop into oil.

Relations to the means of production within the family farm household (*casa*) have never been 'collective' and homogeneous, although a strong ideological component of the cultural concept of *casa* stresses the *common* objective of all the members of the household toward the prosperity of the family farm project. Lines of power and economic prevalence set cleavages between older/younger generations and between the prospective heir (or heiress) and his (her) siblings. Cooperation between spouses is strengthened and the process that drives toward the access to the means of production is a result of both husband's and wife's work. Individual members of the household, therefore, are situated in a field of conflict-laden forces over their present and future means of livelihood.

For the period I have studied (1900–87), different members of the household have always engaged in various non-family farm work and the income generated has been conceptualised through its perceived significance for the *casa*. Before the Spanish Civil War (1936–9) small propertied farmers used to work as day labourers for larger farmers at specific points in the agricultural cycle; young men used to work as day labourers in the village and used to emigrate for specific periods to other local agricultural areas, as well as to engage in odd professions such as 'musician'. Young women also worked as day labourers within the village or as temporary agricultural migrants. Unmarried young girls went to nearby cities such as the coastal Tarragona as domestic servants until they got married. Older women worked at piecework rates peeling almonds for larger farmers, collecting and selling wood, etc.

After the Spanish Civil War this way of making a living was progressively transformed into the present situation. Three main factors have contributed to change the sorts of work people engage in to make a living and to maintain the *casa*. First, the consolidation and expansion of an irrigation infrastructure in the neighbouring *comarques* of Segrià, Garrigues Baixes (this being an irrigated area within the *comarca* of Les Garrigues) and Pla d'Urgell. This situation has permitted capital-intensive agriculture in this area mainly producing fruits and sunflower-seed oil, but also cereal for animal fodder. Temporary use of labour, mainly for fruit collection purposes is met by the neighbouring dry-farming peasants of Garrigues Altes (the dryland of Les Garrigues), and by national and foreign migrants, increasingly North and West African workers. This creates a segmented labour market which contributes to the reduction of labour costs.

The second factor has been the increasing tourist industry in Spain expanding from the mid-1960s onward. Coastal areas were the first to be developed and Tarragona's coast was a prominent tourist resort. Links with this area had been strong before the Spanish Civil War as people of Les Garrigues went to work as agricultural day labourers (men and women) and domestic servants (women). During the 1970s the mountain skiing Pyrenees area was also developed as a tourist area and more temporary jobs in the service sector became available. The tourist service industry has thus created a fairly steady source of work opportunities among people of Les Garrigues. Some young men go to work as temporary workers during the winter season (although this work conflicts with the olive collection period), and young and older men, women, couples work during the longer summer season at seaside resorts.

The third factor has been the decentralisation and expansion into the area of garment manufacturing during the 1970s and increasingly up to the present. The hierarchical subcontracting structure has created a network of small legal workshops, small illegal workshops, middlewomen (some of them self-employed, others in the shadow economy) and hundreds of homeworkers (most of them underground labour, some self-employed). Since the mid-1980s, a few workers' cooperatives have structured garment production around yet another legal framework. In fact most workers are not members of the cooperative, some have no legal contract, others are self-employed while others have temporary or learning contracts. Women of Les Garrigues have provided the flexible labour force that the industry required in order to meet costs in a context of increasingly competitive markets and globalised relations of production.

The present-day situation therefore shows a picture where working people of Les Garrigues enter into very different work relations to make a livelihood. On the one hand households are structured as family farm *casas*, where some members own and/or have access to the means of production, other members provide labour in the fields or as houseworkers and all are meant to be contributing to a common productive endeavour: the bettering of the *casa*. As I have argued elsewhere, however, the *casa* concept has suffered a transformation that has increasingly split the production and reproduction ideas into 'enterprise' and 'family' spheres (Narotzky 1988a). Making a livelihood in this cultural context entails conflicting ideas of what the income generated is meant for: whether it is *for* the *casa* as a productive–reproductive unit; *for* the family as a reproductive unit; *for* the individual as an independent member; *for* the farm enterprise as a productive business venture. And this creates the framework where personal and collective decisions about labour expenditure are made.

In this complex and intertwining context of what working means, we find people working in: first, *agriculture* as small farmer entrepreneurs (owners of the means of production but also investing their labour), as non-wage labourers (close kin) in the family farm, or as temporary day labourers in the neighbouring areas; second, working in the *service sector* (tourism) as temporary wage workers or self-employed workers; third, working in the *garment manufacturing industrial sector* as permanent wage workers (very few cases), temporary wage workers, learning contract wage workers, self-employed (owners of some of the means of production), illegal workshop pieceworkers, underground homeworkers at piecework rates, worker cooperative workers (generally not members, therefore the production relation reverts to one of the previous forms but is ideologically enclosed in a 'cooperative' model; cf. Narotzky 1988b); fourth, working in *domestic reproduction* as houseworkers or Do-It-Yourself home improvement workers. In all, members of households are engaging in at least fourteen different work experiences. Many will be individually experienced, but all will become part of the pool of the family's working experiences.

What is relevant for my discussion here is the fact that there is an enormous diversity in the labour/capital relations present. Some conform to the wage labour 'employee' relationship although only exceptionally do they follow the classic industrial factory model: unwritten contracts are pervasive and temporary and learning contracts are frequent. Others appear as mercantile relations between 'capitalist enterprises' owning the means of production (that is, those selling products or services to other firms), small farm entrepreneurs, self-employed workers. Others are non-contract piecework 'putting out' relations, ideologically situated somewhere between wage and mercantile type relations, where some of the means of production are owned by the worker. Yet others could be questioned as to whether they effectively are labour/capital relations: the farmer's own labour input; his wife's and children's labour on the farm; women's housework for the family and labour power reproduction; men's home improvement work. I personally think they are a labour/capital relation where commodification is not directly realised but indirectly realised via market prices for products or labour (Friedmann 1980; Chevalier 1983; Banaji 1977).

The degree to which individual labour is dependent on commodified relations with capital will vary along the range of these diverse working experiences. 'Independent Producer Figures' (IPFs) such as the farm owner or the self-employed garment worker unquestionably have a stronger 'managerial' position in respect to the organisation of the labour process. In a sense they seem to work in a pre-Taylorised situation, where conception and execution have not been separated and where 'responsibility' for the end-product rests solely in their hands. These individuals own the means of production only in part, however.

Farmers own land, machinery and other inputs necessary to produce olives; but olives are *not* the marketable commodity. Therefore some means of production – the oil mill – are owned collectively through membership in an agricultural cooperative. The oil produced is individually owned but collectively marketed. The market situation, however, is one of virtual monopsony when the largest buyer, an Italian firm, refuses to deal directly with the 'independent producers' through the cooperative but forces sales through a local middleman, thus in fact barring direct producers from the international market. The local middleman, moreover, has a valuable knowledge of the local socioeconomic situation of the farmers and is capable of forcing prices down not on criteria based on the market for the commodity oil, but on particular local circumstances. In this situation of strong monopsony then, farmers may have some 'independence' in the process of production, but are not 'independent' to sell, and the 'commodity' they market is in fact not abstract value at all but remains entangled in multiple social ties that contribute to the formation of its price in the locally mediated transaction. The situation these farmers are in is not yet a 'subcontract' dependent one, but in fact their dependence on agribusiness shapes all major organisation of production decisions. Take, for instance, decisions such as the investment in a new oil mill for the cooperative (which is supposed to give higher quality oil and increase productivity, although both these claims are not unanimously accepted by all farmers), or reduced use of chemicals for a more 'organic' production (therefore increasing crop risks) responding to an increasing demand for such products in the international market. We might conclude, then, that if the labour process remains largely under the management and control of the farmers, the organisation of production as a whole largely escapes the realm of their 'independent' decision-making capacity, although they are at present trying to gain more independence through direct retail marketing. Their labour is not 'free' from the means of production or from the social relations that bind it to the '*casa*' or to the community through the cooperative. As labourers in their own farm, their labour does not enter the labour market as a commodity and is not bound to capital through a 'free' contract. However, the produce of their labour is not 'free' to engage in market transactions as an abstract commodity. Their labour, within its own 'independent producer' framework does *not* produce a commodity, it only produces a commodity when entering into specific social relations with capital. On the other hand their labour cannot be reproduced without entering into these specific social relations with capital. Is then labour related to capital as a commodity? Yes and no. Labour power is not a commodity: it is not sold and bought as labour in the market by capital. Labour power is a commodity in that capital owns its product, really if not formally, by the vertical integration of production through monopsonies, and therefore stands *vis-à-vis* farmers as if it had bought their labour power beforehand, although 'realisation' of this social relation materialises only in the product market (for a Canadian example see Winson 1993).

The dependence of the self-employed garment manufacturer is based in the subcontracting, putting-out type structure of the decentralised garment manufacture industry. These women might own their industrial sewing machines but they are in fact integrated as mere labour power in the organisation of garment production. Upstream firms (frequently international designer names) produce designs, set up quality requirements, productivity minimums through time measurements realised in-firm with the latest technological equipment, set up piecework prices, acquire and cut up material with the latest computerised technology. Downstream packaging and marketing strategies are designed and realised by the firm (parts of these processes might also be subcontracted to smaller service firms). Workers have greater control over the labour process, however, and the individual responsibility they directly assume in such things as quality and time schedules, still points at a certain 'independence' from direct managerial control. Moreover, contractually, self-employed workers have a bizarre status. They *are* 'workers' and therefore must enter in some sort of relationship with capital to become productive; they own some of the means of production and therefore could directly put their labour power into productive use. Being 'self-employed' means the worker remains the owner of his or her own labour power and therefore takes upon him or herself reproduction costs. Therefore the self-employed worker does not sell labour power as a commodity in the labour market. The self-employed worker sells the product of her labour power in the market: garments at piecework rates not work time for wages. Thus incomes earned are supposed to vary according to fluctuations in the product market not in the labour market.

Both these examples of social relations of production point to the need to distinguish control over the labour process from control over the organisation of production. The labour process might in fact remain in direct control of the workers with no *real* loss in the firms' managerial power. The rigid design and framework of the organisation of production (through piecework rates, deadlines and quality control) sets up fairly inflexible limits where 'independent' decisions can be left to workers (Burawoy 1982) or small 'independent' subcontracted firms at small risk.

On the other hand, the detailed analysis of the local cultural context reveals some important links between specific social relations of production, working people's decisions as to income-earning opportunities, the transformation of local concepts such as that of '*casa*', the local meaning of 'communal' structures such as the cooperative, and the ideological use of derived ideas such as 'independence', 'trust', 'cooperation'.

Relations of production and local culture

The concept of '*casa*' is one that pervades the political construction of a Catalan national identity. The President of the Generalitat (Autonomous Government of Catalonia) speaks of Catalonia as '*casa nostra*' and is in fact using a common expression of political identity based on the idea of a social and economic unit which is at once traditional and progressive, solidary and individualistic, moral and contractual. The *casa* is, as we have seen, a hegemonic cultural concept, one which consistently glosses over differentiation and conflict and pictures a long history of a Catalan social organisation of cooperation, common objectives and non-existent class struggle (Vicens Vives 1975 [1954]; Prat 1989; Prats 1988).

But to look at how this cultural concept has been transformed in a specific local context and, moreover, how at different moments it has contributed to structure different and multiple social relations of production, is of particular interest to our discussion. At the beginning of the present century and up to the mid-1950s, the *casa* represents the collective productive–reproductive endeavour of the household members, *bound by contractually set relations of production*. The institution of marriage contracts for all substantial landowners expresses access to the means of production – relations of ownership, of possession, of usufruct – access to and control of the household's members' labour power and sets returns for labour invested in the *casa* venture. The reproduction of the *casa* is only expressed in the heir-to-be's marriage contract and in fact re-establishes privately the cultural assumption of a community of interest, a *casa* identity (that is, all those *belonging* to a certain *casa* even after founding another *casa* in the case of non-heirs), while in fact creating lines of differentiation between generations – predecessors vs. successors in ownership – and between siblings – heir vs. non-heirs. Lines that construct specific power relations and reveal relations of production: what 'working for the *casa*' means for different household members, and what they will get for it.

Starting in the 1960s, with the increase in capital investment in the farm, the *casa* concept comes to hold an ambivalent and split meaning relating to separate realms of production and reproduction. The *casa* is still generally conceived as the common productive–reproductive venture of all the household members, however, the functions of production and reproduction are increasingly perceived within it as different processes. An idea of the 'family' as the exclusive locus of reproduction appears as a new concept ideally organising relations of production according to criteria somewhat different from those at work within the productive–reproductive *casa* cultural construct. At the same time the *casa* comes to refer more and more frequently to the productive realm of the farm-as-enterprise, not encompassing then in its meaning the reproduction of the labour power or congruent responsibility for the household members' livelihood. This is now framed in the 'family' meaning where sexual division of reproductive labour ideally establishes the husband-father as the provider of the material means of subsistence – main income – while the wife-mother is in charge of everyday maintenance, procreation and socialisation of family members.

It is this ambivalent concept of *casa*, no longer institutionalised in marriage contracts or in any other form, that impels different household members to search for different means of livelihood; but also, *within the larger local labour market, it is this ambivalence which enables employers to set specific labour/capital relations in a cultural framework which is acceptable to the workers*. Thus when farmers in the Pla d'Urgell hire local day labourers during the fruit collection, not only are they aware of the general agricultural season as it has affected Les Garrigues, but they can also refer to the main '*casa*' vs. '*malgastos*' (or complementary) incomes as it affects both them and their employees. The more telling example, however, is that of local middlepersons in the garment industry's subcontracting network. Here, reproductive female 'family' responsibilities are alleged, together with '*malgastos*' criteria relating to the *casa* concept showing the complementary nature of both garment work and income, from both the *casa* and 'family' conceptual frameworks' perspective, in an artful play meant to *explain* the local social and economical rationality for very low wages (Narotzky 1990).

Generally, however, convergence rather than shared meaning is at work in the articulation between the search for livelihood and the setting of specific social relations between labour and capital. Thus garment industry firms explain that female workers are bound to accept lower wages and irregular employment on the grounds of their 'family' responsibilities: reproductive work takes priority and they can earn a supplementary income only when necessary. In fact, however, the arguments that impel women of Les Garrigues toward garment production are clearer within the cultural concept of *casa* at work in this area.

Cooperation is another concept that can be traced in the area to the turn of the century. It is a concept that appears as such linked with the attempt by the state to create legal frameworks for agricultural production in the context of small property structures (Pérez Baró 1989), as well as with the nationalist programme to solve the 'social problem'. Significantly, also, even if a majority of internationalist workers' associations were explicitly against cooperatives on the grounds that they produced a bourgeois mentality among workers and impaired solidarity, some workers' leaders such as Peiró from the anarchist CNT (1979 [1925]) defended cooperatives as a form of organisation of production.

It is important to stress that cooperation in this context is based in the farmers' objective of becoming really 'independent' producers with access to the market for the commodity 'olive oil', and also being able to profit from economies of scale in the inputs market and therefore reduce costs. However, this cooperation was not available to everybody and strictly regulated access to membership in the cooperative followed age and gender conflict cleavages within the *casa*'s unequal access to the means of production. It also expressed the existing differentiation between farmers. In fact, although decisions are taken democratically in general assemblies, larger producers have more authority because investments are proportional to the median output of each member – measuring presumed use of services thereof. Therefore, if not explicitly or legally, capital ownership (or shares) does express and condition differential control over the means of production and decision-making processes within the collective endeavour. Conflict may also arise within the cooperative decision-making framework, because the particular 'independent' producers' strategies are different and depend on the structure of the *casa* and on the ways different members within it strive toward making a livelihood, individually and collectively. Thus investment priorities might be very different.

The social structure of cooperation is stranded with unequal and conflicting relations, although, obviously, there is a drive to achieve, through a collective organisation, objectives that would otherwise be impossible to reach: namely, an increased measure of 'independence' as agricultural producers. It is questionable, however, how much of the 'cooperative' spirit in action here is based on a *community* identity or even on a communal pre-existing reciprocity network structure. The basic motors of action behind the formation and development of the agricultural cooperative are linked to the self-interest of a class of peasants that were substantial owners of some of the means of production – land – but lacked the crucial means to transform the primary product (olives) into the marketable commodity (oil) – the oil mill – and also lacked on their own a reasonable scale of production to enter larger markets.

In the context of this experience of cooperation in the area, it is interesting to briefly look at the workers' cooperatives appearing in the garment industry in the 1980s. The ideas of cooperation that converge in the everyday work experience of the women labourers are in part a transformation of the agricultural cooperative local experience, in part an artful mystification of classic capitalist enterprises' ideas, framed in a decentralised and hierarchical industrial network and inserted in a legal, normative concept of what a workers' cooperative is.

In fact the experience of garment workers forced into a 'cooperative' framework generally through a self-employed ('*autónomo*') status (*vis-à-vis* Social Security benefits) is not such an alien participatory experience if we compare it with the agricultural cooperative these women know from their local context. *Self-interest with regard to access to employment* is the main drive toward entering this cooperative organisation of production. Unequal investment in capital confers authority in decision making, and labour, measured by product output, is the measure of income obtained. It is the 'independence' of perceived relations to the work cooperative structure which in fact seems to bring together agricultural cooperative and work cooperative experiences. In fact, in the agricultural cooperative all members stand in the same relationship towards the means of production (whatever their tacit 'share' is) and this gives them real participatory rights; in a sense it enhances their 'independence' *vis-à-vis* each other while strengthening their voluntary collective commitment. In the 'worker cooperative' all women workers, whether in a 'member' status or in an 'employee' status, have *no* relationship to the 'cooperative' means of production and they are barred from decision making and other participatory rights. They are collectively in the same relationship to the means of production in that they are *non-owners* and sellers of their labour power. Nevertheless their experience of previous forms of cooperation tends to enhance their supposed 'independence' *vis-à-vis* each other, therefore fragmenting the perception of a common objective situation.

As in the agricultural cooperative case, it is hard to perceive in the garment worker cooperatives any community-bound solidarity networks or communal social structures in the organisation of these forms of production relations. However, this is not to say that social networks are not at work in the access to the local labour market and in the construction of qualitatively specific, one-to-one personalised labour/capital relations. Here, the concept of 'trust' (*confiança*) is crucial.

'Trust' is the main quality of the employee/employer relation according to employers in the garment production at whatever level of the subcontracting hierarchical structure nodes. Middlemen-entrepreneurs as well as local middlewomen-workers all speak of 'trust' as the building block in the relations of production: one has to trust the local middlewomen or a particular worker, trust her in reference to quality, to delivery deadlines, but more generally, she has to be a 'trustworthy person' (*una persona de confiança*), meaning somebody that will behave as expected (*no et deixará a l'estacada*), that is, that will not cause conflict, somebody, too, that will 'understand' and make hers the employer's interests and views. 'Trust' means that both persons entering a relationship believe in the truthfulness of the other's assertions and intentions. Therefore there is no need to write down or otherwise explicitly state *vis-à-vis* third parties the conditions of truth of the labour agreement. On the other hand, 'trust' relationships are enforced on workers who have no other income-earning opportunities: workers have to rely on 'trust' networks to get a job through local middlewomen; workers have to 'trust' middlemen-entrepreneurs in that they will give work to them and not to other workers in other villages, and 'trust' that he will pay them! 'Trust' relationships rely on personal feelings and past experiences that link employee and employer as unique individuals in a well-known social context. In fact, satisfying production relations can be disrupted when general trustworthiness ends due to other social causes. For example, a good working relationship that had lasted for years between a young woman and the middlewoman manager of a local workshop, was terminated abruptly when the young workers' in-laws got involved in an inheritance dispute with the workshop manager's husband over landownership rights to a big estate. The basis for 'trust' had been broken, although production output and quality standards had been maintained.

Trust sets production relations on an arbitrary ground where employers' feelings and interpretations are the elements that keep up the labour relationship. It is a non-contractual basis and in fact one which is quite different from the contractual and moral building of social relations of production in the *casa*. In a context where work relationships between household members (kin) have been set in written contracts for centuries, 'trust' is a concept that pretends (in words of middlemen-entrepreneurs) to respond to a 'family' type relationship, a 'natural' non-mediated 'traditional' way of constructing a working relationship, but which is, in fact, quite foreign to the local experience of working arrangements (*tractes*) including those between kin. It is interesting to note that workers tend to interpret 'trust' in contractual terms: labour power and goodwill balanced against good piece rates and continuity of employment; whilst employers tend to interpret 'trust' in paternalistic terms: doing favours, caring for the local women's well-being (by offering jobs) is balanced by respect, obedience, quasi-filial 'love' and is expressed in hard work and good work, following the conservative bourgeois nationalist model.

In any event, 'trust'-based relationships do contribute as much as physical dispersion to the construction of a fragmented workforce. Where workers must rely on and accept the individual characterisation of their labour power according to personalised feelings and personal social situations, the homogenisation of social relations of production in everyday experience becomes difficult. No worker, then, appears to be in the same objective relationship with the employer because subjective individual experience seems to be the main stuff of the creation and maintenance of the labour/capital tie.

MODELS OF ANALYSIS FOR A 'NEW ECONOMIC ORGANISATION'

The above case study, however, has to be situated in the increasing body of theoretical analysis of the 'post-Fordist' model of social relations of production, if it is to provide a critical counterpoint to what is becoming an economic model of capitalism with strong ideological and political content.

In Les Garrigues, we have described an uneven proletarianisation where labour power only seldom appears in the classical commodity form ascribed to industrial labour. More frequently labour enters social relations with capital through the form we have loosely termed 'independent producer figures': family farm owners, local subcontracting middlewomen managing small workshops, self-employed workers, homeworkers in informal putting-out networks, members of worker cooperatives. This form embraces distinct labour/capital relations, that is, relations mediated differently as to ownership of the means of production, control of the labour process and of the organisation of production, dependence on particular firms, access to product and labour markets, etc. However, the IPF form defines a common situation where the *labour/capital relations of production are not explicitly stated as a fully commodified relation*, a situation, moreover, where regulation of labour/capital relations by the state has the effect of obscuring commodification of labour while stressing 'independence' and mercantile relations between 'producers'. This raises the issue of the process of proletarianisation. It sets the problem of what we understand by commodification of labour, and whether a specific form of commodified labour/capital relation is at the core of *real* (as opposed to formal) capitalist social relations of production. That is, whether industrial wage work is to be thought of as the *core* labour/capital relation, or whether, by contrast, it would be better to assume diversity as one of the keys to fully developed capitalist relations of production (Roseberry 1983, 1989:138–9, 215–16). I will come back to these problems later.

What I want to bring forward at this point is the way in which recent economic analyses have stressed a *change*, a *deep transformation* in the capitalist world. Models for this new capitalism have been based in analyses of 'developed' European countries such as England, Germany, France, Italy but also the USA and Japan. Different theories have been constructed based on distinct political and ideological positions (Bagnasco 1983, 1991; Boyer 1986; Lipietz 1986; Sabel 1982, 1989; Piore and Sabel 1984; Portes 1983). All agree, however, in seeing a *break* between 'Fordist' labour/capital social relations of production, state regulation policies and consumption strategies and new, different labour/capital relations, regulation policies and consumption strategies. All seem to agree, also, on the importance of *local histories* and specific *cultural contexts* as the key elements behind this new reorganisation of capitalist social relations. Finally, all define the new system as one where dominant social relations of production shift from large-scale to small-scale (or scope) production; from homogenisation to fragmentation (in product and labour markets); from classical employee/employer labour ties to informal ties; from rigidities to flexibilities (in production, in labour relations and regulations); from vertical integration to decentralised factory structures; from dependence of waged labourers (no control of the labour process, no decision-making capacities, etc.) to 'independence' of small producers; from hierarchical managerial power chains to cooperative or non-hierarchical network chains of collaboration; *from abstract 'economic' relations to subjective 'cultural' relations and personal livelihood experiences*.

This coincidence, coming from very different orientations which are purportedly trying to make different accounts of the social and economic organisation of capitalism, seems to open up a relevant discussion. On the one hand we might ask ourselves if what we are now perceiving is really new or if it is mainly our focus of interest which is new (G. Smith 1991); on the other hand we might try exploring how deeply these new social relations transform historical capitalism or if they are meant to transform *our account* of the history of capitalism. Last, but not least, we might ask what political consequences these new models of the economic trends have in structuring government policies, union strategies and individual actions (for critiques of these models see Pollert 1988, 1991; Hyman 1991:267, 278; Williams et al. 1987).

Model I: the industrial districts

The new economic model which seems to have become hegemonic in the context of Western and southern Europe is that of the 'industrial districts' which comes from a theorisation of the Italian analysis of the area described as the Third Italy (Bagnasco 1983; Brusco 1982; Capecchi 1988; Becattini 1990; Benko and Lipietz 1994). This model describes a situation of relatively small independent producers located in relatively circumscribed areas where competition between small firms is limited and cooperation is stressed through networks of non-hierarchical social relations of production, based in previously existing sociocultural links. 'An "Industrial District" is a bundle of social and industrial interdependencies in a specific place' (Becattini 1990:204).

The theory of the industrial district differs from the mere decentralisation of production theory in very crucial aspects:

each of the small firms belonging to an industrial district participates only in one or some of the different stages of the production process. ... These units: a) sell to more than one buyer; b) operate in intermediate and final markets; c) are firms which open themselves to the outside totally or partially (through middlemen and other similar figures) to contract crucial activities such as product design; d) are in essence 'components' of a system and would lose most of their competitive edge outside of it. What unites this group of firms is therefore a network of economic relationships that are external to each firm but internal to the industrial area. (Becattini 1990:210)

Moreover:

Small firms and middlemen effect a kind of *transformation of the cultural potential of a community into goods and services that can be sold in the market.* ... Relationships between members of a small firm don't reach the level of abstraction necessary to the neoclassical concepts of market and enterprise. They are, for example, personalised to the point of deterring opportunistic 'behaviours' [strikes] within the district as well as within the firms. (Becattini 1990:212, emphasis mine)

Referring concretely to the Third Italy (Umbria, Marche, Toscana, Emilia-Romagna and Veneto) the cultural potential that is pointed at as the basis of the new economic transformation into Industrial Districts is constituted by, first, the sudden dismembering of the sharecropping agricultural system of the area, which 'generated a labour force with general skills useful in small firms, a labour force ready to acquire new technological skills, and *which could be trusted* in its work' (Becattini 1990:197–8); second, the importance of the Italian Communist Party (PCI) in the political and social spheres, with a local politics that favours industrialisation; and, third, the creation by the PCI of a system of social institutions, formal and informal. These are 'socialising bodies' which unite persons at work, in the home, at leisure and in many other situations such as the summer party (*Feste de l'Unità*). Through this 'system' of 'socialisation bodies' an idea of life that stresses certain values, that is, 'work and family ethic, collective solidarity above class struggle, etc. has been transmitted from one generation to the next in a non-authoritarian way' (Becattini 1990:197–9).

Many aspects of the construction of this new economic model of the Industrial District seem to be interesting to highlight:

(1) the search for an 'authority', Marshall, who had theoretically constructed such an economic model on the basis of the analysis of economic processes already in existence (Marshall 1964 [1892]:151–5);

(2) the creation of cultural isolates developing into economic isolates (the Industrial District) as opposed to global economic processes transforming and being transformed by local and historical situations (Hadjimichalis and Papamichos 1990);

(3) the stress on social and cultural contexts as opposed to economic contexts especially in defining social relations of production and the organisation of production;

(4) the constant reference to local 'identity' and 'community' as *self-evident* (never analysed) concepts structuring consensual, non-conflictive action within the local economic isolate;

(5) the positing of a *network* structure linking firms within the Industrial District, tacitly *implying non-hierarchical* homogeneous relations between different stages and units of production in a process;

(6) the stress on the 'independence' of the small firms in the input and output product markets as opposed to monopoly and monopsony market relations with other firms;

(7) the stress on *local economic structures of communal solidarity* such as *cooperatives*;

(8) and, generally, the underlying *trust* feelings that structure social relations of production in these cultural and economic local isolates.

Even if the area of Les Garrigues that I have studied would probably not qualify as an Industrial District in a strict sense, my analysis does enable a critique of the oversimplified assumptions of the economic expression of certain cultural local concepts. Moreover, it is interesting to point out that most of the cultural constructs being highlighted in the Industrial District model seem to be present in the area I studied but must not be considered as self-evident or taken at face value. In fact my analysis reveals how cultural concepts become ideological instruments in the organisation of production relations. In the Industrial District model the reverse takes place: *production relations tend to become*

an epiphenomenon of cultural contexts and are *theoretically* dissolved in the
'identity' and 'community' black boxes of consensual mirth.

Model II: Japanisation

A similar trend of de-economisation of social relations of production
is becoming increasingly present in the literature on the Japanese neo-
Fordist (or post-Fordist) organisation of production (Kenney and
Florida 1988; Sayer and Walker 1992). In these analyses we find:

(1)   a renewed stress on individual on-line worker responsibilities for
      quality production and productivity rates;
(2)   a shift of intermediate decision-making capacity from mid-level
      managers to workers;
(3)   an emphasis on cooperation between workers (production teams);
(4)   long-term cooperation between big and small firms;
(5)   a stress on *trust* between workers and management and between
      firms and subcontractors;
(6)   a stress on a common *culture* with shared values (work ethic;
      paternalistic and family values).

   Workers on-line are presented as regaining a certain 'independence'
in respect to their control of the labour process. This aims at decreasing
intermediate managerial costs which have become one of the highest
labour expenses in the Fordist industries. It also aims at creating a certain
professional satisfaction, 'pride', in blue-collar workers, something, in
fact, that highlights skill and at the same time gives *individual personal
value* to each worker's labour and thus justifies individualised rewards.
On the other hand, this means that greater responsibility falls on the
direct worker as opposed to managerial responsibility. This happens,
however, in a context where control of the organisation of production
follows classical strict autocratic hierarchical managerial lines (Burawoy
1985; Ohno 1988; Japan Management Association 1989). It looks as
if the 'independent producer figure' is being imported into the neo-
Fordist factory within a framework that is still basically 'Fordist' in its
organisation, in its aims and in its labour/capital relations. It reminds
us of one of the basic means of 'manufacturing consent' described by
Burawoy (1982) for a typical 'Fordist' factory: giving workers a certain

space for minor decision-making within a very strict hierarchical control framework.

Another point that seems relevant in the Japanese model is the emphasis on *communal social structures of cooperation* – in fact the building of a *community* which is the firm or the group of cooperating subcontracted firms, where differentiation is ideologically obscured; the stress on feelings such as 'trust' as the building block of labour/capital relations – and away from explicit contractual negotiations and deals; the stress on a *cultural context of shared values* between employers and employees – one that seems to preclude the eventuality of class differentiation, as in 'family' relations of production. This cultural rhetoric of 'identity', constructed within exploitative labour/capital relations of production tries to inject an ideology of consensus in a potentially highly conflictive arena.

It is interesting to remark that the Japanese model of social relations of production which is being promoted as the 'other' alternative to the old Fordist model, has many points in common with the Industrial District model. Both stress a certain idea of the benefits of 'independent' workers' responsibility and individuation. Both give a strong emphasis to cultural contexts as contributing the basic elements in the social relations of production, away from exploitative 'economic' relations and power political struggles.

Model III: the 'means of livelihood' approach

A last area of social relations of production which is being put forward as an alternative to classical labour/capital relations emerges from the informal sector literature. Of the three aspects covered by the 'informal' sector definition, that is, unregulated wage labour relationships, criminal activities and communal, self-help and domestic activities, this last area has opened an interesting perspective on economic relations. Scholars such as Gershuny (1988) and Pahl (1984) have stressed the increasing importance of non-wage activities as a means of access to many consumer goods and services. This includes women's housework and young and old dependants' care, but also a wide range of Do-It-Yourself and reciprocal labour exchange in home building construction, car repair, etc. This perspective has permitted a break in the standard work = employment equation and the wage = household income equation.

It has allowed us to perceive a wider range of income-earning activities, to conceive income in a non-monetary way. In essence it has stressed the fact that access to the means of livelihood for individuals and families does not occur in a homogeneous wage employment structure but is a varied, fragmentary, polymorphous arrangement of social relations of production, of life production, that is: reproduction (Mingione 1985, 1987, 1988, 1991).

This new focus on the 'means of livelihood' points, first, to people's experience of work; second, to the way in which social relations other than the strictly 'economic' ones – kinship, neighbourhood, friendship – create an environment where specific non-market relations of production take place; third, to how opportunities relating to employment and other non-wage work are evaluated and how strategies are effected; and fourth, to how flexible degrees of reciprocity as opposed to pre-determined exchange values set the arena where work relations are established.

We find, however, that there is never an analysis of how these non-wage relations of production really work. There seems to be, once more, a self-evident assumption that these relations are based on mutual *trust* as opposed to power, that generalised reciprocity is the norm as opposed to market (labour or product) referred values, that consensus and harmony pervade. The means of livelihood perspective in fact tends to highlight a certain non-conflictual idea of family and community relations where work becomes 'help' or even leisure (as in some DIY activities); where production becomes consumption and where social relations of production disappear into the ambiguous concept of reproduction. This last point is extremely relevant because it obscures not only the structure of the labour process – control, power, decision-making capacities – but the general structure of the organisation of production: it creates, once again, a social isolate – individual, family, household, community. Here, a group of people is involved locally in earning a living but their experience and strategies do not seem to relate to wider political and economic processes outside the local community. For example, the rise of DIY furniture manufacture (or in general home refurbishing) will be related to an increase in income level capacity for the household at a time when cash is scarce, but *not* to the organisation of production in the furniture industry. Therefore a specific structure of social relations between labour and capital is obscured. Social relations of production which are exploitative and affect the structure of the whole industry will be subsumed in the realm of 'self-help', 'means of livelihood' and 'domestic work'.

What is relevant to the discussion is that the 'means of livelihood' model also gives a fragmented image of social relations of production based on the relevance of the 'reproductive' paradigm, on the local community isolate and the pervasiveness in it of 'non-economic' relationships and feelings. It highlights social and cultural dependency links between people but states 'independence' from classical labour/capital relationships, and from classical 'economic' market relationships. It sets these production relations in a framework assumed to be harmonious, non-conflictual and self-evidently preferable to wage employment relations, a framework fading into the 'leisure society' model.

WORK EXPERIENCES AND LABOUR/CAPITAL RELATIONS

We may extract some theoretical conclusions by contrasting the fieldwork analysis with the above models where IPF-type relations of production are increasingly being used in the construction of new models of capitalist organisation of production. I will put forward the following points:

(1) the experience of work is multiple and includes many different forms of labour/capital relationships, not only in reference to different individuals but also in reference to the same individual;

(2) cultural concepts (for example, *casa*) and local communal structures (for example, cooperatives) have to be studied in their historical development, and do not always mean horizontal, egalitarian, non-conflictive relations between the people who constitute them;

(3) concepts such as *trust*, emerging from concepts of identity and propinquity (kin, community), of reciprocal knowledge and participation in the others' interpretations of and decisions about reality, can become useful ideological instruments;

(4) IPFs are imagined in these models as harmonious because more 'natural' and culturally and socially close to people's non-economic life experience;

(5) *cultural* factors, especially 'community identity' and its corollary 'trust', are used in these models as apologetic self-evident

explanations of the advantages of these new – non-proletarianising or de-proletarianising – forms of capitalist relations of production, whereby labour market segmentation appears only as a 'natural' outcome of cultural groupings and network uses.

The first problem is how to explain the non-homogeneous working-class experiences found in fieldwork, because, explicitly or not, this is one of the main motives behind the dismissal of homogeneous 'Fordism' – that is, industrial wage labour relations in a hierarchical organisation of the labour process – as a reality and as a model of labour/capital relations. The classical Marxist position would be that capitalism has specifically been defined as having separated producers from the means of production as well as having cut workers off from the grid of community ties and reciprocities. The first premiss makes labour power a commodity. With the second premiss, by homogenising labour power, by tearing it away from what makes it unique, the commodity labour power can become an abstract value. This second premise of capitalist relations of production is not only a material process but also an ideological one: the departure from values highlighting reciprocity and personalised exchange and the adoption of market values and impersonal exchange relations. We need to question both of these premisses, presenting instead a picture of capitalism based on diversified labour/capital relations and a non-homogeneous working-class experience. This does not preclude the existence of *a* class exploited through different forms while nevertheless based on the same fundamental relationship: that is, the extraction of surplus value through the difference between the value of labour power and the value incorporated in the commodities produced.

The IPFs that we have approached through direct and indirect data are at once pervasive historically and spatially throughout capitalist economies (for statistics on 'persistence' of 'traditional' industrial processes of production see Bairoch 1985:186–7) and contemporary to 'classical' capitalist labour/capital wage relations, that is, are being created at the same time as other 'more' classical-type capitalist relations of production (Marshall 1964:163–4; Berg 1985; Berg et al. 1983; Samuel 1977; cf. also Marx *Capital*, Vol. 1, Ch. 15). Where they have been acknowledged as an important set of economic relations, IPFs have been often explained as a form of 'democratic' capitalism. IPFs, then, are viewed as a *new* development of capitalism in a positive direction. They are pictured as the realisation of the historically lost chance of capitalism (Sabel and Zeitlin 1985) where cooperation (not competition), where equality and autonomy (not differentiation and dependence), where consensus (not conflict), are the norm, and where relations of production are not isolated in an 'economic' sphere but embedded in everyday social relations. What is interesting for the discussion is this understanding of IPFs as an *improved form of capitalism* – something close to an ideal socialist capitalism – since this position actually dismisses the central postulate of Marxist analyses of capitalism: that the owners of capital exploit the owners of labour power (Sabel 1982; Piore and Sabel 1984).

From the Marxist point of view, IPFs are not core forms of capitalist relations of production. IPFs have been explained as a transformation of non-capitalist forms of production in a transitional perspective where labour may be 'formally' but is not yet 'really' subsumed to capital, or as a different mode of production. They are pictured as appearing in the margins or at the interstices of classical labour/capital relations of production, or as relations pertaining to 'other' forms of production articulated in a capitalist social formation. IPFs are either seen as regressions belonging to previous forms of capitalism (merchant, competitive) or as strategies of de-proletarianisation meant to break class solidarity and organised labour action. In either case they are always seen as 'transitional', as something to be seen in reference to 'real' capitalist relations of production, either because they tend toward them, or because they are to be understood as a means to transform the power balance within 'real' capitalist relations: that is, as a means that capital uses to break organised labour and regain absolute power *in* classical labour/capital relations of production. In other words, IPFs are not the stuff that capitalism is made of. Marxist analyses tend to see capitalism as a completed process at the 'centre', which is really expressed in full proletarianisation, that is, separation of direct producers from the means of production and the sale of abstract labour power to capital.

In contrast to either of these positions I think that IPFs are integral and *central* to capitalist relations of production. I see IPFs as forms which are fully subsumed under capital (in Marxist terms 'real subsumption') and hence expressing different yet equivalent processes of 'proletarianisation'. This position rests on the following observations.

First, the various forms I am describing appear simultaneously with 'classical' proletarianisation and are necessary to its accomplishment (they should not be confused with those morphologically similar forms which occur historically in non-capitalist contexts). Moreover they do not seem to decrease in absolute or relative numbers in actually existing capitalism, nor in the national statistics of the working population (if we count *all* working people vs. only *industrial* workers) (Rubery and Wilkinson 1981).

Second, capital has always sought the fragmentation of labour through cultural, formal and spatial means and has fought the construction of a homogenised consciousness even where specific forms of production required the workers' homogenisation (that is, manufacture, factory).

Third, in historical reality a moment never arises in which the capital/labour relation is rendered entirely free of the use of force on the part of capital. Indeed one of the main assets of capital in labour/capital relationships is that labour power is *never* free. On the one hand it is never free from its social and cultural circumstances and capitalism has tended to enhance rather than dissolve such ties of the labour force (in particular 'family' ties). On the other hand it has also often been profitably tied to such means of production as the sewing machine, personal computer, etc.

Fourth, labour power is a 'commodity' of a very specific kind (Polanyi 1971), because it has never entered a *free market* but has always been regulated (even deregulation has always been regulated whether through the Le Chapelier law in Revolutionary France or present-day labour market flexibilisation laws); because it is not free from cultural and social ties and therefore does not have *abstract* value, rather its value is always *tied* to its concrete circumstances; because the contractual freedom of parts in 'classical' labour/capital relations should be seen as an ideological framework working to characterise a forced relation as a free transaction (Reddy 1987); because, historically, labour legislation constructed an ideology of work in which a certain type of labour power became abstract and liable to regulation insofar as it could enter into a specific relation of production with capital: for example, early Spanish labour legislation defines the work being regulated as 'dependent' and taking place away from the domestic sphere (Valverde 1987; Martínez Veiga 1995).

These are just some of the problems. Another one is that the orthodox models based on 'industrial' capitalism marginalise or leave in the shadows many relations of production (and reproduction) which are *integral* to capitalism. Our analytical concepts seem to have inherited the ideological construction present in early labour regulations. Spanish early labour legislation, for example, regulates only industrial work, excluding jobs in agriculture (which are only mentioned in a 1911 Law in reference to the use of machinery) and in family workshops; and services are not contemplated until the 1920s (Valverde 1987; Ley Benot 1873; Ley 1900; Real Decreto 1900; Ley 1911; Real Orden 1920; Martínez Veiga 1995). In fact, as Kautsky pointed out (1974 [1899]), small agricultural family enterprises increase in absolute numbers during the early development of 'industrial' capitalism and are not readily replaced by large-scale 'industrial' agricultural enterprises (Vogeler 1981; Winson 1993). Moreover, although nowadays these IPFs in agriculture seem to be one of the main advantages of agribusiness's organisation of production (so far as agribusiness is concerned), and this same agribusiness is one of the main 'industries' as percentage of its contribution to the GNP of many core capitalist countries (Britain, France, even USA) (Lash and Urry 1987), it is always classified as a 'traditional industry' – never treated as a *key* industrial sector, never a *motor* of the economic development. As a result, the labour/capital relations obtaining therein have always been theoretically marginalised as a *survival* of previous relations of production (in a sense following Redfield's (1960) rural–urban continuum model). The same can be said of the garment apparel industries.

Yet what happens when the electronics industry, a 'key' industry, adopts a structure very similar to the 'traditional' apparel industry? How are these labour/capital relations to be integrated theoretically in a model of capitalism? What happens is that *suddenly* 'capitalist relations of production' are perceived as breaking down or fragmenting; and the organisation of production is seen as decentralising, informalising, etc. Whereas in fact what should really be explained is why the 'industrial' relations model of capitalism became hegemonic and obscured *the majority of people's work relations with capital.* In relative terms the agriculture and service sectors together (both harbouring 'atypical' labour/capital relations) have always been quantitatively larger than the 'industrial' sector, while the industrial sector itself has never fully been proletarianised (for example, such atypical but *key* industries as the 'construction' ones). Also, we must bear in mind that concentration of capital can occur with decentralisation of production. What has been loosely named the 'industrial reserve army' in Marxist analyses was alive and thriving, *living* albeit in the theoretical borders of capitalism, while in fact at its material heart. An army on reserve for what? to break organised labour: once again its existence, its articulation to the economy, appeared in reference to the core industries' labour/capital relations of production, 'pristine proletarianisation'.

Here the 'means of livelihood' perspective has pointed to the often forgotten fact that people eke out their life in many ways, and that work and wage employment are not synonymous. However, the general theoretical impression one gets when reading their analyses is, again, that these work relations are marginal to capital, in fact emerge either against capital or on the margins of capital (or the state in capitalist societies). In a sense they mirror a certain state/civil society debate, where the state/civil society opposition dissolves the class oppositional structure of political action. What these theoretical positions are saying is that outside capitalism, outside the political institutions of the state, people are doing things, in a sense protecting their lives against economic and political formalism. The danger with this perspective is, I think, that it confuses three different problems: first, what people do to earn a living and how they understand their actions (reproduction); second, what capitalists do to increase their benefits and how they try to manage other people's lives (production); and, third, how the articulation of these two problems (social reproduction) can be analysed. In reference to this last point the effort, I think, should be directed so as to: first, find the relations that not only cross-cut particularities, but that are common to working peoples *through* their particularities, in the sense that *diversity in working experiences might be an important part of what labour relations to capital are*, and thus of a *common reality*; and second, try to disentangle the hegemonic 'scientific' discourse from the *real* structure of exploitation which is made of the objective and subjective elements that construct social relations.

RETHINKING PROLETARIANISATION AND CLASS

What I wish to expose here is that the structure of objective positions within the reproduction of capitalist relations of production cannot be separated from the cultural particularities which configure people's experience and actions. This, however, must not be mistaken at a theoretical level with class formation processes and access to class consciousness. Cultural particularities are part of the class structure because they are crucial to the structure of exploitation and they might or might not be pertinent to class consciousness and the meaningful organisation of class identity. If I try to understand subjective elements as part of the structure of labour/capital relations, it is because I aim at transcending fragmentation and want to find out the commonalty of the exploitation link. There is fragmentation – in work experiences, in cultural interpretation – but it is at the core of the specific capitalist scheme: increased accumulation of capital through the appropriation of surplus value. The need to transcend *theoretical* fragmentation by including *real* fragmentation within a specific oppositional structure, implies rethinking the central definition of capitalist relations of production based on the separation of direct producers from the means of production and the subsequent sale of their labour power.

By trying to understand the drive of people to reproduce and at the same time the drive of capitalists to accumulate, we can conclude that it is not the separation from the means of production that forces people into exploitative relations with capital but the *separation from the means of reproduction of their livelihood*, irrespective of the actual 'ownership' status toward certain means of production they might hold. Separation from the means of reproducing a livelihood implies that without entering into specific relations of production there is no life viability. This is expressed very clearly in classical proletarianised wage-earning labour/capital relations, but my argument is that it is *not only* in them.

Small family enterprises, self-employed workers, members of a workers' cooperative, are all forced into exploitative labour relations with capital, be it through the labour market, the financial market, or the product market. Furthermore, social relations which do not enter the market in any of these ways might as well be transformed into specific 'capitalist' relations when causally dependent on other labour/capital relations. We might, for example, think of housework as an income-saving opportunity, as a form of management of scarce resources tied to a male 'family wage' in a context of unequal female competition in the labour market. The same can be true in the case of self-help, reciprocal exchange of labour, or DIY activities in a context of low wages and high unemployment or in a context of high consuming standards and lower relative wages. All of these non-market work forms generate income by non-wage means, lower capital costs and at the same time contribute to capital's accumulation of surplus value.

The result of this line of argument would be that classes in a capitalist society would be defined by the *degree of necessity that impels people into specific labour/capital relations to earn a living, and the degree to which they can choose between different alternative forms of labour/capital relations or other livelihood strategies*. Class would thus be defined by the *articulation between reproduction and production locations*. It is not so much the *property* of the means of production which sets apart and creates conflicts between groups of people in structural terms, but the possibilities of owning one's future.

Theoretically, the extreme form of the class that does not own its future is that of the 'classical' proletarian separated from the means of production and free from their social and cultural ties and thus entering the market as abstract labour power the sale of which is their only chance of survival. This, however, is a theoretical pole: people are rarely free from their social and cultural circumstances. Migrants, for example rely on these ties to get hold of resources (shelter, employment, consumer goods, labour). And capital structures exploitation through the reification of differences (Wolf 1982), though these differences are not transcendently 'given' for capitalism to thrive on. Differences are constructed as significant through both the necessity to earn a living that drives toward espousing an identity in order to enter some form of labour/capital relation *and* capital's necessity to construct an ideology of fragmentation so as to break down homogeneous class action and insure the maximum extraction of surplus value. Nevertheless, underlying the differences is the common reality that working-class people would not earn a living if they did not enter into some sort of dependent and exploitative relation with capital. And this common reality still supports a fairly simple oppositional class structure model.

In addition to this, there is the issue of class consciousness and the process of the formation of class as an organised collectivity that struggles to put forward interests given by positions in the structure of society. Here, as Gramsci insists, the figure of the organic intellectual is fundamental. If cultural particularities can be seen as the framework of what Gramsci calls 'common sense' they should be transcended to arrive at a 'theoretical consciousness' that can become part of political practice (Gramsci 1987:333). It is this theoretical consciousness that he calls an 'organic ideology', 'historically necessary'. These 'historically organic ideologies' '"organise" human masses and create a terrain on which men move, acquire consciousness of their position, struggle, etc.' (1987:376–7). By becoming a coherent homogeneous force ideology gets to be an active component of political action, welded into a unity in a 'historical bloc' (1987:137, 178). Although Gramsci's view of ideology transcends 'common sense', he insists that for it to possess its organic quality it must be worked out from 'the principles and problems raised by the masses in their practical activity' (1987:330). It must be a critique of 'common sense' but must be based on it, if it is to be organic and historically necessary (1987:330–3; 412–13). Therefore Gramsci points to the dialectical relationship between ideology and practice, and because of his preoccupation with political events and actions, he sees a need to transcend 'common sense' so as to render it coherent and capable of establishing collective aims.

Up to this point I have presented the *structural* problems that impair a class understanding of social relations and I have tried to rethink basic definitions so that a class structure analysis could be valuable. The problem remains, however, of the *realisation* of collective identities, based on class interest: the problem of class formation. To address this question it is important, following R. Williams, to distinguish between the spheres of culture, hegemony and ideology. While culture is consciousness engaged in practice related to the 'whole social process', hegemony is 'a culture which has also to be seen as the lived dominance and subordination of particular classes'. Culture and hegemony then pervade a social formation as such. Ideology, by contrast is the practically oriented consciousness of a particular class – as R. Williams puts it: the 'articulate formal system' which is 'the expression or projection of a particular class interest' (Williams 1977:108–10). Ideology is aimed at political action.

There is no doubt that components of local culture could become part of a counter-hegemonic process and I will propose some possible features of this process below. But the uncritical use of 'culture' in economic analyses and models of 'capitalist society' can become simply bourgeois ideology acting to integrate a consciousness of lived experience in the hegemonic culture of Western societies. The conservative nationalist project of the Catalan bourgeoisie at the turn of the century is a good example of this.

The idea of an 'economy' for example could be posited as a fundamental piece of the hegemonic Western culture. It is through the 'economy' that practical consciousness of the whole social process reproduces dominant and subordinate, exploitative and exploited class relations. The experience of livelihood and the experience of work are mediated by an economistic consciousness of social existence. We see everyday decisions about housing, work opportunities, children's education, leisure activities, even love and procreation taking shape mostly from within an 'economic' understanding of life processes. 'Rational' action has much in common with 'economic' rationality in our capitalist societies. In this sense, what might have once appeared as an 'organic bourgeois ideology' must, I think, be understood as a hegemonic culture. It is interesting to note that it was precisely because the economistic framework for consciousness had become hegemonic that an organic ideology of the working-class emerged from within it. A terrain was created in which workers – not only industrial, but also agricultural day labourers and service workers – could imagine themselves as a community bound by common and culturally overarching interests (McClelland 1987). This organic working-class ideology never became a counter-hegemonic culture, however.

In fact counter-hegemonic cultures seem more likely to emerge locally where practical consciousness of the whole social process is experienced through historically specific forms of social relations of production and reproduction. This seems quite obvious when we think of Third World countries, their articulation into capitalist social formations and the political struggles that result. I am suggesting that this might also be the case at the 'centre', in Western capitalist 'developed' societies. The fact that sociologists conceptualise such collective identities as gender, age, ethnicity, etc. as *cross-cutting* and *disrupting* class identity is grounded in the old idea of 'part-societies' and 'local cultures' fragmenting people into particularistic interest groups which are only united in an imaginary realm of image consumption (Lash and Urry 1987; Jameson 1991:318–19, 330; Baudrillard 1974). But we can be more optimistic than this, albeit with caveats.

For counter-hegemonic local cultures to be central in class formation processes, paradoxically, cultural particularism must be transcended. This is the major contemporary problem on which postmodern discussions of 'culture' and the 'new economic organisation' models come together in the form of an ideology of fragmentation put forward by bourgeois 'organic intellectuals' seeking to adapt the 'economic' hegemonic culture into a framework that integrates non-hegemonic practical consciousness.

Let me throw some darts at this picture in the form of a few questions:

(1) Is the contemporary situation in regard to social relations of production *and* to cultural particularities *really more* fragmentary than, let's say, the previous hundred years? Or is it that our theoretical models have become particularly interested in fragmentation (G. Smith, 1991)?

(2) Why is 'local culture' used as a double bind concept where it is supposed to effect two contradictory but complementary movements: first, fragmenting global social relations of productions along boundaries of local cultural isolates and, second, giving a consensual aura to local relations of production by associating them with the positive values of 'community identity'?

(3) Why are the new economic models 'culturalising' the economic domain?

I might venture a tentative answer. The 'economic' hegemonic culture had set the framework for a polarised but negotiable class confrontation where classes were bound by the common project of *making capitalism work* and confronted one another mostly over the distribution of income generated. Against this, from within livelihood experiences which appeared to take place 'in the margins of' or even 'outside' capitalist relations of production, and work experiences which appeared to thrive in contexts qualitatively different from the classical labour/capital 'free' contract, a terrain of counter-hegemonic cultures appear to be arising.

In my view, paradoxically, the practical consciousness of these fragmented livelihoods could be the first step toward a reappraisal of *common* interests of *class* and toward the transcendence of fragmentation and the creation of an organic ideology aimed at political action for the transformation of relations of production. But, if 'local cultures' are integrated into 'economic' hegemonic models in the way I have underlined above, the 'economic' hegemonic culture can appear to be de-economised while in fact consolidating the framework of exploitative production relations. What we get is really just a refined version of the 'economic' hegemonic culture where consensual economic propositions are put forward on the grounds of general human welfare. Now, however, whereas in the previous hegemony this was based on the purely 'economic' logic of increased cooperation between labour and capital – begetting increased productivity begetting increased general welfare – the present-day models seem to favour a 'cultural' and 'sociohistoric' logic where 'community identities' and 'local cultures' become central to successful cooperation between labour and capital (as in the example of nineteenth-century Catalan conservative nationalism). On the one hand, this means favouring non-economic interpretations of social relations of production on the grounds that the economy is embedded in 'other' social relations.

On the other hand social relations of production are said to be strongly determined by cultural and social idiosyncrasies, which, because they are associated with small and closely knit groups are supposedly non-conflictive, and this, I think, is highly questionable. Talking about 'cultural' elements such as 'trust', 'help', 'identity', 'reciprocity' as though they were self-evident, positive and socially harmonious factors in economic relations might be introducing ideology into methodology. The inclusion of local culture in economic models is a move in the right direction. But rendering 'ideal' the material relations of production and reproduction seems to me a move in the wrong direction.

Conclusion

We have seen all along, that, as anthropologists it is very difficult not to take into account cultural and social processes as part of economic processes. Or, put another way: we have to think of economic processes as embedded in social and cultural processes. But as anthropologists, we also know that societies are complex material processes laden with power struggles, conflict, dissent and negotiation; that 'a culture' is never an homogeneous superstructure, or 'essence' or whatever, evenly distributed among a local people. Rather, cultures are real, lived experiences turned into reason, engendering reasons for action and thus embodied in material life and material goods. Then, if we really want to explore how local cultures are entangled in the production and reproduction of material life we should study with care the historical social process of production of cultural concepts. Moreover, we should expect that different social groups, situated in different objective conditions as to their capacity to earn a livelihood, will have distinct experiences giving different meanings to a cultural concept that at first might appear as homogeneous. Culture should not be the easy way out from economic questions: culture is the difficult way into placing economic questions in the larger framework of social reproduction. In the end, in economic anthropology as 'In general, in thinking about society, we start from these people in this place, but it is very unusual to retain this simplicity' (R. Williams 1984 [1961]:121) if only because 'place' has a local and a global dimension and is inscribed with history.

REFERENCES

Althusser, L. (1969) 'El objeto de "El capital"' in L. Althusser and E. Balibar *Para leer El capital*, Siglo XXI, México. [L. Althusser and E. Balibar (1968) *Lire le capital*, François Maspero, Paris.]

Althusser, L. (1974)*Pour Marx*, François Maspero, Paris.

Anderson, B. (1991) *Imagined Communities: Reflections on the Origin and Spread of Nationalism*, Verso, London.

Anderson, M. (1980) *Approaches to the History of the Western Family, 1500–1914*, Macmillan, London.

Anthias, F. (1983) 'Sexual Divisions and Ethnic Adaptation: The Case of Greek-Cypriot Women', in A. Phizacklea (ed.) *One Way Ticket*, London, Routledge and Kegan Paul, pp. 73–94.

Appadurai, A. (ed.) (1986) *The Social Life of Things: Commodities in Cultural Perspective*, Cambridge University Press, Cambridge.

Aristotle (1971) *The Works of Aristotle*, Vol. 2, Encyclopaedia Britannica Inc., Chicago.

Asad, T. (1974) 'The Concept of Rationality in Economic Anthropology', in *Economy and Society*, 3 (2).

Bagnasco, A. (1983) 'La cuestión de la economía informal', in *Sociología del Trabajo*, 9.

Bagnasco, A. (1991) 'El desarrollo de economía difusa: punto de vista económico y punto de vista de la sociedad', in *Sociología del Trabajo*, n.e., Extra.

Bairoch, P. (1985) 'L'énergie et l'industrie manufacturière entre le monde traditionnel et le monde industrialisé: Approche quantitative, 1750–1913' in P. Bairoch and A.M. Piuz (eds) *Les Passages des économies traditionnelles européennes aux sociétés industrielles*, Librairie Droz, Geneva.

Balcells, A. (1992) *Història del nacionalisme Català al origens al nostre temps*, Generalitat de Catalunya, Barcelona.

Balfet, H. (1975) 'Technologie', in R. Cresswell (ed.) *Elements d'ethnologie*, Vol. 2, Armand Colin, Paris.

Balibar, E. (1969) 'Acerca de los conceptos fundamentales del materialismo histórico', in L. Althusser and E. Balibar *Para leer El capital*, Siglo XXI, México. [L. Althusser and E. Balibar (1968) *Lire le capital*, François Maspero, Paris.]

224

Ballard, R. (1987) 'The Political Economy of Migration: Pakistan, Britain, and the Middle East' in J. Eades (ed.) *Migrants, Workers and the Social Order*, Tavistock, London.

Banaji, J. (1977) 'Modes of Production in a Materialist Conception of History', in *Capital and Class*, 3.

Barnes, J.A. (1969) 'Networks and Political Process', in J.C. Mitchell (ed.) *Social Networks in Urban Situations: analyses of Personal Relationships in Central African Towns*, Manchester University Press, Manchester.

Barnes, J.A. (1972) 'Social Networks', in *Addison-Wesley Module in Anthropology*, 26.

Barnes, J.A. (1990) [1954] 'Class and Committees in a Norwegian Island Parish', in J.A. Barnes, *Selected Essays: Models and Interpretations*, Cambridge University Press, Cambridge.

Barrett, M. (1980) *Women's Oppression Today*, Verso, London.

Barthes, R. (1967) *Système de la Mode*, Seuil, Paris.

Baudrillard, J. (1969) *El sistema de los objetos*, Siglo XXI, México. [J. Baudrillard (1968) *Système des objets*, Gallimard, Paris.]

Baudrillard, J. (1974) *Crítica de la economía política del signo*, Siglo XXI, México. [J. Baudrillard (1981) *For a Critique of the Political Economy of the Sign*, Telos Press, St Louis, MO.]

Bauer, P.T. and Yamey, B.S. (1968) 'Economic Progress and Occupational Distribution' in *Markets, Market Control and Marketing Reform*, Weidenfeld and Nicolson, London.

Becattini, G. (1990) 'Italia', in W. Sengenberger, G.W. Loveman and M.J. Piore (eds) *Los distritos industriales y las pequeñas empresas, II: el resurgimiento de la pequeña empresa*, Ministerio de Trabajo y Seguridad Social, Madrid.

Beechey, V. (1980) 'Women and Production: A Critical Analysis of Some Sociological Theories of Women's Work', in A. Kuhn and A.M. Wolpe (eds), *Feminism and Materialism*, Routledge and Kegan Paul, London, pp. 155–97.

Beechey, V. and Perkins, T. (1987) *A Matter of Hours*, University of Minnesota Press, Minneapolis.

Bender, D.R. (1967) 'A Redefinement of the Concept of Household: Families, Co-residence, and Domestic Functions', in *American Anthropologist*, 69.

Beneria, L. and Sen, G. (1982) 'Class and Gender Inequalities and Women's Role in Economic Development – Theoretical and Practical Implications' in *Feminist Studies*, 8 (1).

Benko, G. and Lipietz, A. (eds) (1994) *Las regiones que ganan. Distritos y redes: los nuevos paradigmas de la geografía económica*, Alfons el Magnànim, Valencia. [G. Benko and A. Lipietz (1992) *Les régions qui gagnent. Districts et réseaux: les nouveaux paradigmes de la géographie économique*, Presses Universitaires de France, Paris.]

Berg, M. (1985) *The Age of Manufactures: Industry, Innovation and Work in Britain, 1700–1820*, Fontana, London.

Berg, M., Hudson, P. and Sonenscher, M. (1983) 'Manufacture in Town and Country before the Factory', in M. Berg, P. Hudson and M. Sonenscher (eds), *Manufacture in Town and Country before the Factory*, Cambridge University Press, Cambridge.

Berkner, L. (1972) 'The Stem Family and the Development Cycle of the Peasant Household: An Eighteenth Century Austrian Example', in *American Historical Review*, 77: 398–418.

Berkner, L. (1973) 'Recent Research on the History of the Family in Western Europe', in *Journal of Marriage and the Family*, V.35 pp. 395–403.

Berkner, L. (1976) 'Inheritance, Land Tenure and Peasant Family Structure: A German Regional Comparison', in J. Goody, J. Thirsk and E.P. Thompson (eds) *Family and Inheritance: Rural Society in Western Europe, 1200–1800*, Cambridge University Press, Cambridge, pp. 71–95.

Berry, B., Lobley, J. and Parr, J.B. (1988) [1967] *Market Centers and Retail Location: Theory and Applications*, Prentice Hall, Englewood Cliffs, NJ.

Blau, P.M. (1982) [1964] *Intercambio y poder en la vida social*, Hora, Barcelona. [P.M.Blau (1964) *Exchange and Power in Social Life*, John Wiley and Sons Inc., New York.]

Bloch, M. and Parry, J. (1989) 'Introduction: Money and the Morality of Exchange', in J. Parry and M. Bloch (eds) *Money and the Morality of Exchange*, Cambridge University Press, Cambridge.

Bohannan, P. (1959) 'The Impact of Money on an African Subsistence Economy', in *Journal of Economic History*, 19.

Bohannan, P. and Bohannan, L. (1968) *Tiv Economy*, Longman, London.

Bohannan, P. and Dalton, G. (1971) [1962] 'Markets in Africa: Introduction', in G. Dalton (ed.) *Economic Anthropology and Development*, Basic Books, New York.

Boissevain, J. (1968) 'The Place of Non-groups in the Social Sciences', in *Man* (N.S.), 3.

Boserup, E. (1965) *The Conditions of Agricultural Growth*, Aldine Press, Chicago.

Bott, E. (1975) *Family and Social Network*, Tavistock, London.

Boulding, K.E. (1978) 'Réciprocité et échange: l'individu et la famille dans la société', in A. Michel (ed.) *Les Femmes dans la société marchande*, Presses Universitaires de France, Paris.

Bourdieu, P. (1980) *Le Sens pratique*, Editions de Minuit, Paris.

Bourdieu, P. (1988) *La distinción: Criterio y bases sociales del gusto*, Taurus, Madrid. [P. Bourdieu (1979) *La Distinction*, Editions de Minuit, Paris.]

Boyer, R. (ed.) (1986) *La Flexibilité du travail en Europe*, Editions La Découverte, Paris.

Braverman, H. (1974) *Labor and Monopoly Capitalism*, Monthly Review Press, New York.

Brusco, S. (1982) 'The Emilian Model: Productive Decentralisation and Social Integration', in *Cambridge Journal of Economics*, 6: pp. 167–84.

Burawoy, M. (1976) 'The Functions and Reproduction of Migrant Labor: Comparative Material from Southern Africa and the United States', in *American Journal of Sociology*, 18 (5).

Burawoy, M. (1982) *Manufacturing Consent: Changes in the Labor Process under Monopoly Capitalism*, University of Chicago Press, Chicago.

Burawoy, M. (1985) *The Politics of Production*, Verso, London.

Cameron, A. (1985) 'Bread and Roses Revisited: Women's Culture and Working-class Activism in the Lawrence Strike of 1912', in R. Milkman (ed.) *Women, Work and Protest*, Routledge and Kegan Paul, Boston.

Capecchi, V. (1988) 'Economía informal y desarrollo de especialización flexible', in E. Sanchís and J. Miñana (eds) *La otra economía*, Alfons el Magnànim, Valencia.

Carloni, A.S. (1981) 'Sex Disparities in the Distribution of Food Within Rural Households', SCN, FAO, Rome.

Carneiro, R. (1970) 'A Theory on the Origin of the State', in *Science*, 169.

Casaverde, J. (1981) 'El trueque en la economía pastoril' in J. R. Llobera (ed.) *Antropología Económica*, Anagrama, Barcelona.

Castles, S., Booth, H. and Wallace, T. (1987) *Here for Good: Western Europe's New Ethnic Minorities*, Pluto Press, London.

Charles, N. and Kerr, M. (1987) 'Just the Way It Is: Gender and Age Differences in Family Food Consumption', in J. Brannen and G. Wilson (eds) *Give and Take in Families: Studies in Resource Distribution*, Allen and Unwin, London.

Chayanov, A.V. (1986) [1925] *The Theory of Peasant Economy*, University of Wisconsin Press, Madison, WI.

Chevalier, J.M. (1982) *Civilization and the Stolen Gift: Capital, Kin and Cult in Eastern Peru*, University of Toronto Press, Toronto.

Chevalier, J.M. (1983) 'There is Nothing Simple about Simple Commodity Production', in *Journal of Peasant Studies*, 10 (4).

Christaller, W. (1966) *Central Places in Southern Germany*, Prentice Hall, Englewood Cliffs, NJ.

Clammer, J. (1985) *Anthropology and Political Economy: Theoretical and Asian Perspectives*, Macmillan, London.

Clammer, J. (ed.) (1987) *Beyond the New Economic Anthropology*, Macmillan, London.

Cohen, M.N. (1977) *The Food Crisis in Prehistory*, Yale University Press, New Haven, CT.

Cook, S. (1984) 'Peasant Economy, Rural Industry and Capitalist Development in the Oaxaca Valley, Mexico', in *Journal of Peasant Studies*, 12 (1).

Craig, C., Rubery, J., Tarling, R., and Wilkinson, F. (Labour Studies Group) (1985) 'Economic, Social and Political Factors in the Operation of the Labour Market', in B. Roberts, R. Finnegan and D. Gallie (eds) *New Approaches to Economic Life*, Manchester University Press, Manchester.

Cullá, J. (1977) *El catalanisme d'esquerra*, Curial Edicions, Barcelona.

Curtin, Ph.D. (1992) *Cross-cultural Trade in World History*, Cambridge University Press, Cambridge.

Dalton, G. (1971a) [1965] 'Primitive, Archaic and Modern Economies: Karl Polanyi's Contribution to Economic Anthropology and Comparative Economy', in *Economic Anthropology and Development: Essays on Tribal and Peasant Economies*, Basic Books, New York.

Dalton, G. (1971b) [1961] 'Economic Theory and Primitive Society', in *Economic Anthropology and Development: Essays on Tribal and Peasant Economies*, Basic Books, New York.

De Gaudemar, J.P. (1987) 'Mobilization Networks and Strategies in the Labour Market' in R. Tarling (ed.) *Flexibility in Labour Markets*, Academic Press, London.

De Vault, M. (1991) *Feeding the Family: The Social Organization of Caring as Gendered Work*, University of Chicago Press, Chicago.

Dear, M. and Wolch, J. (1989) 'How Territory Shapes Social Life', in J. Wolch and M. Dear (eds) *The Power of Geography*, Unwin Hyman, Boston.

DiLeonardo, M. (1987) 'The Female World of Cards and Holidays: Women, Families, and the Work of Kinship', in *Signs*, 12 (3).

Douglas, M. and Isherwood, B. (1978) *The World of Goods*, Allen Lane, London.

Dumont, L. (1977) *Homo Aequalis*, Gallimard, Paris.

Durkheim, E. (1933) *On the Division of Labor in Society*, Macmillan, New York.

Eades, J. (1987) 'Anthropologists and Migrants: Changing Models and Realities' in J. Eades (ed.) *Migrants, Workers and the Social Order*, Tavistock, London.

Edholm, F., Harris, O. and Young, K. (1977) 'Conceptualizing Women', *Critique of Anthropology*, 3 (9–10).

Ehrenreich, B. and English, D. (1979) *For Her Own Good: 150 Years of the Experts' Advice to Women*, Anchor Books, Garden City, NY.

Einzig, P. (1966) [1949] *Primitive Money: in its Ethnological, Historical and Economic Aspects*, Pergamon Press, Oxford.

Eisenstein, Z.R. (1984) 'The Patriarchal Relations of the Reagan State', in *Signs*, 10 (2).

Elson, D. and Pearson, R. (1981) 'The Subordination of Women and the Internationalization of Factory Production', in K. Young, C. Wolkowitz and R. McCullagh (eds) *Of Marriage and the Market*, CSE Books, London.

Engels, F. (1975) [1890] 'Engels a Bloch', in K. Marx and F. Engels, *Obras escogidas de Marx y Engels*, tomo II, Fundamentos, Madrid.

Eriksen, T.H. (1993) *Ethnicity and Nationalism: Anthropological Perspectives*, Pluto Press, London.

Evans-Pritchard, E.E. (1940) *The Nuer*, Oxford University Press, London.

Feil, D.K. (1984) *Ways of Exchange: The Enga Tee of Papua New Guinea*, University of Queensland Press, Queensland, Australia.

Figuerola, J. (1991) 'Montserrat, símbol religiós i nacional', in *L'Avenç*, 150.

Figuerola, J. (1994) 'Regeneració religiosa i catalanisme: el cas del bisbe Morgades', in *L'Avenç*, 177.

Fine, B. and Leopold, E. (1993) *The World of Consumption*, Routledge, London.

Firth, R. (1970) 'Themes in Economic Anthropology: A General Comment', in R. Firth (ed.) *Themes in Economic Anthropology*, Tavistock, London.

Fitzpatrick, P. (1987) 'Migration, Resistance, and the Law in Colonial Papua New Guinea', in J. Eades (ed.) *Migrants, Workers and the Social Order*, Tavistock, London.

Flandrin, J.L. (1976) *Familles: Parenté, maison, sexualité dans l'ancienne société*, Hachette, Paris.

Frank, A.G. (1967) *Capitalism and Underdevelopment in Latin America*, Monthly Review Press, New York.

Friedmann, H. (1980) 'Household Production and the National Economy: Concepts for the Analysis of Agrarian Formations', in *Journal of Peasant Studies*, 7 (2).

Fröbel, F., Heinrich, J. and Kreye, O. (1980) *The New International Division of Labour*, Cambridge University Press, Cambridge.

Garner, B. (1971) 'Models of Urban Geography and Settlement Location', in R. Chorley and P. Haggett (eds) *Models in Geography*, Methuen, London.

Gershuny, J.I. (1988) 'Time, Technology and the Informal Economy', in R.E. Pahl (ed.) *On Work: Historical, Comparative and Theoretical Approaches*, Basil Blackwell, Oxford.

Gershuny, J.I. and Miles, I.D. (1985) 'Towards a New Social Economics', in B. Roberts, R. Finnegan and D. Gallie (eds) *New Approaches to Economic Life*, Manchester University Press, Manchester.

Giralt, E. (1986) 'Prólogo' in J. Vicens Vives, *Los Catalanes en el siglo XIX*, Alianza Editorial, Madrid.

Glazer, N. (1984) 'Servants to Capital: Unpaid Domestic Labor and Paid Work', in *Review of Radical Political Economics*, 16 (1).

Godelier, M. (1974) *Rationalité et irrationalité en economie*, Maspero, Paris.

Godelier, M. (1977) *Horizon, trajets marxistes en anthropologie*, tome 1, Maspero, Paris.

Godelier, M. (1978) 'Le Part idéelle du réel: essai sur l'idéologique', in *L'Homme*, 18 (3–4).

Godelier, M. (1984) *L'Idéel et le matériel*, Fayard, Paris.

Goodman, D. and Redclift, M. (1982) *From Peasant to Proletarian: Capitalist Development and Agrarian Transitions*, St Martin's Press, New York.

Gouldner, A. (1960) 'The Norm of Reciprocity: A Preliminary Statement', in *American Sociological Review*, 25 (2).

Graham, H. (1987) 'Being Poor: Perceptions and Coping Strategies of Lone Mothers', in J. Brannen and G. Wilson (eds) *Give and Take in Families. Studies in Resource Distribution*, Allen and Unwin, London.

Gramsci, A. (1987) [1929-35] *Selections from the Prison Notebooks*, International Publishers, New York.

Granovetter, M. (1985) 'Economic Action and Social Structure: The Problem of Embeddedness', in *American Journal of Sociology*, 91 (3) 481–510.

Gregory, C. (1982) *Gifts and Commodities*, Cambridge University Press, Cambridge.

Grierson, Ph. (1978) 'The Origins of Money', in G. Dalton (ed.) *Research in Economic Anthropology*, JAI Press, Greenwich, CT.

Griffen, S. and Griffen, C. (1977) 'Family and Business in a Small City: Poughkeepsie, New York, 1850–1880', in T. Hareven (ed.) *Family and Kin in Urban Communities, 1700–1930*, New Viewpoints, New York.

Grossman, R. (1979) 'Women's Place in the Integrated Circuit', in *South-East Asia Chronicle*, 66.

Gudeman, S. (1986) *Economics as Culture: Models and Metaphors of Livelihood*, Routledge and Kegan Paul, London.

Hadjimichalis, C. and Papamichos, N. (1990) '"Local" Development in Southern Europe: Towards a New Mythology', in *Antipode*, 22 (3).

Haggett, P. (1965) *Locational Analysis in Human Geography*, Edward Arnold, London.

Hamilton Grierson, P.J. (1980) [1903] 'The Silent Trade', in G. Dalton (ed.) *Research in Economic Anthropology*, JAI Press, Greenwich, CT.

Hareven, T. (ed.) (1977a) *Family and Kin in Urban Communities, 1700–1930*, New Viewpoints, New York.

Hareven, T. (1977b) 'Family Time and Industrial Time: Family and Work in a Planned Corporation Town, 1900–1924', in T. Hareven (ed.) *Family and Kin in Urban Communities, 1700–1930*, New Viewpoints, New York.

Harris, C., Lee, R. and Morris, L. (1985) 'Redundancy in Steel: Labour Market Behaviour, Local Social Networks and Domestic Organisation', in B. Roberts, R. Finnegan and D. Gallie *New Approaches to Economic Life*, Manchester University Press, Manchester.

Harris, M. (1986) *Introducción a la antropología general*, Alianza, Madrid. [M. Harris (1971) *Culture, People and Nature: An Introduction to General Anthropology*, 3rd ed, Thomas Crowell, Co.]

Harrison, M. (1975) 'Chayanov and the Economics of the Russian Peasantry', in *Journal of Peasant Studies*, 2 (4).

Harrison, M. (1977) 'The Peasant Mode of Production in the Work of A.V. Chayanov', in *Journal of Peasant Studies*, 4 (2).

Harrison, M. (1979) 'Chayanov and the Marxists', in *Journal of Peasant Studies*, 7 (1).

Hartmann, H. (1981) 'The Family as the Locus of Gender, Class and Political Struggle: The Example of Housework', in *Signs*, 6.

Harvey, D. (1989) *The Condition of Postmodernity: An Enquiry into the Origins of Cultural Change*, Basil Blackwell, Oxford.

Hill, R.P. and Stamey, M. (1990) 'The Homeless in America: An Examination of Possessions and Consumption Bahaviors', in *Journal of Consumer Research*, 17.

Hobsbawm, E. (1984) *Workers: Worlds of Labor*, Pantheon Books, New York.

Hodgson, G.M. (1988) *Economics and Institutions: A Manifesto for a Modern Institutional Economics*, Polity Press, Oxford.

Humphrey, C. and Hugh-Jones, S. (1992) 'Introduction: Barter, Exchange and Value' in C. Humphrey and S. Hugh-Jones (eds) *Barter, Exchange and Value. An Anthropological Approach*, Cambridge University Press, Cambridge.

Humphries, J. (1977) 'Class Struggle and the Persistence of the Working-class Family', in *Cambridge Journal of Economics*, 1.

Hyman, R. (1991) 'Plus ça change? The Theory of Production and the Production of Theory' in A. Pollert (ed.) *Farewell to Flexibility?* Blackwell, Oxford.

Izard, M. (1979) *Manufactureros, industriales y revolucionarios*, Crítica, Barcelona.

Jameson, F. (1991) *Postmodernism, or, the Cultural Logic of Late Capitalism*, Verso, London.

Japan Management Association (1989) *Kanban: Just-in-time at Toyota*, Productivity Press, Cambridge, MA.

Jochim, M.A. (1981) *Strategies for Survival: Cultural Behavior in an Ecological Context*, Academic Press, New York.

Johnson Brown, J. and Reingen, P.H. (1987) 'Social Ties and Word-of-mouth Referral Behavior', in *Journal of Consumer Research*, 14.

Kahn, J. and Llobera, J.R. (1981) 'Towards a New Marxism or a New Anthropology?' in J. Kahn and J.R. Llobera (eds) *The Anthropology of Pre-Capitalist Societies*, Macmillan, London.

Kapferer, B. (1969) 'Norms and the Manipulation of Relationships in a Work Context', in J.C. Mitchell (ed.) *Social Networks in Urban Situations. Analyses of Personal Relationships in Central African Towns*, Manchester University Press, Manchester.

Kautsky, K. (1974) [1899] *La cuestión agraria*, Editorial Laia, Barcelona.

Kenney, M. and Florida, R. (1988) 'Beyond Mass Production: Production and the Labor Process in Japan', in *Politics and Society*, 16 (1).

Kessler-Harris, A. (1982) *Out to Work: A History of Wage-earning Women in the United States*, Oxford University Press, Oxford.

Kessler-Harris, A. (1985) 'Problems of Coalition-Building: Women and Trade Unions in the 1920s', in R. Milkman (ed.) *Women, Work and Protest*, Routledge and Kegan Paul, Boston.

Kurimoto, S. (1980) 'Silent Trade in Japan', in G. Dalton (ed.) *Research in Economic Anthropology*, JAI Press, Greenwich, CT.

Laclau, E. (1971) 'Feudalism and Capitalism in Latin America', in *New Left Review*, 67.

Lamphere, L. (1987) *From Working Daughters to Working Mothers: Immigrant Women in a New England Industrial Community*, Cornell University Press, Ithaca, NY.

Land, H. (1980) 'The Family Wage', in *Feminist Review*, 6.

Lash, S. and Urry, J. (1987) *The End of Organized Capital*, Polity Press, Oxford.

Leacock, E. (1978) 'Women's Status in Egalitarian Society: Implications For Social Evolution', in *Current Anthropology*, 19 (2).

Lee, R.B. (1979) *The !Kung San. Men, Women, and Work in a Foraging Society*, Cambridge University Press, Cambridge.

Lenin, V.I. (1977) [1899] *The Development of Capitalism in Russia*, Progress Publishers, Moscow.

Leo XIII (1959a) [1878] 'Quod Apostolici Muneris', in F. Rodriguez (ed.) *Doctrina pontificia: documentos sociales*, BAC, Madrid.

Leo XIII (1959b) [1891] 'Rerum Novarum', in F. Rodriguez (ed.) *Doctrina pontificia: documentos sociales*, BAC, Madrid.

Lewis, J. (1984) *Women in England 1870–1950: Sexual Divisions and Social Change*, Wheatsheaf Books, Sussex.

Lewis, J. (1986) 'The Working-class Wife and Mother and State Intervention, 1870–1918', in J. Lewis (ed.) *Labour and Love: Women's Experience of Home and Family, 1850–1940*, Blackwell, Oxford.

'Ley [Benot] de 24 de julio de 1873: Condiciones de trabajo en las fábricas, talleres y minas' (1987) in A. Valverde (ed.) *La legislación social en la historia de España de la revolución liberal a 1936*, Congreso de los Diputados, Madrid.

'Ley de 17 de julio de 1911: Contrato de aprendizaje' (1987) in A. Valverde (ed.) *La legislación social en la historia de España de la revolución liberal a 1936*, Congreso de los Diputados, Madrid.

'Ley de 30 de enero de 1900: Accidentes de Trabajo' (1987) in Valverde, A. (ed.) *La legislación social en la historia de España de la revolución liberal a 1936*, Congreso de los Diputados, Madrid.

Lipietz, A. (1986) *Mirages et miracles: problèmes de l'industrialisation dans le tiers monde*, Editions La Découverte, Paris.

Löfgren, O. (1984) 'Family and Household: Images and Realities: Cultural Change in Swedish Society', in R.M. Netting, R.R. Wilk and E.S. Arnould *Households: Comparative and Historical Studies of the Domestic Group*, University of California Press, Berkeley.

Lösch, A. (1954) *The Economics of Location*, Yale University Press, New Haven, CT.

McClelland, K. (1987) 'Time to Work, Time to Live: Some Aspects of Work and Re-formation of Class in Britain, 1850–1880', in P. Joyce (ed.) *The Historical Meanings of Work*, Cambridge University Press, Cambridge.

MacCormack, C.P. (1982a) 'Biological, Cultural and Social Adaptation in Human Fertility and Birth: A Synthesis', in C.P. MacCormack (ed.) *Ethnography of Fertility and Birth*, Academic Press, London.

MacCormack, C.P. (ed.) (1982b) *Ethnography of Fertility and Birth*, Academic Press, London.

McDonogh, G.W. (1989) *Las buenas familias de Barcelona*, Barcelona, Ediciones Omega SA. [G.W. McDonogh (1986) *Good Families of Barcelona: A Social History of Power in the Industrial Era*, Princeton University Press, Princeton, NJ].

McKee, L. (1987) 'Households during Unemployment: The Resourcefulness of the Unemployed', in J. Brannen, and G. Wilson, (eds) *Give and Take in Families: Studies in Resource Distribution*, Allen and Unwin, London.

McLaren, A. (1984) *Reproductive Rituals: The Perception of Fertility in England From the Sixteenth Century to the Nineteenth Century*, Methuen, London.

Malinowski, B. (1961) [1922] *Argonauts of the Western Pacific*, Dutton and Co, New York.

Malinowski, B. (1977) [1935] *El cultivo de la tierra y los ritos agrícolas en las islas Trobriand*, Labor, Barcelona. [B. Malinowski (1935) *Coral Gardens and their Magic. Soil-tilling and Agricultural Rites in the Trobriand Islands*, Allen and Unwin Ltd, London.]

Malthus, Th. (1982) [1798] *An Essay on the Principle of Population*, Penguin Books, Harmondsworth.

Marceau, J. (1989) *A Family Business? The Making of an International Business Élite*, Cambridge University Press/MSH, Cambridge.

Marshall, A. (1964) [1892] *Elements of Economics of Industry*, Macmillan, London.

Martínez Alier, J. (1973) 'Relaciones de producción en las haciendas andinas del Perú', in *Los huachilleros del Perú*, Ruedo Ibérico, Paris.

Martínez Alier, J. (1992) *De la economía ecológica al ecologismo popular*, Icaria, Barcelona.

Martínez Alier, J. (1993) 'Valoración económica y valoración ecológica', in J.M. Naredo and F. Parra (eds) *Hacia una ciencia de los recursos naturales*, Siglo XXI, Madrid.

Martínez Veiga, U. (1995) *Mujer, trabajo y domicilio: los orígenes de la discriminación*, Icaria, Barcelona.

Marx, K. (1950) [1847] *Misère de la philosophie en réponse à la philosophie de la misère de M. Proudhon*, Alfred Costes Editeur, Paris.

Marx, K. (1952) *Capital*, V.1, Encyclopaedia Britannica Inc., Chicago.

Marx, K. (1970a) [1844] *Manuscritos: economía y filosofía*, Alianza Editorial, Madrid.

Marx, K. (1970b) [1859] 'Prólogo', in *Contribución a la crítica de la economía política*, Alberto Corazón Editor, Madrid.

Marx, K. (1970c) [1859] 'Prefacio', in *Contribución a la crítica de la economiá política*, Alberto Corazón Editor, Madrid.

Marx, K. (1972) [1859] [*Grundrisse*] *Los fundamentos de la crítica de la economía política*, Vol.1, Alberto Corazón Editor, Madrid.

Marx, K. (1976) [1893] *Le Capital*, 3 vols, Editions Sociales, Paris.

Marx, K. and Engels, F. (1975) *Obras escogidas*, Tome 2, Editorial Fundamentos, Madrid.

Marx, K. and Engels, F. (1992) [1845-6] *La ideología alemana*, Universitat de València, Valencia.

Mauss, M. (1990) [1923-4] *The Gift: The Form and Reason for Exchange in Archaic Societies*, Routledge, London. [M. Mauss (1968) [1923-24] 'Essai sur le don: forme et raison de l'échange dans les sociétés archaïques' in *Sociologie et anthropologie*, Presses Universitaires de France, Paris.]

May, M. (1982) 'The Historical Problem of the Family Wage: The Ford Motor Company and the Five Dollar Day', in *Feminist Studies*, 8 (2).

Mazumdar, D. (1987) 'Rural–Urban Migration in Developing Countries', in E.S. Mills (ed.) *Handbook of Urban Economics*, Vol.2, Elsevier, New York.

Meijer, F. and van Nijf, O. (1992) *Trade, Transport and Society in the Ancient World: A Sourcebook*, Routledge, London.

Meillassoux, C. (1978) 'Kinship Relations and Relations of Production', in D. Seddon (ed.) *Relations of Production: Marxist Approaches to Economic Anthropology*, Frank Cass, London.

Meillassoux, C. (1982) [1975] *Mujeres, graneros y capitales*, Siglo XXI, Madrid. [C. Meillassoux (1975) *Femmes, greniers, capitaux*, François Maspero, Paris.]

Mies, M. (1986) *Patriarchy and Accumulation on a World Scale: Women in the International Division of Labour*, Zed Books, London.

Millán, J. (1991) 'Contrarevolució i mobilització a l'Espanya contemporània', in *L'Avenç*, 154.

Miller, D. (1987) *Material Culture and Mass Consumption*, Basil Blackwell, Oxford.

Miller, D. (1995) 'Consumption as the Vanguard of History: A Polemic by Way of an Introduction', in D. Miller (ed.) *Acknowledging Consumption*, Routledge, London.

Mingione, E. (1985) 'Social Reproduction of the Surplus Labour Force: The Case of Southern Italy', in N. Redclift and E. Mingione (eds) *Beyond Employment*, Blackwell, Oxford.

Mingione, E. (1987) 'Economic Development, Social Factors and Social Context: Comparative Analysis of Economic Development and Family/Social Survival Strategies', paper given at the American Sociological Association, Chicago.

Mingione, E. (1988) 'Underground Economy and Irregular Forms of Employment (Travail au Noir): The Case of Italy', Study no. 87929 for the Commission for European Communities, DG V.

Mingione, E. (1991) *Fragmented Societies: A Sociology of Economic Life Beyond the Market Paradigm*, Blackwell, Oxford.

Mintz, S.W. (1986) *Sweetness and Power: The Place of Sugar in Modern History*, Penguin, New York.

Mitchell, J.C. (1969) 'The Concept and Use of Social Networks', in J.C. Mitchell (ed.) *Social Networks in Urban Situations: Analyses of Personal Relationships in Central African Towns*, Manchester University Press, Manchester.

Mitter, S. (1994) 'On Organising Women in Casualised Work: A Global Overview', in S. Rowbotham and S. Mitter (eds) *Dignity and Daily Bread*, Routledge, London.

Mitterauer, M. and Sieder, R. (1979) 'The Developmental Process of Domestic Groups: Problems of Reconstruction and Possibilities of Interpretation', in *Journal of Family History*, Fall.

Moniot, H. (1976) 'En France: une anthropologie d'inspiration marxiste', in F. Pouillon (ed.) *L'Anthroplogie économique: courants et problèmes*, Maspero, Paris.

Mozo, C. (1995) '*Sexuación y generización en el ámbito de los seguros*', Doctoral Thesis, Universidad de Sevilla, Spain.

Nadal, J. (1979) *El fracaso de la Revolución Industrial en España, 1814–1913*, Ariel, Barcelona.

Naredo, J.M. (1987) *La economía en evolución*, Siglo XXI, Madrid.

Narotzky, S. (1988a) 'The Ideological Squeeze: "Casa", "Family" and "Co-operation" in the Processes Of Transition', in *Social Science Information*, 27 (4):559–81.

Narotzky, S. (1988b) 'Worker Cooperatives, Women's Work and Food Security in a Catalan Rural Area', in *Journal of Rural Cooperation*, 16 (1–2).

Narotzky, S. (1988c) 'El conreu de l'olivera; la producció de l'oli a les Garrigues', in *L'Avenç*, 111.

Narotzky, S. (1989) '*Ideas That Work: Ideologies and Social Reproduction in Rural Catalunya and Beyond*', PhD Thesis, New School For Social Research, New York.

Narotzky, S. (1990) '"Not to be a Burden": Ideologies of the Domestic Group and Women's Work in Rural Catalonia', in J.L. Collins and M. Gimenez (eds) (1990) *Work Without Wages: Comparative Studies of Domestic Labor and Self-employment*, State University of New York Press, Albany.

Narotzky, S. (1991) 'La renta del afecto: ideología y reproducción social en el cuidado de los viejos', in J. Prat, U. Martínez, J. Contreras and I. Moreno (eds) (1991) *Antropología de los pueblos de España*, Taurus, Madrid.

Nash, J. (1979) *We Eat the Mines and the Mines Eat Us*, Columbia University Press, New York.

Nash, J. and Fernández-Kelly, M.P. (eds) (1983) *Women, Men and the International Division of Labor*, State University of New York Press, Albany.

Nelson, N. (1987) 'Rural–urban Child Fostering in Kenya: Migration, Kinship Ideology and Class', in J. Eades (ed.) *Migrants, Workers and the Social Order*, Tavistock, London.

Ohno, T. (1988) *The Toyota Production System: Beyond Large-scale Production*, Productivity Press, Cambridge, MA.

Oresmes, N. (1989) *Traité des monnaies*, La Manufacture, Lyon.

Ortiz, S. (ed.) (1983) *Economic Anthropology: Topics and Theories*, University Press of America, Lanham, MD.

Ottenberg, S. and Ottenberg, Ph. (1968) 'Afikpo Markets. 1900–1960', in P. Bohannan and G. Dalton (eds) *Markets in Africa*, NorthWestern University Press, Evanston, IL.

Pahl, R.E. (1984) *Divisions of Labour*, Oxford, Basil Blackwell.

Pahl, R.E. and Wallace, C.D. (1985) 'Forms of Work and Privatisation on the Isle of Sheppey', in B. Roberts, R. Finnegan and D. Gallie *New Approaches to Economic Life*, Manchester University Press, Manchester.

Pala, A.O. (1979) 'Women in the Household Economy: Managing Multiple Roles', in *Studies in Family Planning*, 10 (11–12).

Parra, F. (1993) 'La ecología como antecedente de una ciencia aplicada de los recursos y del territorio', in J.M. Naredo and F. Parra (eds) *Hacia una ciencia de los recursos naturales*, Siglo XXI, Madrid.

Parry, J. (1989) 'On the Moral Perils of Exchange', in J. Parry and M. Bloch (eds) *Money and the Morality of Exchange*, Cambridge University Press, Cambridge.

Peiró, J. (1979) *Trayectoria de la CNT: sindicalismo y anarquismo*, Ediciones Júcar, Madrid.

Pérez Baró, A. (1989) *Història de les cooperatives a Catalunya*, Barcelona, Crítica.

Phillips, A. and Taylor, B. (1980) 'Sex and Skill: Notes Towards a Feminist Economics', in *Feminist Review*, 6.

Phizacklea, A. (ed.) (1983) *One-Way ticket: Migration and Female Labour*, Routledge and Kegan Paul, London.

Pi i Margall, F. (1854) *La reacción y la revolución: estudios políticos y sociales*, Imprenta Rivadeneyra, Madrid.

Pi i Margall, F. (1973) [1876] *Las nacionalidades*, Editorial Cuadernos para el Diálogo, Madrid.

Pi i Sunyer, C. (1983) [1927] *L'aptitud econòmica de Catalunya*, La Magrana, Barcelona.

Picchio, A. (1992) *Social Reproduction: The Political Economy of the Labour Market*, Cambridge University Press, Cambridge.

Piore, M. and Sabel, C. (1984) *The Second Industrial Divide: Possibilities for Prosperity*, Basic Books, New York.

Plakans, A. (1984) *Kinship in the Past: An Anthropology of European Family Life, 1500–1900*, Blackwell, Oxford.

Plattner, S. (1989) 'Economic Behavior in Markets', in S. Plattner (ed.) *Economic Anthropology*, Stanford University Press, Stanford, CA.

Plattner, S. (ed.) (1985) *Markets and Marketing*, University Press of America, Lanham, MD.

Polanyi, K. (1957) 'The Economy as Instituted Process', in K. Polanyi, C. Arensberg and H. Pearson (eds) *Trade and Market in the Early Empires: Economies in History and Theory*, The Free Press, New York.

Polanyi, K. (1971) [1944] *The Great Transformation*, Beacon Press, Boston.

Pollert, A. (1988) 'Dismantling Flexibility', in *Capital and Class*, 34.

Pollert, A. (1991) 'The Orthodoxy of Flexibility', in A. Pollert (ed.) *Farewell to Flexibility?* Blackwell, Oxford.

Portes, A. (1983) 'The Informal Sector: Definition, Controversy, and Relations to National Development', in *Cultures et Développement*, 15 (2) 295–315.

Prat, J. (1989) 'El pairalisme com a model ideològic', in *L'Avenç*, 132.

Prats, Ll. (1988) *El mite de la tradició popular*, Edicions 62, Barcelona.

Price, J.A. (1980) 'On Silent Trade', in G. Dalton (ed.) *Research in Economic Anthropology*, JAI Press, Greenwich, CT.

Rapp, R. (1978) 'Family and Class in Contemporary America: Notes Toward an Understanding of Ideology', in *Science and Society*, 42 (3).

Rapp, R. (1987) 'Toward a Nuclear Freeze? The Gender Politics of Euro-American Kinship Analysis', in J. Collier and S. Yanagisako (eds) *Gender and*

Kinship: Essays Toward a Unified Analysis, Stanford University Press, Stanford, CA.

Rappaport, R. (1968) *Pigs for the Ancestors: Ritual in the Ecology of a New Guinea People*, Yale University Press, New Haven, CT.

'Real decreto de 13 de noviembre de 1900: Reglamento para la aplicación de la ley de 13 de marzo de 1900' (1987) in A. Valverde (ed.) *La legislación social en la Historia de España de la Revolución liberal a 1936*, Congreso de los Diputados, Madrid.

'Real orden de 15 de enero de 1920: Normas para la aplicación de la jornada máxima' (1987) in A. Valverde (ed.) *La legislación social en la historia de España de la revolución liberal a 1936*, Congreso de los Diputados, Madrid.

Rebel, H. (1983) *Peasant Classes: The Bureaucratization of Property and Family Relations under Early Habsburg Absolutism, 1511–1636*, Princeton University Press, Princeton, NJ.

Reddy, W.M. (1987) *The Rise of Market Culture*, Cambridge University Press/Maison des Sciences de l'Homme, Cambridge.

Redfield, R. (1960) *The Little Community/Peasant Society and Culture*, University of Chicago Press, Chicago.

Reid, M. (1934) *Economics of Household Production*, John Wiley, New York.

Reid, M. (1968) 'Consumers: Levels and Standards', in *International Encyclopedia of the Social Sciences*, Vol. 3, pp.335–42, Crowell Collier and MacMillan Inc., New York.

Rey, P.Ph. (1971) *Colonialisme, néo-colonialisme et transition au capitalisme*, Editions La Découverte, Paris.

Ricardo, D. (1959) [1821] *Principios de Economía Política y Tributación*, Fondo de Cultura Económica, México. [D. Ricardo (1950) *The Works and Correspondence of David Ricardo*, Vol.I . *On the Principles of Political Economy and Taxation*, Cambridge University Press, London.]

Roberts, B. (1978) *Cities of Peasants: The Political Economy of Urbanization in the Third World*, Edward Arnold, London.

Roig i Rosich, J.M. (1993) 'La dictadura de Primo de Rivera i Catalunya', in J. Ferrer et al., *Les bases de Manresa 1892–1992: Cent anys de catalanisme*, Generalitat de Catalunya, Barcelona.

Roigé, X. (1989) 'Els juristes i la família Catalana', in *L'Avenç*, 132.

Roseberry, W. (1983) *Coffee and Capitalism in the Venezuelan Andes*, University of Texas Press, Austin.

Roseberry, W. (1988) 'Political Economy', in *Annual Review of Anthropology*, 17.

Roseberry, W. (1989) *Anthropologies and Histories: Essays in Culture, History and Political Economy*, Rutgers University Press, New Brunswick, NJ.

Rubery, J. and Wilkinson, F. (1981) 'Outwork and Segmented Labour Markets', in F. Wilkinson (ed.) *The Dynamics of Labour Market Segmentation*, Academic Press, London.

Rubin, G. (1975) 'The Traffic in Women: Notes on the "Political Economy" of Sex', in R. Reiter (ed.) *Toward an Anthropology of Women*, Monthly Review Press, New York.

Rule, J. (1987) 'The property of Skill in the Period of Manufacture', in P. Joyce (ed.) *The historical Meanings of Work*, Cambridge University Press, Cambridge.

Sabel, Ch. (1982) *Work and Politics*, Cambridge University Press, Cambridge.

Sabel, Ch. (1989) 'Flexible Specialization and the Re-emergence of Regional Economies', in P. Hirst and J. Zeitlin (eds) *Reversing Industrial Decline? Industrial Structure and Policy in Britain and Her Competitors*, Berg, Oxford.

Sabel, Ch. and Zeitlin, J. (1985) 'Historical Alternatives to Mass Production: Politics, Markets and Technology in XIXth-century Industrialization', in *Past and Present*, 108.

Sahlins, M. (1965) 'On the Sociology of Primitive Exchange', in M. Banton (ed.) *The Relevance of Models for Social Anthropology*, Tavistock, London.

Sahlins, M. (1972) *Stone Age Economics*, Aldine-Atherton Inc., Chicago.

Samuel, R. (1977) 'Workshop of the World: Steam Power and Hand Technology in Mid-Victorian Britain', in *History Workshop*, 3.

Sassen-Koob, S. (1981) 'Exporting Capital and Importing Labor: The Role of Caribbean Migration to New York City', in *Occasional Papers*, 28 New York University.

Sayer, A. and Walker, R. (1992) *The New Social Economy: Reworking the Division of Labor*, Blackwell, Cambridge, MA.

Scott, J.W. (1988) 'Work Identities for Men and Women: The Politics of Work and Family in the Parisian Garment Trades in 1848', in *Gender and the Politics of History*, Columbia University Press, New York.

Service, E. (1966) *The Hunters*, Prentice Hall, Englewood Cliffs, NJ.

Sewell, W.H. Jr (1980) *Work and Revolution in France: The Language of Labor from the Old Regime to 1848*, Cambridge University Press, Cambridge.

Sharp, J. (1987) 'Relocation, Labour Migration, and the Domestic Predicament: Qwaqwa in the 1980s', in J. Eades (ed.) *Migrants, Workers and the Social Order*, Tavistock, London.

Skinner, G.W. (1985) 'Rural Marketing in China: Revival and Reappraisal', in S. Plattner (ed.) *Markets and Marketing*, University Press of America, Lanham, MD.

Smith, A. (1982) [1776] *The Wealth of Nations*, Penguin Books, Harmondsworth.

Smith, C. (1983) 'Regional Analysis in World-system Perspective: A Critique of Three Structural Theories of Uneven Development', in S. Ortiz (ed.) *Economic Anthropology: Topics and Theories*, University Press of America, Lanham, MD.

Smith, C. (1985) 'How to Count Onions: Methods for a Regional Analysis of Marketing', in S. Plattner (ed.) *Markets and Marketing*, University Press of America, Lanham, MD.

Smith, G. (1989) *Livelihood and Resistance: Peasants and the Politics of Land in Peru*, University of California Press, Berkeley.

Smith, G. (1991) 'Writing for Real: Capitalist Constructions and Constructions of Capitalism', in *Critique of Anthropology*, 11 (3).

Smith, J. (1984) 'The Paradox of Women's Poverty: Wage-earning Women and Economic Transformation', in *Signs*, 10 (2).

Soldevila, F. (1978) *Síntesis de historia de Cataluña*, Destino, Barcelona.

Spooner, B. (1986) 'Weavers and Dealers: The Authenticity of a Persian Carpet' in A. Appadurai (ed.) *The Social Life of Things*, Cambridge University Press, Cambridge.

Stack, C. (1975) *All our Kin: Strategies for Survival in a Black Community*, Harper and Row, New York.

Stavrakis, O. and Marshall, M.C. (1978) 'Women, Agriculture and Development in the Maya Lowlands: Profit or Progress?', paper presented at Conference on the Role of Women in Meeting Basic Food and Water Needs in Developing Countries, 8–11 Jan.

Stichter, S. (1985) *Migrant Laborers*, Cambridge University Press, Cambridge.

Strathern, A. (1971) *The Rope of Moka. Big-men and Ceremonial Exchange in Mount Hagen, New Guinea*, Cambridge University Press, Cambridge.

Strathern, A. (1980) 'The Central and the Contingent: Bridewealth Among the Melpa and the Wiru', in J.L. Comaroff (ed.) *The Meaning of Marriage Payments*, Academic Press, London.

Strathern, M. (1972) *Women in Between: Female Roles in a Male World*, Seminar Press, London.

Sweezy, P.M. (1964) [1942] *The Theory of Capitalist Development*, Monthly Review Press, New York.

Swift, A. (1993) *Global Political Ecology: The Crisis in Economy and Government*, Pluto Press, London.

Tabet, P. (1985) 'Fertilité naturelle, reproduction forcée', in N.C. Mathieu (ed.) *L'Arraisonnement des femmes: Essais en anthropologie des sexes*, Editions de l'Ecole des Hautes Etudes en Sciences Sociales, Paris.

Tardits, C. and Tardits, C. (1968) 'Traditional Market Economy in South Dahomey', in P. Bohannan and G. Dalton (eds) *Markets in Africa*, NorthWestern University Press, Evanston, IL.

Taussig, M. (1980) *The Devil and Commodity Fetishism in South America*, University of North Carolina Press, Chapel Hill.

Taylor, F.W. (1970) [1911] *Management científico*, Oikos-Tau, Barcelona. [F.W. Taylor (1947) *The Principles of Scientific Management*, Harper and Row, New York.]

Termes, J. and Colomines, A. (1992) *Les bases de Manresa de 1892 i els orígens del catalanisme*, Generalitat de Catalunya, Barcelona.

Terradas, I. (1984) *El món històric de les masies*, Curial, Barcelona.

Terradas, I. (1995) *La qüestió de les colònies industrials: l'exemple de l'Ametlla de Merola*, CEB, Manresa.

Terray, E. (1969) *Le Marxisme devant les sociétés 'primitives': deux études*, Maspero, Paris.

Thomas, N. (1991) *Entangled Objects: Exchange, Material Culture and Colonialism in the Pacific*, Harvard University Press, Cambridge, MA.

Thompson, E.P. (1966) *The Making of the English Working Class*, Vintage, New York.

Thompson, E.P. (1978) *The Poverty of Theory and Other Essays*, Merlin, London.

Tilly, L. and Scott, J.W. (1978) *Women, Work and Family*, Holt Rinehart and Winston, New York.

Trías, J. (1975) *Almirall y los orígenes del catalanismo*, Siglo XXI, Madrid.

Turbin, C. (1987) 'Beyond Conventional Wisdom: Women's Wage Work, Household Economic Contribution, and Labor Activism in a Mid-nineteenth-century Working-class Community', in C. Groneman and M.B. Norton (eds) *'To Toil the Livelong Day': American Women at Work, 1780–1980*, Cornell University Press, Ithaca, NY.

Unió Catalanista (1993) [1904] *El catalanisme y'l problema social*, Eumo Editorial, Vic.

Valentine, B. (1978) *Hustling and Other Hard Work: Life Styles in the Ghetto*, Free Press, New York.

Valls-Taberner, F. (1954) *Obras selectas*, V.2. *Estudios histórico-jurídicos*, Consejo Superior de Investigaciones Científicas, Madrid.

Valverde, A. (1987) 'Estudio preliminar: la formación del derecho del trabajo en España', in A. Valverde, (ed.) *La legislación social en la historia de España de la revolución Liberal a 1936*, Congreso de los Diputados, Madrid.

Vicens Vives, J. (1975) [1954] *Notícia de Catalunya*, Edicions Destino, Barcelona.

Vicens Vives, J. (1986) *Los catalanes en el siglo XX*, Alianza Editorial, Madrid.

Vilar, P. (1982) [1962] *La Catalogne dans l'Espagne moderne*, 3 vols, Le Sycomore/Editions de l'EHESS, Paris.

Vogeler, I. (1981) *The Myth of the Family Farm: Agribusiness Dominance of US Agriculture*, Westview Press, Boulder, CO.

Walker, K.E. (1978) 'La Mesure du temps consacré aux activités domestiques des familles américaines', in A. Michel (ed.) *Les Femmes dans la société marchande*, Presses Universitaires de France, Paris.

Wallendorf, M. and Arnould, E.S. (1991) '"We Gather Together": Consumption Rituals of Thanksgiving Day', in *Journal of Consumer Research*, 18.

Wallerstein, I. (1974) *The Modern World-system, Vol. 1: Capitalist Agriculture and the Origins of the European World-economy in the Sixteenth Century*, Academic Press, New York.

Wallerstein, I. (1980) *The Modern World-system, Vol. 2: Mercantilism and the Consolidation of the European World-economy, 1600–1750*, Academic Press, New York.

Wallerstein, I., Martin, W. and Dickinson, T. (1982) 'Household Structures and Production Processes', in *Review*, 3 (Winter).

Weber, J.L. (1993) 'Tener en cuenta(s) la naturaleza (bases para una contabilidad de los recursos naturales)', in J.M. Naredo and F. Parra (eds) *Hacia una ciencia de los recursos naturales*, Siglo XXI, Madrid.

Weiner, A.B. (1976) *Women of Value, Men of Renown: New Perspectives in Trobriand Exchange*, University of Texas Press, Austin.

Weiner, A.B. (1978) 'The Reproductive Model in Trobriand Society', in *Mankind*, 11 (3).

Weiner, A.B. (1980) 'Reproduction: A Replacement For Reciprocity', in *American Ethnologist*, 7 (1).

Weissner, P. (1982) 'Risk, Reciprocity and Social Influences on !Kung San Economics', in E. Leacock and R. Lee (eds) *Politics and History in Band Societies*, Cambridge University Press, Cambridge.

Whitten, N.E. Jr. and Wolfe, A.W. (1973) 'Network Analysis', in J.J. Honigmann (ed.) *Handbook of Social and Cultural Anthropology*, Rand McNally, Chicago.

Wilk, R.R. and Netting, R.M. (1984) 'Households: Changing Forms and Functions', in R.M. Netting, R.R. Wilk and E.S. Arnould (eds) *Households: Comparative and Historical Studies of the Domestic Group*, University of California Press, Berkeley.

Williams, K., Cutler, T., Williams, J. and Haslam, C. (1987) 'The End of Mass Production?' in *Economy and Society*, 16 (3).

Williams, R. (1977) *Marxism and Literature*, Oxford University Press, Oxford.

Williams, R. (1984) [1961] *The Long Revolution*, Penguin Books, Harmondsworth.

Wilmsen, E.N. (1989) *Land Filled with Flies. A Political Economy of the Kalahari*, University of Chicago Press, Chicago.

Wilson, G. (1987) 'Money: Patterns of Responsibility and Irresponsibility in Marriage', in J. Brannen and G. Wilson (eds) *Give and Take in Families: Studies in Resource Distribution*, Allen and Unwin, London.

Winson, A. (1993) *The Intimate Commodity: Food and the Development of the Agro-Industrial Complex in Canada*, Garamond Press, Canada.

Wolf, E.R. (1982) *Europe and the People without History*, University of California Press, Berkeley.

Author's note: As I am a Spanish scholar living in Spain, it would be unreasonable to suggest that I should read and give all my references in English. Although I try to read texts in their original version (English or otherwise), this is not always possible. Where I can, I have put in brackets the English title and publisher and edition so that the reference can be easily located by English-speaking readers. If any are missing (as in the case of English editions of Marx's works) it is only because I have been unable to locate the English editions in the libraries available to me.

Index